PRAISE FOR *CROSS-BORDER LOGISTICS OPERATIONS*

'Drawing on his many years as a trade facilitation practitioner and academic in the field, including as a contributor to the WCO's PICARD Programme, Andrew Grainger's book provides a comprehensive and valuable look at cross-border logistics, the players involved, the challenges faced and even offers glimpses of what the future could look like. This book should be on the reading list for anyone in the public or private sector whose work touches on cross-border logistics and desires a deeper understanding of how and why it all works.'

Kunio Mikuriya, Secretary General, World Customs Organization (WCO)

'Building on personal experience, a thorough literature review and years of project practice, Andrew Grainger gets one key message across: successful trade facilitation helps achieve both better controls and – at the same time – easier trade. And the book shows you how to do it.'

Dr Jan Hoffman, Chief, Trade Logistics Branch, United Nations Conference on Trade and Development

'This book deals with a topic that is of global importance and affects the economic development of all countries. Cross-border logistics is the basis of international trade. As the subtitle of the book points out, it is about making trade facilitation and border management effective. The author covers all the important aspects of cross-border logistics and also points out the future development. Dr Grainger has produced a refreshingly well-written, seminal book that will serve scholars, students and practitioners for years to come.'

Professor Dr Hans-Michael Wolffgang, Institute of Customs and International Trade Law, University of Münster

'This book unravels the mysteries of cross-border trade, offering an expansive but digestible overview of cross border commerce. Andrew Grainger explains the rules and conventions that define how goods are moved around the globe and in a language that does not assume an in-depth knowledge of the subject. This is a useful guide that should be on the bookshelf of anyone involved in international trade, whatever your role and experience.'

Steven Pope, Group Head Trade Facilitation, Go Trade, Deutsche Post DHL Group

'Trade facilitation, or how to ease the flow of goods across borders, is a much-discussed but generally poorly understood topic. It has long been as important – if not more important – than tariffs for most goods in developed country trade and is of vital importance for developing economies wishing to engage in international trade. This volume is a must-read for anyone wishing to understand the processes and challenges involved in goods crossing borders.'

Dr Stephen Woolcock, Associate Professor of International Relations, London School of Economics

'This book gives an excellent overview of how cross-border logistics can be improved by the simplification and harmonization of customs procedures, often referred to as trade facilitation. It provides a thorough, scientific analysis of these issues, explaining the latest developments in regulation, policy making and IT innovations that foster trade facilitation. Combined with the extensive experience of the author in trade facilitation consulting, it provides a rich set of guidelines and best practices that can inspire customs officers and logistics professionals to realize the full potential of trade facilitation.'

Professor Yao-Hua Tan, Professor of Information and Communication Technology, Delft University of Technology

'In a time when cross-border operations are becoming increasingly complex and the need for customs and trade compliance is greater than ever, Andrew Grainger's book is a timely and extremely useful view of this rapidly changing landscape and should be a reference of choice for any professional operating in this area.'

Mark Corby, National UK Customs and Trade Compliance Manager, Kuehne+Nagel

'Kudos to Andrew Grainger for such a comprehensive book, covering all aspects of cross-border trade from logistic operations and customs compliance to coordinated border management and supply chain integrity. It seems he responded to the challenge "if you don't see the book you want on the shelf, write it". An essential go-to resource for all its readers.'

Dr Mohammad Saeed, Senior Adviser, Trade Facilitation and Policy for Business, International Trade Centre

'Unlike most supply chain and logistics books, which deal with it as a footnote, this book unveils every inch of cross-border operations; an increasingly important and urgent subject governing the international flow of goods which should be taught at every business school. By focusing on the "missing link" and overcoming friction between business operators and border agencies, Dr Grainger, a worldwide trade facilitation expert, has produced a much-needed, insightful and up-to-date book that is worth every page.'

Professor Cristiano Morini, Faculty of Applied Sciences, FCA/UNICAMP, University of Campinas, Brazil

'A spot-on contribution to the field of cross-border logistics management, the role of customs and other border agencies, as well as the facilitation of global trade. I warmly recommend Dr Grainger's book as a key learning and reference resource for students, executives, researchers and policy makers worldwide.'

Dr Juha Hintsa, Founder, Cross-border Research Association, Switzerland

'What a great book! There is so little useful literature in our field, and this book fills that gap. I recommend this book to all practitioners and academics in the field of cross-border logistics.'

Professor Dr Albert W Veenstra, Professor of Trade and Logistics, Rotterdam School of Management, Erasmus University Rotterdam

'Organizations moving goods across international borders face a multitude of challenges and risks, including successfully dealing with national administrations and negotiating the diverse range of rules and regulations. In this book, Andrew Grainger provides an insightful overview of compliance activities for cross-border logistics, addressing the spectrum of issues that need to be considered, including customs administration, declarations, prohibitions, compliance and coordination. The book discusses the role of customs and other border agencies within the wider context of logistics and supply chain management, the importance of trade facilitation, the institutions that contribute to making international trade work, and concludes with a look at the impact on the movement of goods in crisis situations. These insights are drawn from Andrew's extensive career in trade facilitation both operationally and academically. The world of customs and trade facilitation is made understandable, and will be useful to students, policy makers and practitioners. The absence of textbooks covering this subject means that this book is both the first of its kind, and an essential text for anyone interested in trade facilitation, customs operations and cross-border logistics.'

Professor Stephen Pettit, Logistics and Operations Management, Cardiff Business School

'What an impressive book! An essential resource for anyone involved in cross-border logistics operations, as well as those who seek to mitigate the impact of borders on international commerce. For nearly 30 years I have been an active proponent of semantic data harmonization to encourage digitalization of global supply chain communications as a migration path from paper, and for progression towards single window environments. This book supports these ambitions for enhanced trade facilitation.'

Sue Probert, Chair, United Nations Centre for Trade Facilitation and Electronic Business (UN/CEFACT)

Cross-border Logistics Operations

Effective trade facilitation and border management

Andrew Grainger

KoganPage

Publisher's note

Every possible effort has been made to ensure that the information contained in this book is accurate at the time of going to press, and the publishers and author cannot accept responsibility for any errors or omissions, however caused. No responsibility for loss or damage occasioned to any person acting, or refraining from action, as a result of the material in this publication can be accepted by the editor, the publisher or the author.

First published in Great Britain and the United States in 2021 by Kogan Page Limited

2nd Floor, 45 Gee Street
London
EC1V 3RS
United Kingdom
www.koganpage.com

122 W 27th St, 10th Floor
New York, NY 10001
USA

4737/23 Ansari Road
Daryaganj
New Delhi 110002
India

Kogan Page books are printed on paper from sustainable forests.

ISBNs

Hardback 978 1 78966 673 1
Paperback 978 1 78966 672 4
Ebook 978 1 78966 674 8

British Library Cataloguing-in-Publication Data

A CIP record for this book is available from the British Library.

Library of Congress Cataloging-in-Publication Data
Names: Grainger, Andrew, author.
Title: Cross-border logistics operations : effective trade facilitation and border management / Andrew Grainger.
Description: London, United Kingdom ; New York, NY : Kogan Page Limited, 2021. | Includes bibliographical references and index.
Identifiers: LCCN 2021022637 (print) | LCCN 2021022638 (ebook) | ISBN 9781789666724 (paperback) | ISBN 9781789666731 (hardback) | ISBN 9781789666748 (ebook)
Subjects: LCSH: Customs administration. | Business logistics.
Classification: LCC HJ6609 .G75 2021 (print) | LCC HJ6609 (ebook) | DDC 352.4/48–dc23
LC record available at https://lccn.loc.gov/2021022637
LC ebook record available at https://lccn.loc.gov/2021022638

Typeset by Integra Software Services, Pondicherry
Print production managed by Jellyfish
Printed and bound by CPI Group (UK) Ltd, Croydon, CR0 4YY

To my wife and son, without whom this book would never have been written.

CONTENTS

LIST OF FIGURES AND TABLES

FIGURES

TABLES

ABOUT THE AUTHOR

Professor Dr Andrew Grainger is a trade facilitation practitioner, expert and academic with over 20 years of experience. As the Director of Trade Facilitation Consulting, he helps government agencies, companies and international organizations cut red tape in international trade. Andrew is also an Adjunct Professor at the Centre for Customs and Excise Studies (CSU, Australia) and an Honorary Associate Professor at the University of Nottingham (UK). On many occasions he has provided consultancy services to the World Bank Group and the United Nations family of organizations. He has given witness to the UK Parliament's Select Committees and provided research services to the European Parliament.

Andrew also was the Deputy Director Trade Procedures at SITPRO, the UK's former trade facilitation agency. His PhD thesis was awarded the prestigious Palgrave Macmillan Prize for best PhD in Maritime Economics and Logistics 2005 08. For over 10 years Andrew taught transport and logistics at the University of Nottingham and spent longer visiting stints at Technical University Delft (Netherlands), Shanghai Customs College (China), the University of Canberra (Australia), the University of New South Wales (Australia), the University of Münster (Germany), amongst others. Andrew is an active member of the International Network of Customs Universities (INCU). Much of his work is freely available and has been published by leading academic journals and various international organizations.

PREFACE

This book has been a long time in the making. My first encounter with a border, as far as I can remember, was in the back seat of my parents' tiny car. I could not have been much older than four and it was somewhere high up in the Alps – too young to remember exactly where. My Mum reaches out from the front to take her handbag as we roll up to what must have been a very quiet border post. A man in uniform walks over to us and motions my Dad to switch the engine off. Mum takes a few booklets from her handbag, which I now know were our passports, and hands them through the car window to the uniformed man. The officer then takes a closer look at the back seat where I am sitting – window wide open.

He motions me to hand over my precious, somewhat empty, kindergarten satchel that rests beside me. I do not quite understand; my parents explain that he wants to take a closer look to see if there is anything inside. I give him the satchel only to witness him disappear with it. A few minutes later he returns from a small house and returns the passports to my Mum. He then walks to my window, smiles, and hands me my satchel. What was before an almost empty satchel was now full to the brim with sweets! What strange things borders are: you must stop the car, present some papers, loan your satchel to a uniformed stranger and in return, you're presented with more sweets than your parents think is good for you!

Later on in life I learnt that the outcome of border inspections is not normally quite so bountiful. In my early career, as a fairly inexperienced freight forwarder in Southeast Asia, for example, I heard the phrase 'stuck in customs' being frequently uttered as an excuse for all manner of border-related delays. I myself spent many unhappy hours dealing with pre-shipment inspections (PSI, Chapter 3). Based in Singapore, I was tasked over a period of many months with presenting container loads of disassembled construction equipment to PSI inspectors before onward shipment to Indonesia. Most of that equipment was used and had been consolidated from construction sites around the world. A satisfactory PSI inspection outcome was necessary to ensure compliance with Indonesia's import customs procedures.

Unfortunately, the inspection process was seldom straightforward and necessitated each container being unpacked box by box. Moreover, each single part had to be matched against reams of accompanying commercial documents. The required effort was tremendous and often took weeks to prepare, especially since the original paperwork was often shoddy. Occasionally, even with the best of care, goods were damaged during unpacking and repacking. More often than not, inspection outcomes resulted in rejection and goods could not be shipped. Fortunately, to the best of my knowledge, such strict PSI measures for most imports into Indonesia no longer apply.

As an undergraduate at Cardiff University, I was taught that logistics management is about getting the right goods to the right place at the right time at the right price and in the right condition. The lesson that I painfully learnt in Singapore was how quickly that mission can be undermined by adverse regulatory requirements. Their impact on logistics operations and cost is significant. I could not help but reflect that my education – although good – was incomplete.

Five years later, after completing an MA in International Political Economy, a keen interest in the politics of international trade and a stint at PricewaterhouseCoopers, I found myself working for SITPRO (which was the UK trade facilitation agency) as their Deputy Director Trade Procedures. My job was to work with the UK business community to pinpoint the many sources of friction that they may have with various government agencies at ports and borders. Collaboratively we would then make recommendations for their remedy. Often, standard solutions to cutting trade-related red tape are very straightforward and can be quickly implemented. But many of the more ambitious trade facilitation solutions require changes to the governing legislation and guidelines – which is a considerably more demanding undertaking.

Most trade and customs procedures are embedded in wider international frameworks, such as those of the World Trade Organization (WTO). Many countries choose to align their rules and procedures even deeper, for example, within the context of regional trade and cooperation agreements. The solution to operational impediments thus requires international cooperation. I spent a lot of time in Brussels lending input into what has now become the Union Customs Code. Frequently, I also participated in the work of the World Customs Organization (WCO) and the committees of the United Nations Centre for Trade Facilitation and Electronic Business (UN CEFACT).

I treasure the many first-hand insights gained at SITPRO, not to mention a wonderful team of colleagues and mentors. Somehow, I also managed to complete a part-time PhD at Birkbeck, University of London, that reflected on my activities at SITPRO. My academic aim was to link the subject of trade facilitation to that of logistics and supply chain management. Much of the resulting PhD thesis has since been published and formed the basis of most of my academic activities.

Fifteen years have passed since finalizing that PhD thesis. I have worked as an academic at the University of Nottingham, as short-term consultant for many international organizations, and I also co-founded Trade Facilitation Consulting Ltd. So much more has been learnt. It is also wonderful to have witnessed the considerable policy strides in aid of making improvements to the trade and customs environment. Trade facilitation – the cutting of red tape in international trade – is now a central theme within contemporary trade policy. In February 2017, for example, the WTO Trade Facilitation Agreement came into force, and commits countries worldwide to implement various measures to help make trade easier.

Yet, border formalities might still be dismissed by some as just a bit of paperwork and a few checks. Regulatory demands and compliance practices are far more complex. Solutions to help make things easier require a lot of effort. The use of technology is dependent on standards. Commercial and regulatory procedures need to be aligned. Most modern border management practices are based on trust and cooperation, which needs to be earned and cultivated – whether it is between border agencies, between business partners up and down the supply chain or between business operators and the border agencies. It requires a broad skill set that extends significantly beyond knowing how to fill in a form or check a vehicle.

The management of cross-border logistics operations places demands upon knowledge in the applied interplay between law, technology, operations, economics, safety and security, and global trade politics. The need for professionalism and comprehensive knowledge is made explicit in the World Customs Organization's professional standards defined by its Partnership in Customs Academic Research and Development (PICARD) programme. Skill and training requirements might also be made explicit for the career development of border officials. In some countries, the private sector might have similar training frameworks for the development of border compliance specialists (Chapter 6).

Often, though, the career path is undefined, perhaps even accidental and 'on the job'. Contemporary training in logistics and supply chain management, especially at universities, often (not everywhere) only covers border-specific operations in the margins, if at all. There is an emerging need for more advanced and comprehensive training which this book aims to serve. Inspired by the WCO PICARD Standard it focuses on the challenges associated with moving goods across the border and the controls that are associated with them.

This book aims to serve both students and professionals, whether working in the private sector or with cross-border regulatory agencies, including Customs. It recognizes that some readers may be new to the subject and in need of a broad induction. It also suits readers familiar with the subject but in need of a comprehensive overview. As such, it may be used as a textbook or as a compendium. The book would also suit readers tasked with implementing trade facilitation-type initiatives and making improvements to the trade and customs environment.

Much has changed from the days when I first encountered border management in practice. I cannot promise sweets covertly smuggled between the pages, but I do hope the content will provide for bountiful reading.

ACKNOWLEDGEMENTS AND DISCLAIMER

Many people have helped me in my professional journey and thus indirectly with writing this book. They are colleagues, fellow travellers and peers, mentors, supervisors, students and friends – more than I can list. However, I do wish to explicitly thank Mark Corby, David Widdowson and Cristiano Morini for their helpful comments for some of the chapters. I also wish to thank Adam Cox at Kogan Page for editorial guidance and support. Like so many things in life, this book would not have been possible without the love, patience and support of my family.

All mistakes and errors are of course my own. I also need to stress that any referenced rules and procedures are subject to change. The purpose of this book is educational.

LIST OF ABBREVIATIONS

AAP	Australian Associated Press
ACTS	ASEAN's Customs Transit System
AEO	Authorized economic operator
APHA	Association of Port Health Authorities
ASEAN	Association of Southeast Asian Nations
ASYCUDA	Automated system for customs data
ASYREC	Automated system for relief consignments
B2B	Business to business
B2G	Business to government
BEST	Border Enforcement Security Task Force
BIS	Department for Business, Innovation and Skills
BREXIT	British Exit from the European Union
BTI	Binding tariff information
BTWC	Biological and Toxin Weapons Convention
C-TPAT	Customs and Trade Partnership against Terrorism
CACM	Central American Common Market
CAN	Andean Community
CARICOM	Caribbean Community and Common Market
CBP	United States Customs and Border Protection
CCC	Customs Co-operation Council
CCES	Centre for Customs and Excise Studies
CCSA	Committee for the Coordinating of Statistical Activities
CE	*Conformitė Europėenne*
CEEC	Committee for European Economic Co-operation
CEFTA	The Central European Free Trade Agreement
CEMAC	Economic and Monetary Community of Central Africa
CFR	Cost and freight
CIF	Cost, insurance and freight
CIP	Carriage and insurance paid

CITES	Convention on International Trade in Endangered Species of Wild Fauna and Flora
CMAA	Customs Mutual Assistance Agreements
CN	Combined nomenclature
CN22	Customs declaration form for packages sent by post
COMESA	Common Market for Eastern and Southern Africa
CPT	Carriage paid to
CPTPP	Comprehensive and Progressive Agreement for Trans-Pacific Partnership
CR	Continuous replenishment
CWC	Chemical Weapons Convention
DAfTF	*Deutsche Alliance für Trade Facilitation*
DAP	Delivered at place
DDP	Delivered duty paid
DIT	United States Department for International Trade
DPU	Delivered at place unloaded
DTI	Direct trader input
DVSA	Driver and Vehicle Standards Agency
EAC	East African Community
EAEC	Eurasian Economic Community
EAEU	Eurasian Economic Union
EAR	Export Administration Regulation
EBRD	European Bank for Reconstruction and Development
ECOWAS	Economic Community of West African States
ECR	Efficient consumer response
EDI	Electronic data interchange
EFTA	European Free Trade Area
EIDR	Entry in the declarant's records
EIN	Employer identification number
EORI	Economic Operators Registration and Identification
EPOS	Electronic point of sale
EU	European Union
EXW	Ex works
FAL	Facilitation of Maritime Traffic
FAO	Food and Agriculture Organization
FAS	Free alongside ship

FAST	Free and secure trade
FCA	Free carrier
FCC	Federal Communications Commission
FDA	United States Food and Drug Administration
FMCSA	United States Federal Motor Carrier Safety Administration
FMVSS	Federal Motor Vehicle Safety Standards
FOB	Free on board
FSA	Food Standards Agency
FSANZ	Food Standards Code (Australia/New Zealand)
FTA	Free trade agreements
FTA	Freight Transport Association
G2B	Government to business
G2B2B2G	Government-to-business-to-business-to-government
G2G	Government-to-government
GATT	The General Agreement on Tariffs and Trade
GCC	Gulf Cooperation Council
GDP	Gross domestic product
GIR	General Interpretative Rules
GIZ	*Deutsche Gesellschaft für Internationale Zusammenarbeit*
GSP	General System of Preference
GSSA	Global service and sales agent
GST	Goods sales tax
HCOC	Hague Code of Conduct against Ballistic Missile Proliferation
HMG	Her Majesty's Government (Government of the United Kingdom)
HMRC	Her Majesty's Revenue and Customs Services
HS	Harmonized System
IATA	International Air Transport Association
ICAO	International Civil Aviation Organization
ICC	International Chamber of Commerce
ICT	Information and communication technology
IFRC	International Federation of Red Cross and Red Crescent Societies

IMF	International Monetary Fund
IMO	International Maritime Organization
INCU	International Network of Customs Universities
INTERPOL	International Criminal Police Organization
IPPC	International Plant Protection Convention
IPU	Inter-Parliamentary Union
IRS	Inland Revenue Service
IRU	International Road Transport Union
ISO	International Organization for Standardization
ISPM	International Standards for Phytosanitary Measures
ISPS	International Ship and Port Facility
ITC	International Trade Centre
IUU	Illegal, unreported and unregulated fishing
JCCC	Joint Customs Consultative Committee
JHUM	John Hopkins University and Medicine
JIT	Just-in-time
KP	Kimberley Process
KPI	Key performance indicator
LTP	Lao PDR Trade Portal
MERCOSUR	Common Market of the South
MFN	Most favoured nation
MHRA	Medicines and Healthcare Products Regulatory Agency
MoU	Memorandum of understanding
NCTS	European Union's New Computerized Transit System
NGO	Non-governmental organization
NOP	United States National Organic Program
NPT	Treaty on the Non-Proliferation of Nuclear Weapons
NVOCC	Non-vessel operating common carriers
OCHA	Office for the Coordination of Humanitarian Affairs
OECD	Organisation for Economic Co-operation and Development
OIE	World Organization for Animal Health
OSCE	Organization for Security and Cooperation in Europe
PICARD	Partnership in Customs Academic Research and Development

PPE	Personal protective equipment
PSI	Pre-shipment inspections
SACU	Southern African Customs Union
SAD	Single Administrative Document
SAFE(WCO)	Framework of Standards to Secure and Facilitate Global Trade
SCBD	Secretariat of the Convention on Biological Diversity
SCM	Supply chain management
SDR	Special drawing rights
SITPRO	Simplifying International Trade Procedures (the UK's former trade facilitation agency)
SOLAS	International Convention for the Safety of Life at Sea
SOP	Standard operating procedure
SPS	Sanitary and phytosanitary
STDF	Standards and Trade Development Facility
TARIC	Integrated Tariff of the European Union
TECRO	Taipei Economic and Agricultural Representative Office
TFEU	Treaty of the Functioning of the European Union
TIR	*Transports Internationaux Routiers*
TRACES	Trade control and expert system
TRIPS	Trade-related aspects of intellectual property rights
UN CEFACT	United Nations Centre for Trade Facilitation and Electronic Business
UN ESCAP	United Nations Economic and Social Commission for Asia and the Pacific
UNCTAD	United Nations Conference on Trade and Development
UNDP	United Nations Development Programme
UNECE	United Nations Economic Commission for Europe
UNEP	United Nations Environment Programme
UNESCO	United Nations Educational, Scientific and Cultural Organization
UNODC	United Nations Office on Drugs and Crime
UPU	Universal Postal Union
USCBP	United States Customs and Border Protection
USGS	United States Geological Survey

USITA	United States International Trade Administration
USPB	United States Customs and Border Protection
WAEMU	West African Economic and Monetary Union
WCO	World Customs Organization
WTO	World Trade Organization

FOREWORD

I have known Professor Andrew Grainger for many years. Our academic interests are very similar, but while my background is in government regulation, his is in international trade, logistics and commerce, and so over the years we have approached our debates on cross-border issues from different perspectives. I think it is fair to say that we have both found this to be very refreshing, and it has helped us both to broaden our thinking on what Andrew describes in his delightfully plain English style as 'the challenges associated with moving goods across the border and the controls that are associated with them'.

In *Cross-border Logistics Operations* Andrew has managed to capture the way in which public and private sector objectives meet at the regulatory touchpoint of international trade – the point at which the international trading community must satisfy agencies responsible for border management of the legitimacy of their cross-border transactions. In doing so, he highlights the need to weed out the friction that often occurs at this intersection of public and private sector interests and he points to the way in which such friction can undermine competitiveness and the economic growth that international trade could otherwise generate. An underlying theme of this compendium is the evident lack of knowledge and skills required to alleviate such friction by more effectively navigating the complexities of regulatory requirements in this important area of business activity.

This timely publication represents a significant milestone in addressing this emerging need for knowledge and skills development. After firstly setting the scene of how, why and where government and commercial interests intersect, it takes the reader on a journey of the regulatory policies, practices and procedural requirements associated with cross-border trade in a comprehensive yet remarkably concise fashion. While maintaining a clearly commercial perspective of international trade that is founded on the theory and practice of logistics and supply chain management, the reader is provided with a thorough introduction to the intricacies of the cross-border regulatory environment, some of which are quite technical in nature. As Andrew rightly says, 'the challenge in global cross-border logistics is not just one of transporting goods at a low cost, but also one of managing the necessary compliance requirements'.

I admire the way in which Andrew has managed to present a comprehensive coverage of this complex subject in such a readable fashion. The style in which he firstly introduces and then explores the various topics enables a relative novice to understand the concepts under discussion, while at the same time providing the more knowledgeable reader with an insightful coverage of the subject matter. Indeed, Professor Grainger is to be congratulated for providing us with this excellent tome, which represents a significant and timely contribution to the body of knowledge in this important area of economic growth. Written from the perspective of one whose livelihood depends on knowing the rules, it will become a 'must-have' text for practitioners from both the public and private sectors, as well as students and others who wish to learn why border formalities are more than 'just a bit of paperwork and a few checks'.

Professor David Widdowson
President, International Network of Customs Universities
Chief Executive Officer, Centre for Customs and Excise Studies, Charles Sturt University

01

Cross-border logistics operations

On most maps borders between countries are easy to find. They are depicted as lines separating one country from the other. Political maps add even more contrast by using different colours to highlight the space that is commanded by the respective countries around the world. The legends of maps and atlases provide yet further context; for example, by explaining that thick lines depict international boundaries and dotted lines the state (federal) and provincial boundaries (Informa, 2019). Google Maps uses solid grey lines for undisputed international boundaries, while dashed grey lines are used for treaty boundaries (which are defined by a treaty or similar agreement, but not finalized in law), de facto boundaries (not set by treaty but used by all states involved), and disputed boundaries (Google, 2021). Thus, when viewing maps, we have become accustomed to viewing borders as boundaries which set countries apart.

However, those very same maps also depict geographic features such as rivers and oceans. These types of boundaries, in our modern world, do not have to divide, and are the backbone to global trade. About 80 per cent (by volume) of global trade is carried by sea (Benamara *et al*, 2017). Oceans and rivers – just like roads, railway lines, tunnels, bridges and airports – connect. The easier and cheaper connections are, the greater are the trade opportunities. And connecting businesses that trade with each other is what logistics and transport operations are about. Goods in the hands of sellers are converted into items of value in the hands of buyers. Without logistics and transport, trade would not take place. Without goods finding themselves in the right amount, in the right condition, at the right place, at the right time and at the right cost, there would be no sale!

A key principle within economic geography is that the lower the costs for moving goods are, the greater the catchment of the market. With increasing size and scope for competition this in turn helps bring down the price of goods sold on that market. Adam Smith, for example, writes that:

> Good roads, canals and navigable rivers, by diminishing the expense of carriage, put the remote parts of the country more nearly upon a level with those in the neighbourhood of the town. They are upon that account the greatest of all improvements.
>
> SOURCE Smith, 1776, Book 1, Chapter XI, Part 1

However, markets are normally subject to rules that must be followed to gain access. Moving on from the time of Smith, even today market inspectors in towns across the world are likely to check that stall operators use weights and measures correctly, follow sanitation and hygiene guidelines, and that relevant fees and taxes have been paid. Crucially, though, in today's modern state, the trade rules that once might have been associated with individual market towns, and thus local in nature, now tend to be part of a body of rules that apply to the entire country. Trade and customs tariffs, amongst many other aspects of business regulation, apply.

Subsequently, the challenge in global cross-border logistics is not just one of transporting goods at a low cost, but also one of managing the necessary compliance requirements. Commonly these are enforced at the borders. The image that comes to mind is one of a boom barrier, where authorities such as Customs stop traffic and only let goods through once satisfied that all regulatory requirements have been met. Indeed, the United Nation's Convention on Road Signs and Signals (UN, 1968) recommended sign for border controls is a black horizontal line framed within a red circle, notifying any driver approaching a border that they may not pass without stopping at the Customs' boom barrier. Logistics practitioners around the world, with very little prompting, are usually able to share stories of significant border-related delays. Likewise, customs and border officials are often quick to highlight success stories, where they have managed to intercept illegal trades – the media frequently celebrates such stories (AAP, 2020).

However, as countries move together, not all borders are the same. Trade agreements between countries help bring down trade obstacles. This has a direct impact on the border arrangements. Some borders, such as those between the members of the European Union, are without any border control facilities at all. In line with global efforts towards trade-led economic growth there is also a lot of attention on trade and border formalities. Associated costs are to be reduced in the form of trade facilitation. Likewise, the enforcement of shared rules should be effective and in line with good border management practice.

Compliances requirements

The regulatory requirements that apply to the trade in goods between countries can be extensive. The World Trade Organization (WTO), however, sets two fundamental principles that apply to all of its members – which at more than 160 member states encompasses all of the world's largest markets – to make sure that trade is fair:

- The first is the Most Favoured Nation (MFN) principle for the trade in goods. It holds that countries cannot normally discriminate between their trading partners (GATT, 1947, Article 1). Any favours granted to one partner must be extended to all other WTO members – they are as such all 'most favoured'. But exceptions within the framework of more comprehensive preferential trade agreements (including free trade agreements, FTAs) are allowable (Trebilcock *et al*, 2013); and with another 300 of them in place, they are a key feature in today's global business environment (WTO, 2020).
- The second principle is 'national treatment', where any imported and locally produced goods should be treated equally (GATT, 1947, Article 3).

Despite these principles, trade is seldom 'free'. Import tariffs frequently apply to protect certain industries from foreign competition.

Most countries also have concerns about safety and security and will seek to protect themselves from risks that are associated with the cross-border movement of goods. These can, to give a few examples, relate to the smuggling of arms or to making sure that the vehicles used to carry goods are safe and operated in line with national transport legislation (Lowe and Pidgeon, 2020). Likewise, most countries enforce strict measures to safeguard against environment- and health-related risks. Such measures frequently apply to foods, products of animal origin and of the soil. Compliance requirements with such sanitary and phytosanitary requirements can be particularly complex. Inspections along with tests and mandatory border checks are often necessary. Many types of business regulations concerning market and consumer protection frequently spill over into border compliance requirements, too (see Box 1.1).

BOX 1.1

Regulatory regimes frequently applied at national borders: examples

The collection and payment of import tax, including tariffs

- Customs tariffs, which are usually a percentage figure based on the value and origin of the goods.
- Value added tax (VAT), which applies in many countries around the world and requires businesses to pay tax when selling goods, including imports (so-called Import VAT); VAT regimes often also allow businesses to claim back VAT that has been paid on inputs and zero-rate (ie not charge VAT) when exporting goods.
- Excise duties, which are additional taxes that apply to some types of goods and need to be paid when sold to customers whether domestically produced or imported; the range of goods subject to excise duties depends on the country concerned, but typically includes mineral oils (like petrol), tobacco and alcohol products.

Tariff quotas and restrictions (economic trade policy measures)

- Anti-dumping and countervailing measures which are designed to offset the advantages of unfairly priced imported goods; for example, because they are sold for export at prices lower than at home, or where the manufacturer has benefited unfairly from financial subsidies.
- Tariff quotas, where importers may temporarily benefit from tariff suspensions or tariff rates that are below the normal rate. These are subject to application and often come into play where domestic production can bear some limited competition from foreign producers, or where goods are seasonal, and the protection of domestic production conferred through customs tariffs is not required when out of season.

Safety and security

- Export controls and licences that are often enforced by countries that seek to restrict or prohibit certain types of exports. Often this applies to goods that can have military uses (even if designed for civilian use) or are at risk of being diverted to countries against which trade sanctions have been imposed; they often also apply to goods of national heritage.
- Interventions to stop clandestine and deliberately mis-declared cross-border traffic.
- Immigration controls, to make sure the operators of vehicles moving goods are compliant with applicable immigration conditions.
- Vehicle checks and procedures to make sure that the vehicles moving goods are safe. The requirements and practices will differ significantly from one type of transport mode to the next as well as one country to the next. Objects of control will often extend to vehicle and operator licensing, weight constraints and insurance certification.
- Radiological checks, which might be enforced routinely to intercept illegal trade in radioactive materials; but also specialist checks to identify radioactive contaminations in goods such as soil and metals that have been exposed to nuclear disasters (eg the Chernobyl and Fukushima disasters).
- Dangerous goods procedures, to make sure that goods that are hazardous (eg because they are explosive, gasses, flammable, oxidizing, toxic, infectious, radioactive or corrosive) are appropriately handled.

Environment and health

- Phytosanitary controls that apply to 'products of the soil' with the aim of protecting against pests harmful to plants and plant products. The extent of control can differ significantly from country to country. A subset of phytosanitary controls are those specific to wood packing – including wooden pallets, crates and dunnage – that are widely used in international trade operations.
- Veterinary controls that apply to living animals as well as 'products of animal origin' (eg meat, bone and leather). The aim of these controls is to prevent the spread of animal-borne diseases to both livestock and humans.
- Quarantine controls, which is an umbrella term used in many countries for both phytosanitary and veterinary controls; often the acronym SPS – standing for sanitary and phytosanitary – is used.
- Live animal controls concerning safeguards to ensure animal welfare.
- Food controls that range from conditions about hygiene and handling to safeguards against 'high risks', such as aflatoxins in nuts, pesticides in farmed goods, traces of antibiotics in farmed fish and meat, illegal dyes in chilli products, and any other food contaminants.
- Endangered species of wild flora and fauna controls, especially those falling under the Convention on International Trade in Endangered Species of Wild Fauna and Flora (CITES, 1973).
- Ships' waste, which in many parts of the world needs to be accounted for at so-called 'port reception facilities'.
- Ozone-depleting substances, such as chlorofluorocarbons used in older refrigeration systems and halons used in older fire extinguishers, are subject to strict prohibitions or licensing requirements.

Market and consumer protection

- Strict product safety standards for electronics, toys and cosmetics, which for the European market includes the CE label that must be attached to applicable products.
- Product labelling requirements, including details about product ingredients and product descriptions – including compliance with so-called geographic indicators like 'Scotch whisky' or 'Parma ham'.

- Intellectual copyright and trademark protection, where border agencies have been tasked with intercepting breaches, including the importation of counterfeit and pirated goods.
- Horticulture and marketing standards, which apply to the description of quality for fruit and vegetables and are subject to official inspections – which in many countries also apply to importers.

The steps to clear goods can be extensive, especially when considering the fact that most borders have two sides and that both export and import procedures apply. Many import procedures are also conditional on requirements that must be met in the country of export. For instance, if businesses wish to take advantage of preferential or free trade agreements (see Chapter 2), they must normally provide proof that their goods are eligible by reference to the applicable 'preferential origin rules' (Box 2.2). Without that proof the importer would have to pay the full import tariff rate and is likely to procure from elsewhere. Additional transport and logistics conditions can (but not in all agreements) apply, such as the need for direct shipment and non-alteration as well as restrictions on handling, including splitting cargo into multiple consignments.

The volume of trade-related paperwork – or its electronic equivalent – can also be extensive. The BBC, for example, reported that 71 pages of paperwork is necessary for the export of one lorry load of fish from the United Kingdom (UK) to the European Union (EU) (Jones *et al*, 2021). Although the trade in fish is particularly prone to paperwork, the described procedures will be recognizable to seafood traders elsewhere in the world, too (Figure 1.1). Next to the commercial arrangement between the exporter and buyer (including transport), arrangements also need to be made for health certificates, catch certificates (to prove fish is not illegally fished from depleted stocks – a requirement in the UK and EU), preferential origin documents to prove eligibility to free trade arrangements, customs export documents, import inspection documents and customs import clearance documents.

FIGURE 1.1 Documentary requirements commonly required for the trade in fish products

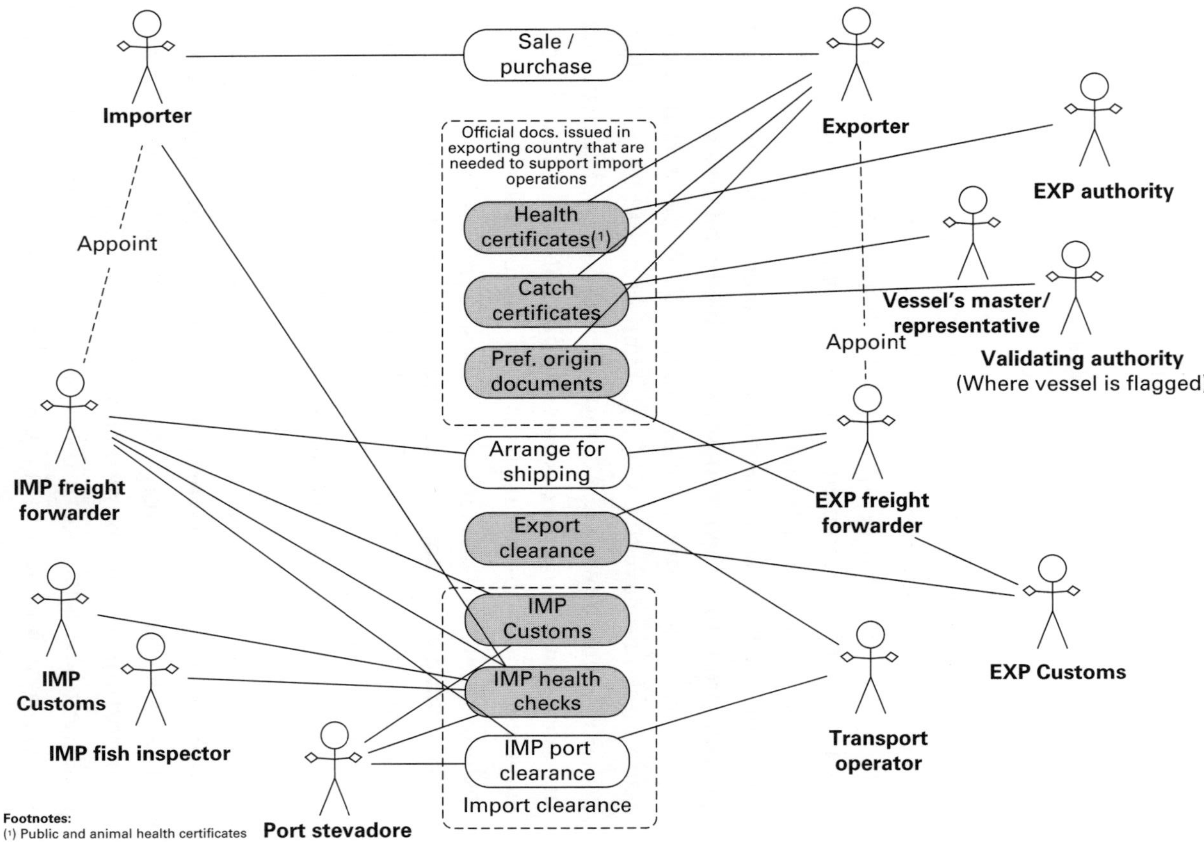

Footnotes:
(1) Public and animal health certificates

SOURCE © Trade Facilitation Consulting Ltd

The example of trade in fish is one of many. Important to note is that each procedure and document might have additional requirements. For example, Customs along with other border agencies in the country of import, such as the Fish Health Inspectorate, need to be notified that the goods are coming (see Chapter 3). Arrangements for the payment of duties and fees need to be put in place. Subscriptions to electronic compliance systems are often necessary. Usually, copies of relevant documents (or their electronic equivalent) need to be retained. Some procedures are also subject to post-clearance controls. Each agency involved is likely to have its own specific additional requirements (see Chapter 4).

Seldom is one single party responsible for all compliance aspects. Usually, the seller and buyer will agree who is responsible for export formalities and who is responsible for import formalities – along with applicable transport and logistics obligations – when agreeing the sale. Often this will be done by applying standard terms, such as the International Chamber of Commerce's (ICC) Incoterms® 2020 (see Chapter 6). Figure 1.1 already touches upon the operators and government agencies involved in the trade in fish products. In most trades there are more parties involved. These include:

- customs brokers, agents and freight forwarders to help prepare and submit customs declarations on behalf of the importer or exporter;
- transport and shipping companies who transport goods from one country to the next and inevitably need to present those goods to authorities at the border facilities. In many countries the transport operator also has to lodge the customs pre-notifications – telling authorities that cargo is about to come so that they can make decisions about inspections before the cargo arrives;
- terminal operators and cargo-handling companies, especially at seaports and airports, who load and offload cargo from ships or aircraft, and are also relied upon to take cargo to the inspection facilities;
- banks, who arrange for the payment of inspection-related charges – especially those incurred by the transport operators, cargo-handling companies and terminal operators in conjunction with clearing goods;

- official laboratories, that are used to conduct tests – especially those concerning veterinary and phytosanitary controls;
- transit shed and terminal operators, who may hold goods in temporary storage until goods are cleared by the authorities.

Sophisticated electronic systems are often relied upon to help coordinate compliance and handling operations. In some cases, much of the interaction between business operators and the regulatory agencies is highly automated (see Chapter 3). Goods may clear at the speed it takes for one computer to talk to another. However, such operations require preparation. Obtaining all the data required to complete the necessary notifications and declarations – along with any additional certificates, licences or permits that apply to goods subject to prohibitions and restrictions (Chapter 4) – can be an extensive operational undertaking.

Border agencies and control

Typically, the main agency at the border is Customs. One of its main tasks – next to trade facilitation (Chapter 9) and the protection of society – is the collection of revenue (WCO, 2019b). Institutional arrangements, as discussed in Chapter 2, can differ depending on the country concerned. The customs administration might be constituted as a dedicated agency and enjoy a significant degree of autonomy. The customs function might be performed by a specialist ministerial department (often the finance ministry). Customs-related activities might be part of the responsibilities of a dedicated revenue authority tasked with collecting all taxes, including those due on goods when crossing borders. Some countries may also distinguish between administrative type activities – such as processing import and export declarations – and border enforcement activities. In the UK, for example, the former falls under the remit of HM Revenue and Customs while the latter is the responsibility of UK Border Force, which is also responsible for immigration checks. In many countries certain border enforcement-type activities might also be the responsibility of a dedicated border police or border guard.

Other, non-customs agencies with an interest in the border controls include:

- immigration authorities;
- national trade boards or trade ministries;
- a wide range of specialist agencies with expertise in the enforcement of vehicle controls;
- a wide range of specialist agencies with focus on quarantine as well as food and hygiene measures, such as plant health, veterinary and sanitary inspectors;
- a wide range of agencies with concern for product specific standards and safety;
- export and import licensing agencies;
- police authorities;
- intelligence agencies;
- national statistics offices.

In addition to the above, traders themselves might conduct certain types of tests and inspections – eg to confirm product quality or compliance with voluntary standards, such as those relating to organic produce.

The mix of border management objectives is broad, and in part reflects the forces that drive the many regulatory regimes that underpin them. Logistics and transport operators generally have to worry about compliance with procedures governing the control of goods along with those that impact on the movement of those goods, especially those relating to transport, but also those concerning immigration rules for drivers and crews. Border agencies need to make sure that their operations do not unnecessarily impede wealth generating trade, but yet also need to make sure that regulatory objectives are met by safeguarding against various threats to society (see Chapter 7, Figure 7.1). To give a few examples, these include threats to:

- national income (revenue), arising from uncollected taxes and duties;
- the market, arising from unfair competition by non-compliant businesses;

- public policy, arising from illegal imports of prohibited goods (eg drugs and weapons);
- public security, arising from uncontrolled trades in arms and weapons;
- health and life of humans, arising unsafe goods;
- the health of animals and plants, arising from illegal imports of diseased and high-risk goods;
- the environment, arising from the illegal trade in regulated pollutants, such as waste and ozone-depleting substances;
- national and international treasures, arising from illegal trade in cultural artefacts;
- industrial and commercial property, arising from loss of intellectual property rights.

Prevailing trade and customs policy

Trade, including its rules, has a long history. For example, trade from boats around the Mediterranean can be dated back to around 7000 BC (Curtin, 1984). There are several accounts of ancient trade treaties, including those between Carthage and Rome in 509 BC (Mann, 1986). Evidence of ancient customs law as applied in Rome can still be viewed today. The Monument from Ephesus on display at the Ephesus Archaeological Museum in Selçuk, Turkey, is one such example (Cottier *et al,* 2008). Today, many cities will still maintain public reference displays of standard weights and measures. In London, for example, public reference locations for the imperial measurements of inches, yards, links, perches and poles can be found in Trafalgar Square (placed in the north terrace wall), in the Great Hall of the Guildhall and outside the Royal Observatory in Greenwich.

Many of the contemporary institutions which define today's global economic environment have their roots in the 1944 Bretton Woods Agreement (Stubbs and Underhill, 1994), which concerned the post-World War II reconstruction of market economies, designed to generate prosperity and secure peace through interdependence and trade. The International Monetary Fund (IMF) and the World Bank Group were brought into existence. As highlighted in Chapter 9 (see Box 9.1), other key institutions such as the World Trade Organization and the World Customs Organization can also trace their roots to post-World War II reconstruction efforts through trade-led growth and co-dependence.

A global production structure has unfolded (Dicken, 2011). It is characterized by low trade and customs tariffs for most types of goods; but still with significant tariffs in some industries (Chapter 2). It is also characterized by the liberalization in finance that has allowed for funds to move freely, including for foreign direct investment. Markets now tend to be viewed from a more global perspective (Levitt, 1983; Prahalad and Doz, 1986; Douglas and Wind, 1987). This has also been aided by revolutionary innovations in transport and logistics technology, especially the humble shipping container. In the 1960s ships still spent about 60 per cent of their time laid up in ports (Goss, 1968). Today, a modern container vessel many times larger can be turned around within hours! The cost of international shipping has come down markedly (Levinson, 2006). Competition now takes place between firms that are part of global supply chains (Chapter 8).

For border agencies the growing volumes in trade have created several challenges. With only finite resources at their disposal, rapidly increasing trade volumes require new control approaches. Innovation, for example by using electronic systems, has become necessary. New control practices, such as risk management, have become necessary, too (Chapter 2). These allow for differentiation between business operators that are likely to be compliant and those that are not. Available control and inspections resources are focused on the latter; coercions and sanctions are applied to help improve compliance behaviour. Access to business partnership programmes (Chapter 7) and authorizations conferring access to advantageous customs treatment (eg customs warehousing, duty deferment) can provide further incentives for virtuous behaviour.

However, there still remains widespread concern about the regulatory burden created by trade and customs procedures. Overly heavy-handed border management practices and compliance requirements add to business costs. They undermine business competitiveness; affected business communities are less able to take part in the global economy. When compared to the demise in trade tariffs – the average applied tariff rate worldwide has been at or less than 3 per cent since 2006 (UNCTAD, 2019) – trade-related compliance costs experienced by business operators, which some suggest might be many times more (OECD, 2009), seem disproportionate. The international trade policy community thus has placed more and more effort on such non-tariff barriers.

Many ideas and measures to help bring down compliance costs and facilitate trade without undermining control objectives have been developed (Grainger, 2011) and is the subject of trade facilitation (Chapter 9). Key trade facilitation ideas draw on notions of cooperation and coordination – either between compliant business operators and the border agencies or between Customs and other border agencies to help streamline operations and avoid duplication (Chapter 7). The main ideas tend to concern the simplification, harmonization, standardization and modernization of trade and customs procedures (UNECE, 2012). Since February 2017 many standard trade-facilitation ideas have become formal commitments in the form of the WTO Trade Facilitation Agreement (WTO, 2017). Subsequently many trade-facilitation-focused reform projects have been launched in most countries around the world. Developing countries may, under WTO mechanisms, access funds to support their efforts (WTO, 2021).

Challenges in cross-border logistics operations

Inevitably, the operational requirements and practices differ between the many organizations involved. For government administrations, the guiding rationale might be to safeguard regulatory objectives that apply to goods as they move across the border. For business operators it would be to ensure compliance whilst taking advantage of global trade opportunities. Both stakeholder groups within the cross-border environment have an interest in managing cost: be it to make best use of scarce resources in the administration of trade and border controls; or be it to ensure that goods move across borders as efficiently as possible. There is a lot of common ground between those that seek to enforce controls and those that want to be compliant. The trick is to provide for an operational framework that accommodates those respective needs.

The supply chain metaphor – where operations are depicted as a string of activities – features strongly within cross-border logistics operations. For government agencies there is an emerging awareness that borders might not always be the best place for controls. It is worth reaching out across horizontal lines with relevant parties in the country from which goods originate and with relevant parties at the final destination. Those parties might be colleagues across the border, they might be business operators that have been suitably incentivized to take on some of the control burden themselves, for example, in order to take advantage of preferential or fast-track treatment at the border. It is also worthwhile for government agencies to reach out across vertical lines, to make sure that the various agencies with an interest in cross-border operations work together as efficiently as possible (Chapter 7).

The supply chain metaphor is important for business operators, too. Compliance responsibilities are frequently subcontracted to specialists, such as freight forwarders and customs brokers. They are also shaped by the commercial arrangements agreed between sellers and buyers that concern transport, risk and regulatory compliance for export, transit and import (Chapter 6). Compliance mistakes give rise to fines and penalties. They also have an impact on business relationships, especially where goods cannot be delivered on time, and on the relationship with the border agencies, including access to any preferential treatment. Inevitably, competitiveness is undermined.

However, operational performance in cross-border logistics is also of concern to trade and customs policy makers. If business competitiveness is undermined, it will also spill over into wider economic performance. Taxes may not be paid; businesses may choose to forgo export markets; foreign direct investment may be less forthcoming; businesses and consumers do not benefit from global market opportunities. Yet policy makers also need to worry about making sure that regulatory objectives are met, including those that protect business from unfair competition, consumers from unsafe products, the environment from undesirable trades, and over societal needs, such as security. As such, cross-border operations should not just be understood as a transaction challenge between business operators and border agencies. It is also about the forces that govern the wider regulatory environments, including the form and shape of governing laws, regulations and procedures.

The latter is in constant flux. For example, subsequent to the 9/11 attacks in the United States, supply chain security and partnership arrangements between border agencies and with business operators became a priority for many customs administrations (Widdowson *et al,* 2014). Some countries may alternate between a liberal and protectionist trade policy outlook, depending on political sentiments and the specific needs of their citizens and business communities. Many countries agree to deeper collaboration by aligning applicable rules and procedures; often also agreeing to how their respective authorities can best work together in the administration of applicable trade and customs procedures. The Comprehensive and Progressive Agreement for Trans-Pacific Partnership (CPTPP) signed in March 2018 by 11 economies across the Pacific is one such example, but there are hundreds of others (WTO, 2020). Some countries may, as was the case between the UK and the EU, choose to take different paths – replacing access to a single market with that of a partnership agreement (EU and UK, 2020). Thus, cross-border operations are deeply entangled in this interplay between trade and customs policy. The subject, therefore, is at once political and operational, but also has – as discussed in this book – significant administrative, legal, technological, commercial and economic dimensions.

Skills needed

The skills needed for cross-border logistics operations depend in part on the organizations involved and how they manage customs-related functions. Customs managers within large multinational companies, for example, focus their efforts on three areas (Grainger, 2016):

1. The first relates to logistics support, to ensure that goods clear borders as planned and on time.
2. The second area relates to supply chain management, where least cost options are explored to mitigate customs and duty liabilities – for example, by procuring goods from countries that benefit from preferential (lower) duty rates or equivalence agreements, where regulations in the non-custom area benefit from a lower regulatory compliance burden.
3. The third part of their job, and perhaps the most significant, is also to make sure that the company has appropriate compliance systems in place to protect the company's reputation with the authorities, reduce its exposure to harshly applied border controls, and give consumers (and shareholders) confidence that their company operates within the parameters of regulatory expectations.

In order to do their job effectively customs managers:

- require advanced knowledge of the applicable trade and customs procedures, know when to refer to specialist third parties (eg customs agents and brokers) and monitor the services that they provide;
- have systems in place to make sure that the company overall, wherever their locations are, has robust compliance capabilities;
- need to ensure their company complies with reporting and training requirements, which can differ from country to country.

In some countries staff making customs declarations are required (or are strongly encouraged) to pass official qualifications, such as a customs broker's exam. In some places, they also need to be licensed by Customs to make a customs declaration. Often, customs managers also need to develop a good rapport with the border agencies. This is not just to help make sure that any operational challenges can be quickly addressed, but also to help lend input into the form and shape of applicable rules and procedures. More and more countries around the world will actively seek their input – for example via so-called National Trade Facilitation Committees (Grainger, 2014) – to make sure that any impediments to trade through poorly applied procedures can be adequately addressed.

The job of a border official requires extensive expertise. Most officers will be specialists in specific aspects of their role, whether operational, legal, administrative, technical or policy. Border officials, such as customs officers, often need to complete extensive training (European Commission, 2019). Many countries around the world provide that training at dedicated customs universities or academies. Several of them also offer programmes open to students from outside of Customs. Several of those institutions also subscribe to the professional standards recommended by the WCO's Partnership in Customs Academic Research and Development (PICARD) programme (WCO, 2019a). The standard requires that professionals should have detailed knowledge of a wide range of issues (Box 1.2). Some – such as that of legal systems, economics, change and project management, human resource management, media and communications – have well established literatures, along with dedicated text books. Most are more specialist in nature for which this book aims to provide a detailed overview.

BOX 1.2

Customs knowledge requirements listed in the WCO PICARD standard

1. The customs business, including revenue collection, trade compliance, the protection of society, safety and security, and protection against unfair trade.
2. The interactions between Customs and other government agencies.
3. Customs policy.
4. The judicial and legal systems.
5. The international supply chain.
6. International economics.
7. Strategic planning.
8. Change management.
9. Project, programme and portfolio management.

10 Risk management.

11 Information/knowledge management.

12 Emerging technologies.

13 Financial management.

14 Human resource management.

15 Customs instruments.

16 Customs management.

17 Public and media relations, and communication.

Summary of this book

Chapter 1 'Cross-border logistics operations' aims to give a broad overview of the subject by setting the scene. It gives a broad summary of the many regulatory compliance requirements and parties involved. It also gives an account of the forces that have brought the contemporary global productions structure to life within which cross-border logistics operations take place.

Chapter 2 'Customs administration, tariffs and other taxes' touches upon the customs business with specific focus on the institutional arrangements, import duties and the classification, valuation and origin rules for calculating applicable trade tariffs. The chapter also elaborates on special customs arrangements that allow for customs duties and other import taxes to be suspended or deferred.

Chapter 3 'Customs declarations and control' focuses on the steps necessary for business operators to submit declarations and for customs officers to assess and process those declarations. It also elaborates on risk assessment practices along with cargo inspection and the payment of import taxes. The chapter also introduces how such arrangements might be electronically facilitated. Procedures for transit are outlined, too, as are customs business support activities.

Chapter 4 'Prohibitions, restrictions and other border procedures' considers those goods that are subject to additional control requirements, often enforced by other government agencies in cooperation with Customs.

Chapter 5 'Border facilities: Operations and design' takes a close look at the operational practices at the border and elaborates further on the required border facilities and their operations. It also considers various factors that shape their design, including service needs and spatial considerations.

Chapter 6 'International trade and customs compliance management' focuses on the practices of businesses involved in international trade. It draws particular attention to compliance practices, including the commercial arrangements (Incoterms®, 2020) between sellers and buyers. The chapter details the role of customs brokers and agents along with other service providers frequently relied upon in international trade. The chapter also discusses in detail some of the more practical aspects of the customs manager's work.

Chapter 7 'Coordinated border management and supply chain security' considers how the various border agencies might work together at home. It also considers the scope for coordination and cooperation across borders along with support trade and customs policy. This chapter also considers the subject of supply chain security, where customs administrations seek to develop partnership arrangements with suitably trusted business operators to extend controls beyond the confines of border posts.

Chapter 8 'Logistics, supply chain management and borders' provides a review of current theories and practices in logistics and supply chain management. It builds on this review to highlight the relevance of borders to contemporary logistics and supply chain management thinking. It also considers the costs experienced by business operators with Customs and other government agencies at the border, along with models for how those costs might be addressed through trade and customs policy.

Chapter 9 'Trade facilitation' follows on from the previous chapter by reviewing contemporary trade and customs policy measures that seek to reduce the costs experienced by business operators whilst still safeguarding regulatory control objectives. The reviewed trade facilitation ideas are then discussed by reference to their objectives, which are: to make international trade more efficient, less costly and easier; to harness data-sharing technologies to best effect; to improve coordination and cooperation between the various parties involved in cross-border logistics operations; and to assess and evaluate frictions in cross-border logistics operations, hold the relevant parties accountable to their promises and obligations, and to learn and innovate.

Chapter 10 The final chapter in this book focuses on 'Borders and disaster relief logistics operations'. As such it offers a practical illustration of logistics operations and border management practices along with yet more pressing and urgent demands for trade facilitation.

> ACTIVITIES AND DISCUSSION POINTS
>
> 1 Type 'goods stuck at border [country of your choice]' into an internet news search engine. What are the main news stories and what are the reported issues causing those delays? Discuss.
>
> 2 Repeat the above for the terms 'border officials seized' and 'customs stopped'. By reference to the main news stories discuss why border controls are necessary.
>
> 3 Consider the forces that give shape to global production and how inefficient border practices might undermine global supply chain operations. Discuss.

References

AAP (2020) Two charged after police seize yacht off NSW coast allegedly packed with drugs, *The Guardian,* 19 April, www.theguardian.com/world/2020/apr/19/two-charged-after-police-seize-yacht-off-nsw-coast-allegedly-packed-with-drugs (archived at https://perma.cc/Y6C7-J7BF)

Benamara, H, Hoffmann, J and Youssef, F (2017) Demand, supply and freight rates: the shipping of global trade, in *International Freight Transport,* pp 13–56, eds A Beresford and S Pettit, Kogan Page, London

CITES (1973) Convention on International Trade in Endangered Species of Wild Fauna and Flora (as amended), United Nations, Washington, DC

Cottier, M, Crawford, M, Crowther, C, Ferrary, J, Levick, B, Salomies, O and Wörrle, M (2008) *The Customs Law of Asia*, Oxford University Press, Oxford

Curtin, PD (1984) *Cross-Cultural Trade in World History*, Cambridge University Press, Cambridge

Dicken, P (2011) *Global Shift: Mapping the changing contours of the world economy*, Los Angeles, CA, SAGE, London

Douglas, SP and Wind, Y (1987) The myth of globalization, *Columbia Journal of World Business,* **22** (4), p 19

European Commission (2019) The CustComp[eu], EU Customs Competency Framework, European Union, Brussels

EU and UK (2020) Trade and Cooperation Agreement between the European Union and the European Atomic Energy Community, of the one part, and the United Kingdom of Great Britain and Northern Ireland, on the other part, *Offical Journal of the European Union,* **63** (L444), pp 14–1462

GATT (1947) The General Agreement on Tariffs and Trade, World Trade Organization

Google (2021) Google Maps Help, support.google.com/maps/answer/3145721?hl=en-GB (archived at https://perma.cc/NDK5-3YQE)

Goss, RO (1968) *Studies in Maritime Economics*, Cambridge University Press, Cambridge

Grainger, A (2011) Trade Facilitation: a conceptual review, *Journal of World Trade,* **45** (1), pp 39–62

Grainger, A (2014) The WTO Trade Facilitation Agreement: Consulting the private sector, *Journal of World Trade,* **48** (6)

Grainger, A (2016) Customs management in multinational companies, *World Customs Journal,* **10** (2)

Informa (2019) 2018–19 Lloyd's Maritime Atlas of World Ports and Shipping Places, 30th edn, Informa Publishing Group, Colchester

Jones, L, Bailey, D and Huynh, L (2021) Brexit: 71 pages of paperwork for 1 lorry of fish, BBC, London, https://www.bbc.co.uk/news/business-55887043 (archived at https://perma.cc/457D-3G7C)

Levinson, M (2006) *The Box: How the shipping container made the world smaller and the world economy bigger,* Princeton University Press, Princeton, NJ

Levitt, T (1983) The globalization of markets, *Harvard Business Review,* **61** (3), p 92

Lowe, D and Pidgeon, C (2020) *Lowe's Transport Manager's and Operator's Handbook 2020,* Kogan Page, London

Mann, M (1986) *The Sources of Social Power,* Cambridge University Press, Cambridge

OECD (2009) Overcoming border bottlenecks: The costs and benefits of trade facilitation. Organisation for Economic Co-operation and Development, Paris

Prahalad, CK and Doz, Y (1986) *The Dynamics of Global Competition*, Free Press

Smith, A (1776) *The Wealth of Nations: Books I-III*, Penguin Classics (1997)

Stubbs, R and Underhill, GRD (1994) *Global Issues and Historic Perspectives. Political economy and the changing global order,* pp 145–62, Macmillan, London

Trebilcock, MJ, Howse, R and Eliason, A (2013) *The Most Favoured Nation Principle. The regulation of international trade,* pp 54–82, Routledge, London

UN (1968) Convention on Road Signs and Signals, 8 November 1968 (2006 consolidated version), United Nations Economic Commission for Europe, Geneva

UNCTAD (2019) Key statistics and trends in trade policy 2018, United Nations Conference on Trade and Development, Geneva

UNECE (2012) Trade facilitation: principles and benefits, 16 February, United Nations Economic Commission for Europe, tfig.unece.org/details.html (archived at https://perma.cc/7AH5-T8SB)

WCO (2019a) PICARD Professional Standards, World Customs Organization, Brussels

WCO (2019b) Strategic Plan 2019–2022, World Customs Organization, Brussels

Widdowson, D, Blegen, B, Kashubsky, M and Grainger, A (2014) Review of accredited operator schemes: an Australian study, *World Customs Journal,* 8 (1), pp 17–34

WTO (2017) WTO's Trade Facilitation Agreement enters into force, 22 February, World Trade Organization, www.wto.org/english/news_e/news17_e/fac_31jan17_e.htm (archived at https://perma.cc/5SAH-TZ9V)

WTO (2020) Regional Trade Agreements Database, 13 May, World Trade Organization, rtais.wto.org/UI/PublicMaintainRTAHome.aspx (archived at https://perma.cc/A76E-SWV4)

WTO (2021) Trade Facilitation Agreement Facility, World Trade Organization, www.tfafacility.org (archived at https://perma.cc/6YHH-L6BN)

02

Customs administrations, tariffs and other taxes

Customs

Customs administrations are specialists in the control of trade in goods. In most countries, the customs administration is the most visible government agency at the border and any goods moved across a border must be declared and placed under customs control until they have been formally released (Chapter 3). A key function of the customs administration is to collect all relevant import duties and other taxes, such as import VAT and excise duties. This understanding of customs is also reflected in the *Oxford English Dictionary*, which highlights that one of the historic uses of the word 'customs' refers to 'any tax or tribute paid to a lord or ruler' (*OED*, 2019).

However, Customs do not only serve revenue collection purposes; there is also a wide range of non-revenue specific control objectives (De Wulf, 2005). They concern the enforcement of prohibitions and restrictions (Chapter 4) and supply chain security, which seeks to safeguard against threats from organized criminals and terrorists (Chapter 7). In most countries, customs officers have extensive executive powers that allow them to stop and detain goods, for example: as part of an ongoing investigation into the parties involved in the trade; where there is good reason to believe that the goods have been smuggled; or where the correct procedures have not been followed. Furthermore, customs officers also play a prominent role in the enforcement of trade prohibitions and restrictions in concert with colleagues from other regulatory agencies. The list of goods subject to prohibitions and restrictions is generally long, and ranges from endangered species to anything that could be used in the manufacture of weapons for mass destruction. Examples of trades frequently impacted by restrictions include most medicines as well as most products of animal and plant origin (Chapter 4).

Inevitably, the administration of customs procedures is entangled in trade policy, be it to ensure that protectionist measures like trade tariffs are correctly applied or by ensuring that the bureaucratic requirements of customs administrations do not unnecessarily inhibit international trade opportunities (Chapters 8 and 9). And customs administrations are also expected to support legitimate businesses in their cross-border trade operations, for example, by giving access to special customs treatments and encouraging compliant behaviour, such as by giving compliant businesses with a good track record preference over businesses that have been found to be less compliant (Widdowson, 2005).

As experts in the control of goods, customs officers need to serve a wider range of regulatory regimes that often draw on different sources of national and international law. The activities of customs officers concern:

- revenue collection;
- the protection of business from unfair foreign competition;
- supply chain security;
- the prevention of trade in prohibited and unsafe goods;
- the enforcement of any export controls and restrictions;
- combatting illicit trades;
- provision of support to other, non-customs, government agencies;
- offering business support and trade facilitation.

The job of a customs officer might be **administrative**, where the focus is on processing declarations made by businesses – ideally, as efficiently and effective as possible. The job might also be in an **executive** capacity, where it is about holding and detaining goods. Usually, given the broad range of activities and technical nature of the governing regulatory regimes and supporting procedures, customs officers tend to specialize. Senior officers are likely to have gained knowledge of a wide range of technical and non-technical areas. Likewise, private-sector customs and trade managers who interact with customs officers need to be expert in the various compliance requirements specific to the goods and logistics operations for which they are responsible (Chapter 6).

Institutional arrangements

The institutional arrangements for customs tend to fall into one of four models (WCO, 2019b). The customs administration might be:

1. an autonomous 'customs agency' (even if affiliated to a ministry) – as is the case, for example, in China, Russia, Germany, Algeria and France;
2. a 'revenue authority' where the customs administration is part of an agency in which customs and tax authorities are integrated – as is the case, for example, in Poland, Kazakhstan, Ukraine, Bangladesh and Pakistan;
3. a 'ministerial department' where the customs administration is a department, bureau or division within a ministry, such as the ministry of finance or the ministry of the interior – as is the case, for example, in India, Indonesia, Turkey, Libya and Malaysia;
4. a 'border protection service' where the customs administration is, in addition to its customs portfolio, also responsible for immigration services, such as visa verification at borders service – as is the case, for example, in the United States, Australia and Canada.

The United Kingdom differs somewhat from the four standard models (Grainger, 2015). While import duties are collected by customs officers working for the UK's revenue authority – Her Majesty's Revenue and Customs Service (HMRC) – frontline enforcement staff responsible for the control of goods and people at the border (including immigration controls) are under the command of UK Border Force. UK Border Force is a separate body reporting to the Home Office (the UK's ministry responsible for home affairs such as security, law and order, policing and immigration).

When enforcing import and export controls, customs officers are also often relied upon to support colleagues in other government agencies, (Chapters 7). These often include the ministry/ies responsible for:

- finance;
- home affairs or the interior;
- trade and business;
- agriculture, environment, food and farming;
- health;
- defence;
- police services and border guards;
- military services... and others.

Much of the institutional cooperation relates to the enforcement of prohibitions and restrictions (Chapter 4).

Customs law

Customs law itself, to a large part, focuses on the collection of trade tariffs and making sure that goods are controlled by Customs before entering or leaving the country. The treaty 'Concerning the Creation of an International Union for the Publication of Customs Tariffs' that was signed in 1890, and then amended in 1950 (UN, 1950), is an early example of modern customs legislation. The League of Nations' 'International Convention relating to the Simplification of Customs Formalities' (League of Nations, 1923) is another.

Much of contemporary customs law is tied in with that of international trade law, especially within multilateral trade instruments such as those of the World Trade Organization (WTO) and its General Agreement on Tariffs and Trade (GATT, 1947, 1994b), but also within regional and bilateral trade and customs agreements. The corresponding responsibilities and procedures for customs administrations have become the focus on the Brussels-based Customs Cooperation Council, which in 1994 renamed itself as the World Customs Organization (WCO).

Most customs administrations around the world now work towards procedures that follow the recommendations of the WCO's Kyoto (Customs) Convention (WCO, 2019a). This convention serves as a blueprint for contemporary customs procedures (Box 2.1). It first came into force in 1976 and was then replaced by the current Revised Kyoto (Customs) Convention (WCO, 2006). Many of the provisions within the Revised Kyoto Convention are also made binding by the WTO's Trade Facilitation Agreement (WTO, 2014), which was adopted in 2017 to help reduce the bureaucratic burden that may arise between businesses and border agencies such as Customs (Chapter 9). Subsequently, customs procedures around the world benefit from a large degree of harmonization.

BOX 2.1

Revised Kyoto Convention: content and principles

The Convention's General Annex has 10 chapters:

Chapter 1: General Principle

Chapter 2: Definitions

Chapter 3: Clearance and Other Customs Formalities

Chapter 4: Duties and Taxes

Chapter 5: Security

Chapter 6: Customs Control

Chapter 7: Application of Information Technology

Chapter 8: Relationship Between the Customs and Third parties

Chapter 9: Information, Decisions and Ruling Supplied by the Customs

Chapter 10: Appeals in Customs Matters

In addition, the Convention's 10 specific annexes concern:

A. arrival of goods in a customs territory;

B. importation;
C. exportation;
D. customs warehouses and free zones;
E. transit;
F. processing;
G. temporary admission;
H. offences;
I. special procedures;
J. origin.

The underlying principles of the Convention seek to ensure that customs procedures:

- are transparent and predictable;
- are standardized and simplified;
- confer preferential treatment to suitably trusted individuals or companies;
- make maximum use of information technology;
- require minimal effort from the customs administration to ensure that businesses are compliant with applicable regulations;
- utilize risk management techniques, and audit-based controls;
- are developed and applied in partnership with the business community;
- are coordinated, along with any subsequent operational interventions, with other (non-customs) border agencies.

SOURCE Adapted from the Revised Kyoto Convention (WCO, 2006)

The WCO has also helped create a wide range of additional instruments, including the Harmonized System for the Classification of Goods (WCO, 2006), which drew on an earlier Customs Cooperation Council classification convention from 1959 and first came into force in 1988. It serves as the main classification system against which applicable customs tariffs are referenced. WTO valuation rules are used to work out the value upon which customs tariffs are to be based (GATT, 1994a). The WCO seeks to coordinate customs policy in other areas, too – especially with regard to supply chain security (see Chapter 7) and trade facilitation (Chapter 9).

Customs law will also be defined by national requirements, including the specification of the powers held by customs officers and the specific details for business compliance arrangements (Chapter 3). Customs laws is usually published in the form of a single Regulation (or Act) or a collection of Regulations (or Acts). Additional directives or implementing provisions may give specific details about how the regulations are to be applied. Often customs administrations may also publish administrative guidelines that set out how customs officers and the business community should interpret the body of customs law. Memoranda of Understanding (MoUs) are frequently relied upon to set out how the customs administration should work together with other border agencies. Demands from the business community to help make compliance simpler and without unnecessary friction (Chapter 9) – including provision for national electronic trade and customs systems – also increasingly feature within national customs legislation and policy.

It is difficult to generalize, but customs law in most countries will have substantive and procedural components. Substantive components largely concern the collection of import duties and taxes, including reference to the trade tariff and underpinning tariff classification, origin and valuation rules. Procedural elements concern customs control (Chapter 3), including import, export and transit formalities. In addition, there will be sections and provisions detailing: the powers of a customs officer; arrangements for fines and penalties; the right to appeal; and other related administrative and executive issues.

Import duties and taxes

As mentioned earlier, customs responsibilities are often placed within the revenue authority or under the jurisdiction of the finance ministry, thus emphasizing the collection of import duties and taxes as a central customs activity. A common distinction for the collection of taxes is between direct and indirect taxes. Direct taxes are those levied on the income or profit and are paid in the form of corporation or business taxes and income tax. Indirect taxes are taxes paid on goods or services and their consumption, such as value added taxes (VAT), sales taxes (GST), excise duties and customs duties. Customs administrations are normally always responsible for the collection of customs duties, but are often also tasked with the collection of other indirect taxes, especially import-related VAT and excise duties (WCO, 2019b).

How high are custom duties?

Customs duties can represent a significant source of income in some countries. For a few countries the share is as much as 20–30 per cent of the total tax income (eg Andorra, Bermuda, Cape Verde, Côte d'Ivoire, Guinea, Liberia and Vanuatu). In a number of economies, it is between 10 and 20 per cent (eg Iran, Pakistan or Bangladesh). For the majority of countries, however, revenue from customs duties represents a relatively small share of the total tax income – especially amongst the worlds' more developed economies (Table 2.1). Thus, customs duties are often not designed as a source of revenue, but more as a trade protection measure to safeguard certain business sectors from foreign competition.

Applicable customs duty rates are listed in the country's international trade tariff (often also referred to as customs tariff). Tariff rates are referenced against tariff classification numbers (frequently also referred to as customs or commodity codes) using the WCO's Harmonized System (HS System). The amount of customs duty due is listed as a percentage figure – an *ad valorem* rate – that is to be applied to the customs value.

All WTO member states, which with over 160 members includes most major markets, subscribe to the Most Favoured Nation (MFN) principle. This means that their respective trade tariffs must be made available to all members of the WTO without any discrimination. In 2018 the simple average MFN tariff rate amongst the world's largest economies ranged between 3.5 per cent for the United States and 17.1 per cent for India (Table 2.2). However, WTO rules (GATT,

TABLE 2.1 Customs duties in tax revenue (%): reported in bands against WCO member countries

Band	Countries
> 30%	None reported
>=20% and <30%	Andorra, Bermuda, Cape Verde, Côte d'Ivoire, Guinea, Liberia, Vanuatu
>=10% and <20%	Angola, Antigua and Barbuda, Bahamas, Bangladesh, Benin, Cambodia, Cameroon, Ecuador, Fiji, Guinea-Bissau, Haiti, Iran, Kazakhstan, Kyrgyzstan, Madagascar, Malawi, Maldives, Mali, Nepal, Pakistan, Paraguay, Samoa, Senegal, Suriname, Togo
>=5% and <10%	Algeria, Argentina, Armenia, Belize, Bolivia, Brazil, Dominican Republic, Egypt, Gabon, Guyana, India, Jamaica, Kosovo, Mongolia, Panama, Rwanda, Sri Lanka, Tanzania, Tonga, Uganda, Union of Myanmar (Republic of the), Zambia, Zimbabwe
>=0% and <5%	Australia, Bhutan, Botswana, Bulgaria, Canada, Chile, China, Colombia, Comoros, Costa Rica, Cyprus, Czech Republic, Denmark, El Salvador, Estonia, Eswatini, Finland, France, Georgia, Germany, Greece, Guatemala, Hong Kong (China), Hungary, Iceland, Indonesia, Ireland, Israel, Italy, Japan, Korea (Republic of), Latvia, Lithuania, Luxembourg, Malaysia, Malta, Mauritius, Mexico, Moldova, Morocco, Mozambique, Netherlands, New Zealand, North Macedonia, Palestine, Peru, Philippines, Poland, Portugal, Romania, Serbia, Seychelles, Singapore, Slovakia, Slovenia, South Africa, Spain, Sweden, Switzerland, Thailand, Tunisia, Turkey, Ukraine, United Kingdom, United States, Uruguay

SOURCE Extracted from WCO, 2019

1994a) do allow member countries to set lower preferential tariffs under certain conditions (Trebilcock *et al*, 2013). For example, WTO members may agree to free trade or regional trade agreements that apply only to goods traded amongst members of that free trade agreement. WTO members may also choose to offer preferential tariffs to developing countries without the expectation reciprocity, as is the case with the General System of Preference (GSP) (UNCTAD, 2021).

Moreover, any trade agreements must be notified to the WTO; and in 2020 more than 300 such agreements were in place (WTO, 2020b). Thus, by taking advantage of the lower duties available under such trade agreements, the average applied tariff rates paid by businesses is less than the average MFN tariff rates offered under WTO arrangements. When taking the volume of trade and use of lower preferential duty rates into account, the average 2018 applied tariff rates amongst the world's largest markets (ie the average tariff rate paid by traders) ranged between 1.7 per cent for the USA and 8.6 per cent for Brazil. But despite such low averages, a number of business sectors do benefit from significant tariff protection. For some goods the tariff rates are as high as 723 per cent in Japan, 549 per cent in Canada and 350 per cent in the United States (Table 2.2).

Moreover, Table 2.3 shows that the average MFN tariff rates for some types of product groups are significantly greater than in others. Dairy products in Canada and in the European Union, for example, are subject to particularly high average MFN rates (248.9 per cent and 43.6 per cent respectively). In both cases, domestic producers

TABLE 2.2 Simple average MFN rate, applied weighted mean tariff rate, range of MFN rates (2018)

Rank	Country	Simple average of the MFN *ad valorem* duty rates (2018)	Tariff rate, applied, weighted mean, all products (%) (2017)	Range of MFN tariff rates (2018)
1	United States of America	3.5	1.7	0–350
2	China	9.8	3.8	0–65
3	Japan	4.4	2.5	0–723
4	Germany	5.2	1.8	0–235
5	United Kingdom	5.2	1.8	0–235
6	France	5.2	1.8	0–235
7	India	17.1	5.8	0–150
8	Italy	5.2	1.8	0–235
9	Brazil	13.4	8.6	0–35
10	Canada	4.0	1.5	0–549

SOURCE Extracted from WTO datasets

thus benefit from significant protection from foreign competition. The level of tariff protection in other sectors, such as non-electrical machinery and transport equipment in Japan, is non-existent or less pronounced.

Which goods are protected and which goods are not is a political process that manifests itself in trade policy. Low or zero tariffs are commonly associated with an economic liberal outlook and the expectation of significant economic growth that is achieved through trade (Sally, 2008). But increased exposure to foreign competition can have an immediate adverse impact for some domestic producers. Such short-term pain may not always be easily squared with the anticipated long-term economic benefits derived from trade (George, 2010). Trade tariffs thus provide policy makers with a tool to help moderate any immediate adverse impacts of trade.

TABLE 2.3 MFN: simple average duty by product group (%) (2018)

Product/Sector	United States of America	Japan	India	European Union	China	Canada	Brazil
Animal products	2.3	13.2	32.5	17.9	14.2	24.4	8.3
Dairy products	19.6	95.1	34.8	43.6	12.3	248.9	18.3
Fruits, vegetables, plants	4.7	10.5	32.4	10.7	14.8	2.3	9.7
Coffee, tea	3.0	14.7	56.3	5.9	14.9	10.1	13.3
Cereals and preparations	3.1	37.5	37.1	14.9	23	20.6	10.7
Oilseeds, fats, oils	7.3	7.8	54.1	5.5	10.8	3.1	8.0
Sugars and confectionery	14.5	26.0	51.5	27.5	28.7	3.5	16.5
Beverages and tobacco	18.4	15.0	74.7	19.8	23.7	3.6	17.3
Cotton	5.0	0	26.0	0	18.0	0	6.4
Other agricultural products	1.1	3.9	29.0	3.3	11.8	6.1	7.7
Fish and fish products	0.7	5.6	30.0	11.6	10.9	0.9	10.3
Minerals and metals	1.8	1.0	11.0	2.0	7.8	1.0	10.1

(Continued)

TABLE 2.3 (Continued)

Product/Sector	United States of America	Japan	India	European Union	China	Canada	Brazil
Petroleum	1.8	0.7	9.2	2.5	5.3	0.9	0.1
Chemicals	2.8	2.1	10.2	4.5	6.7	0.7	8.1
Wood, paper, etc	0.6	0.9	10.0	0.9	4.1	1.0	10.4
Textiles	8.0	5.3	20.7	6.5	9.6	2.3	23.3
Clothing	11.7	9.0	20.5	11.5	16.1	16.5	35.0
Leather, footwear, etc	3.9	10.3	12.1	4.1	13.2	3.8	15.8
Non-electrical machinery	1.2	0	7.8	1.8	8.1	0.4	12.8
Electrical machinery	1.5	0.1	8.8	2.4	8.4	0.9	13.9
Transport equipment	2.9	0	31.1	4.7	12.3	5.5	19.0
Manufactures not elsewhere specified	2.2	1.1	11.1	2.2	11.6	2.5	15.2

SOURCE Extracted from WTO data

Other types of tariff measures

Trade protection may also result from how the tariff is structured. Often higher-value goods are subject to tariff rates that are higher than those of their inputs. In the European Union, for example, the MFN rate for unroasted coffee beans in 2020 was 0 per cent whereas the rate for roasted beans was 7.5 per cent (European Commission, 2020). It thus might make economic sense for coffee roasters to be located within the European Union instead of roasting the coffee in the country where it is grown. Unless, of course, the country of supply benefits from preferential trade agreements with the European Union, as is the case for coffee beans from GSP countries like Kenya (2.6 per cent) and some Central American countries (0 per cent) (European Commission, 2020).

Within the framework of WTO rules, countries can also levy **anti-dumping duties.** In line with international rules governments sometimes use these to protect businesses from 'dumped' imports. Dumping complaints can arise in instances where a foreign company exports goods at prices significantly below those at home and material injury to businesses (eg inability to sell) has been or is likely to be caused. Governments may also seek to protect their business communities from foreign competitors who have benefited from unfair subsidies and subsequently are able to compete on more favourable terms. In such instances **countervailing duties** may be levied. **Safeguard actions** (eg additional tariffs or quantitative restrictions) can come into play as an emergency measure when a sudden surge of imports causes or threatens to cause serious injury to businesses at home.

Many countries also allow importers to apply for **tariff suspensions.** If granted, applicable import duties are temporarily waived. Applications for tariff suspensions can normally only be made for goods that domestic manufacturers are unable to sufficiently provide. In the European Union, for example, the tariff suspensions can be requested for such goods and materials on the condition that there are no suppliers from within the EU and Turkey and that there are no similar or competing products available (see Article 31 of the Treaty of the Functioning of the European Union (TFEU); European Union, 2012). Following the tariff suspension application, trade officials check that relevant conditions are fulfilled. Once the tariff suspension is granted, importers are allowed to import the goods falling under the suspension free from customs duties. Another example is that of the United States. During the coronavirus pandemic in 2020 it, along with many other countries, temporarily suspended import tariffs for certain medical supplies, protective equipment, apparels and light trucks (Politi and Williams, 2020).

How are customs duties calculated?

The basis for assessing the correct amount of customs duties is the published customs tariff; often also called the trade tariff (Table 2.4). Some countries may (and some may not) publish electronic versions of their tariff with cross-references to other tariff measures, such as: anti-dumping and countervailing duties; preferential duty rates (that depend on origin); import licensing requirements (see Chapter 4); quantitative limits and restrictions; tariff quotas; surveillance measures; temporary suspensions of duties; VAT rates; excise duties; and cross-references to SPS controls.

Customs tariff publications (online or paper-based) usually reference tariff rates against tariff classification codes. The first step in working out the correct amount of customs duty is thus finding the correct tariff classification code. Most tariffs will be listed as percentage figures that are to be applied to the value of the goods (*ad valorem*). Occasionally, there may be variances from the *ad valorem* approach and duty rates are based on weight (eg kg or tonne), volume (eg litres), length (eg cm or m) or a combination of the three (eg volume and alcohol content). The next step in working out the correct amount of customs duty relates to determining the correct value of the goods. Where goods benefit from preferential treatment, eligibility is subject to relevant preferential origin rules. These need to be checked in order to work out whether the imported goods can benefit from any free trade or preferential trade type agreements.

For most countries the correct classification of goods is governed by the WCO's Harmonized System. The correct assessment of the customs value is based on the WTO's General Agreement of Trade and Tariffs' Article 7 (GATT, 1994b) and supporting customs valuation rules (GATT, 1994a). Preferential origin rules are normally defined in the text of relevant trade agreements. Tariff classification, valuation and origin rules can be very technical and will be briefly discussed in the next few sections. For most customs practitioners the task of working out the correct tariff classification, value and origin of goods represents a key aspect of their day-to-day work.

TABLE 2.4 Weblinks to the customs tariffs of the worlds' largest economies

Country	Electronic Trade Tariff
European Union (common customs tariff for all 27 Member States)	ec.europa.eu/taxation_customs/dds2/taric/taric_consultation.jsp?Lang=en
Germany	auskunft.ezt-online.de/ezto
France	www.douane.gouv.fr/service-en-ligne/tarif-douanier-communautaire-et-national-rita

(continued)

TABLE 2.4 (Continued)

Country	Electronic Trade Tariff
Italy	aidaonline7.adm.gov.it/nsitaricinternet/
United States of America	hts.usitc.gov
China (PDF download)	gss.mof.gov.cn/gzdt/zhengcefabu/201912/t20191230_3452186.htm
Japan	www.customs.go.jp/english/tariff/index.htm
United Kingdom	www.gov.uk/trade-tariff
India	www.icegate.gov.in/Webappl/
Brazil (MS Excel download)	www.camex.gov.br/tarifa-externa-comum-tec/tec-listas-em-vigor
Canada	www.cbsa-asfc.gc.ca/trade-commerce/tariff-tarif/current-actuel-eng.html

TIP

The International Trade Centre maintains an online database that gives access to applied tariff information for over 150 countries. This resource can be freely accessed at www.macmap.org.

Readers with internet access in the European Union can utilize its Access2Market tool. It lists customs tariff details for over 110 countries along with descriptions about applicable import formalities in each of them. See trade.ec.europa.eu/access-to-markets/en/content.

Other countries offer similarly comprehensive information, including, for example:

- the UK on its gov.uk website, www.check-duties-customs-exporting-goods.service.gov.uk/; and
- the United States on the website of its International Trade Administration, www.trade.gov/ccg-landing-page.

TARIFF CLASSIFICATION

A key prerequisite to looking up the correct trade tariff is the tariff classification number. Most countries – over 200 – use the WCO's Harmonized System (HS) for this purpose. The Harmonized System is structured in 21 sections containing 97 chapters (WCO, 2017b).

Chapters 98 and 99 are reserved for non-harmonized national additions. Each chapter is subdivided into headings and subheadings – yielding an HS tariff classification code consisting of:

- the first two digits, which represent the chapter number (ie 01–97);
- the third and fourth digits, representing the heading within the chapter; and
- the fifth and sixth digits, representing a further subdivision of the heading number, the so-called subheading.

In total, the Harmonized System provides for close to 5,500 subheadings (6-digit numbers). However, most countries do not find the classification into 6-digit numbers to be sufficient and will add their own additional subdivisions. In the European Union, to give one example, this includes: a seventh and eight digit representing the so-called CN code (Combined Nomenclature); and a ninth and tenth digit, representing the so-called TARIC (Integrated Tariff of the European Union) code against which the applicable import duty rate is referenced.

A key principle of the Harmonized System is that there is always only one correct reference number that the declarant is permitted to use. In order to identify that number, the HS's General Interpretative Rules (GIR) are to be applied (see Box 2.2). These are supported by the WCO's extensive explanatory notes that provide further guidance on interpretation (WCO, 2017a). Many countries (or Unions) may publish additional explanatory notes to assist with the correct tariff classification (European Commission, 2019). Court and tribunal rulings may occasionally need to be relied upon as well (Courts and Tribunals Judiciary, 2020).

BOX 2.2

Abridged General Interpretive Rules for the WCO's Harmonized System

The first rule of the Harmonized System (HS), **General Interpretative Rule 1** (GIR1), is that tariff classification must be in accordance with the description of the heading (ie the first four digits). Section notes, found at the beginning of each of the Harmonized System's 21 Sections, along with Chapter notes, are to be used in support of identifying the most appropriate tariff heading. Once the HS heading has been found, the most appropriate HS subheading must be selected. A pure-bred horse, for example, is correctly classified within Chapter 01 'Live Animals' under the heading 0101 'Live horses, asses, mules and hinnies'. If the horse is a pure-bred breeding horse it subsequently falls under the subheading 0101.21; any other type of live horse would fall under 0101.29 (ie 'other'):

Heading	H.S. Code	
01.01		**Live horses, asses, mules and hinnies.**
		– Horses:
	0101.21	– Pure-bred breeding animals
	0101.29	– Other
	0101.30	– Asses
	0101.90	– Other

Rule 2 (GIR2) is designed for incomplete or unfinished goods and mixtures. It has an (a) and (b) component:

- 2(a) states that reference in a heading to an *article* shall also apply to: incomplete and unfinished articles with the essential character of the complete or finished article; and articles in an unassembled or disassembled state.
- 2(b) states that reference in a heading to a material or substance shall include mixtures and combinations containing that material. It also states that goods made of a specific material include goods consisting wholly or partly of that material. However, where Rule 2(b) indicates two or more headings, Rule 3 applies.

Rule 3 (GIR3) is the rule by which decisions are made. It states that where goods are prima facie classifiable in two or more headings, the following principles apply:

a. The heading which provides the most specific description shall be preferred to headings providing a more general description. However, all headings relating to only part of the goods are equally specific.
b. Mixtures, composite goods and sets are to be classified according to material giving them their essential character.

c. Goods not classifiable under (a) or (b) are to be classified under the last applicable heading (ie the higher number).

Rule 4 (GIR4) (a catch-all rule that is rarely used) states that goods not classifiable under Rules 1–3 are to be classified as the goods to which they are most akin.

Rule 5 (GIR5) concerns the classification of cases and packaging materials and has an (a) and (b) component:

- 5(a) states that cases, boxes and similar containers intended to fit and be sold with particular articles are to be classified with such articles unless the container gives the article its essential character.
- 5(b) states that subject to Rule 5(a), packing materials and containers are to be classified with the goods therein unless clearly suitable for repetitive use.

Rule 6 (GIR6) relates to subheadings and confirms that Rules 1–5 apply equally to both headings and subheadings; that only subheadings of comparable status can be considered; and that Section and Chapter notes apply to subheadings unless the context requires otherwise.

NOTE *The full unabridged GIRs (Rules 1–6) can be found in the preamble of the HS Nomenclature (WCO, 2017b; Weerth, 2008).*

CUSTOMS VALUATION RULES

Customs valuation rules, used to determine the value upon which customs duties are levied, are based on Article 7 of the GATT (1994b) and defined in the supporting customs valuation rules (GATT, 1994a). Although standardized within the framework of WTO law, they can be technically demanding. As a principle, the customs value upon which customs duties are levied has to be based on actual quantifiable data. When possible the customs value is to be based on the so-called 'transaction value', which is the 'price actually paid or payable for the goods when sold for export to the country of importation' (GATT, 1994a). This transaction value approach is also referred to as the Customs Valuation Method 1.

If the Customs Valuation Method 1 cannot be applied, Methods 2 to 6 need to be considered in sequence (Box 2.3). Routinely, customs administration will ask declarants to provide detailed information about the customs value. In cases where parties are not related (eg trade between sister companies) this often includes requests for a copy of the commercial invoice plus details about the transport arrangements (usually found in standard transport documents like the airwaybill or shipping note). Customs officers may also ask for a detailed valuation declaration – especially in cases where standard commercial documents like the invoice are not available (eg because they have been imported before the sale has been made), when goods are of high value, or where contracting parties are related and thus able to influence the price of the goods. When making a valuation declaration the declarant usually needs to give a detailed account of how the value of the goods has been determined by reference to the applicable customs valuation methods that have been abridged in Box 2.3.

Important to note is that customs officers are not only worried about under-declared transaction values. Uncharacteristically high customs values can be a strong indicator for cross-border crimes, such as circumvention of foreign exchange controls and money laundering. If the value is thought to be too high, customs officers may, in cooperation with direct tax colleagues, be concerned about aggressive tax avoidance schemes. For example, companies in high cooperation tax jurisdictions could be tempted to shift profits to sister companies in low tax jurisdictions, for example by overstating the value of goods shipped to the sister company.

BOX 2.3

Abridged valuation methods: adapted from the WTO Customs Valuation Agreement (GATT, 1994a)

Method 1

Method 1, the default method, requires that there is evidence of sale (eg a commercial invoice, contract, purchase order), that the buyer and seller are not related (eg as might be the case with inter-company sales and transactions between sister companies) unless Customs are satisfied that the relationship did not influence the price, and that there are no restrictions on the disposition of the goods to the buyer (though exceptions can be made for restrictions required by law, that limit the geographic area in which the goods may be resold, or do not affect the value of goods).

In many countries the transaction value also includes the cost of transport, handling and insurance costs up to the point of importation, as is the case for European Union Member States. In some countries those costs do not form part of the customs value, as is, for example, in the case of the United States (Homeland Security, 2006; WTO, 2020a).

If not part of the price at which the goods were sold, the transaction value also includes:

- commissions and brokerage (excluding buying commissions);
- the cost of containers if classified as part of the goods;
- packing costs for both packaging materials and labour;
- royalties and licence fees related to the goods that are not already included in the price of sale;
- the value of proceeds of resale, use or disposal that accrue to the seller.

Any manufacturing 'assists' of the following nature, if not already captured in the price paid for the goods, must also be included apportioned as appropriate, to the transaction value:

- materials, components, parts and similar items incorporated in the imported goods;
- tools, dies, moulds and similar items used in the production of the imported goods; and materials consumed in production (eg catalysts);
- any engineering, development, artwork, design work, plans and sketches.

But the transaction value does not include:

- the cost of transport and handling after importation;
- charges for construction, erection, assembly or maintenance of plant and machinery;
- interest payable under a finance arrangement related to the imported goods;

- charges for the right to reproduce the imported goods;
- buying commissions; and
- import duties and other taxes or charges payable on import or sale (eg VAT, excise and port fees).

Where a transaction value is not available, for example, because the price was influenced by the relationship between the parties, alternative valuation methods are to be applied in hierarchical order.

Method 2

Method 2, 'Transaction value of identical goods', where the transaction value is determined in the same manner by reference to identical goods. The identical goods used for determining the customs value must be sold for export to the same country and sold at or about the same time. Importantly, they must have the same physical characteristics, quality and reputation as the goods under valuation. If these conditions cannot be met, Method 3 applies.

Method 3

This method, 'Transaction value of similar goods', is used where the transaction value is calculated by reference to similar goods on the condition that:

- they resemble the goods being valued in terms of component materials and characteristics;
- are able to perform the same functions; and
- are commercially interchangeable with the goods being valued.

Moreover, they must be produced in the same country by the same manufacturer as the goods being valued. As with Method 2, they also must be exported to the same country and sold at or about the same time.

Method 4

This deductive method applies if a transaction value cannot be agreed by reference to identical or similar goods. In this case the transaction value shall be determined by reference to the unit price at which the imported goods (or similar or identical goods) were sold to unrelated parties in the greatest aggregate quantity in the country of importation. Conditions apply.

Method 5

This computed method is based on a calculation that considers the production costs, profits and general expenses (eg legal) and other expenses (eg transport and handling). The cost of packaging, containers and assists usually also need to be considered.

Method 6

This fall-back method comes into play when the respective requirements for Methods 1 to 5 cannot be met. Instead, it allows Methods 1 to 5 to be applied in a flexible but reasonable manner, and on the basis of available data.

FOR INFORMATION

Switzerland is the only WTO member that sets customs duties exclusively by reference to their volume, weight or length. For example, lipstick imported from the United States with the tariff classification number 3304.10.00 is subject to CHF 115.00 (about US $118.00) in customs duties per 100 kg. Shampoo imported into Switzerland in 2020 with the tariff classification number 3305.10.00 was subject to CHF 65.00 (about US $67.00) in customs duties per 100 kg. The Swiss customs tariff can be accessed at xtares.admin.ch/tares?l=en.

Other countries occasionally also use specific customs rates for certain types of goods. One such example is the European Union's MFN rate for wine (classified under 2204.29.22.90), which in 2020 was €12.10 per hectolitre (about US $13.50 per 100 litres). Likewise, cider (classified under 2206.00.31.00) was €19.20 per hectolitre (about US $21.45 per 100 litres). The European Union's customs tariff can be browsed at ec.europa.eu/taxation_customs/dds2/taric/taric_consultation.jsp?Lang=en

NOTE *Tariff rates are subject to change; rates given applied in April 2021.*

ORIGIN RULES

Where goods come from is important when country-specific restrictions or conditions apply, as might be case for: anti-dumping duties, tariff quotas and other trade policy measures; marking and labelling rules; and trade-specific political or economic measures. The determination of origin is also important where importers seek to take advantage of preferential duty rates that are specific to the countries within the supporting trade agreement. Unfortunately, origin rules to work out where goods come from – so-called 'non-preferential rules of origin' – are not necessarily the same as those that confer eligibility for preferential tariff treatment – so-called 'preferential origin rules'.

Despite considerable efforts to harmonize rules, rules for non-preferential and preferential origin can still differ from one country and trade agreement to the next. Negotiations at the WTO to harmonize origin rules are still ongoing (WTO, 2020c). To help keep track of non-preferential origin rules WTO members are required to notify them to the WTO Secretariat. Likewise, WTO member countries are also required to notify the WTO of any preferential trade agreements which can be accessed via WTO databases for reciprocal trade preferences (rtais.wto.org/) and non-reciprocal trade preferences (ptadb.wto.org). In 2019 there were more than 300 notified agreements.

Often, preferential rules that confirm eligibility to lower (preferential) duty rates within the framework of a preferential or free trade agreement are defined by reference to the HS heading (ie first four digits of the tariff code). Common criteria for preferential origin rules may consider whether the declared good has been 'produced wholly in a given country', where the most value has been added, or where there has been a substantial transformation (Inama, 2009). The text of free trade agreements often also makes reference to product specific rules (Box 2.4). Free trade and preferential trade agreements also set conditions, such as the requirement for goods to be shipped directly or that goods cannot benefit from Duty Drawback procedures (a special customs procedure where the duties and taxes paid on goods that are imported in the manufacture of exports can be reclaimed). However, many regional trade agreements will allow for 'cumulation' where goods originating in one of the countries signed up to the agreement may be considered as originating if used by another country signed up to the agreement. This can be useful in instances where origin rules set requirements for minimal national content.

BOX 2.4

Examples of preferential origin rules

Substantial transformation

The USA–Australia Free Trade Agreement specifies that 'Wood and articles of wood; wood charcoal' originate where 'a change to heading 4401 through 4421 from any other heading' has taken place (USA and Australia, 2004). Thus, a wooden frame for a painting classifiable under HS heading 4414 would originate in the country where the wood has been manufactured (transformed) into a frame.

Product specific rules

The China–Peru Free Trade Agreement specifies that rice classified under HS subheadings 1006.10 (rice in the husk), 1006.20 (husked brown rice), 1006.30 (semi-milled or wholly milled rice, whether or not polished or glazed) and 1006.40 (broken rice) originate in the country where goods have been 'harvested, picked or gathered' (China and Peru, 2009). Thus, in the case of 1006.30, any milling, polishing or glazing processes would not have any bearing on where the goods originate.

Value added/national content

The EU–UK Trade and Cooperation Agreement stipulates that a grand piano (classified under the HS code 9201.20) can only benefit from the agreed zero preferential tariff if no more than 50 per cent of the ex-works value of its parts (eg timber, strings, keys, fittings, etc) come from outside the EU or the UK (EU and UK, 2020).

Produce wholly in a given country

The MERCOSUR–SACU Preferential Trade Agreement (between Argentina, Brazil, Paraguay, Uruguay, Botswana, Lesotho, Namibia, South Africa and Eswatini) states that all 'meat and edible meat offal' falling under HS Chapter 2 (HS headings 0101 through to 0110) shall be deemed to originate where wholly obtained. The term 'wholly obtained', by reference to Annex III, Article 4 (d) of the agreement, encompasses all products from live animals raised in the signatory countries (MERCOSUR and SACU, 2008).

Where businesses need to prove to Customs the origin for non-preferential origin purposes the Certificate of Origin is commonly requested. Accredited Chambers of Commerce are frequently relied upon to provide such certificates; fees apply. Procedures can vary from country to country and there may be special arrangements within the framework of preferential trade and customs cooperation arrangements. In many countries it is also possible to obtain electronic certificates of origin.

Preferential origin documents can often be requested from the customs administrations or from third parties appointed by Customs (which in some countries might also be the Chamber of Commerce). Often trade agreements also allow trading businesses to issue their own preferential origin documents. In trade agreements with the European Union, for example, it is usually possible to make a preferential origin declaration – stating conformity with applicable rules – on the commercial invoice. Where goods are of a higher value, authorizations from Customs to make such an invoice declaration may be necessary.

For trade with some countries, often amongst least developed countries, it is sometimes necessary to obtain a so-called consular invoice, which must be obtained prior to import from the consulate of the country to which the goods are destined. When issuing the document, officials at the consulate will seek to verify the value, quantity and nature of the shipment. Fees apply and the process might take time.

Other indirect taxes

As already mentioned, customs administrations are often tasked with collecting other types of indirect taxes, too. These are designed as a revenue generating measure and unlike customs duties are not designed to protect businesses from foreign competition. Such taxes include value added and sales taxes (eg VAT and GST) as well as excise duties.

VAT and GST regimes can differ significantly from one country to the next and apply to both goods and services. Amongst developed countries within the OECD the average VAT rate in 2018 was 19.3 per cent (OECD, 2018). In some countries, such as Sweden and Denmark (25 per cent) or Hungary (27 per cent) the VAT rates can be considerably higher. VAT is normally collected by the seller of goods and services and then credited towards the national revenue authority (which in some countries incorporates the customs administration). But sellers are normally able to claim back any VAT paid on their supplies. The tax burden thus passes on to the end consumer.

In the case of imports, import VAT is due and needs to be paid on top of the applicable customs duties. However, some countries, like the UK, Ireland and Poland, have recently implemented postponed import VAT arrangements that allow import VAT to be accounted on the VAT return (eg every two or three months). Any import VAT can normally be claimed back as long as the goods are sold on by the importer to another VAT registered business. The principle of passing on the tax burden to the end consumer thus remains. Where goods are exported, goods can usually (subject to documented evidence) be zero-rate, ie no VAT needs to be charged to the foreign buyer.

Excise duties are additional taxes for specific types of goods. They are collected (unlike VAT) at the stage of consumption, ie when they reach the final consumer. Until then businesses manufacturing or trading excisable goods may keep those goods under an excise bond. This is a financial security upon which authorities can draw in the event that any excisable goods are unaccounted (eg went missing or were stolen). For some goods, like cigarettes, excise duties can be above 80 per cent of the retail price (as is the case in Chile, Finland, France, Greece, Israel, Poland, Turkey and the United Kingdom). For premium unleaded gasoline, excise duties plus VAT exceed 100 per cent of pre-tax prices in all of the OECD counties except Australia, Canada, Chile, Japan, Mexico, New Zealand and the United States (OECD, 2018).

Customs administrations in many parts of the world are tasked with managing the control of excisable goods, especially when imported for domestic consumption or exported and the trader needs Customs to confirm their export (and release the trader from any financial excise bond or security). Given the very high excise

TABLE 2.5 Revenue collected by Customs in top 10 economies by GDP (2018)

Rank	Country	Share of customs duties in tax revenue (%)	Revenue collected by Customs in tax revenue (%)
1	United States of America	1.3	1.4
2	China	3.3	23.1
3	Japan	1.6	13.8
4	Germany	0.7	18.4
5	United Kingdom	0.6	Not reported
6	France	0.7	28.0
7	India	6.1	43.5
8	Italy	0.5	3.6
9	Brazil	8.8	10.0
10	Canada	2.5	12.7

SOURCE Extracted from WCO, 2019

rates in many parts of the world, goods subject to excise duties are attractive to smugglers and counterfeiters. Subsequently, a significant part of Customs' anti-smuggling activities can have a bias towards excisable goods.

Compared to import duties, other indirect taxes tend to have a significantly greater share in the customs administration's contribution to the national revenue. Amongst the world's largest economies India's customs administration was responsible for collecting almost half (43.5 per cent) of the national revenue in 2018 (Table 2.5).

Special customs procedures with financial benefits

The WCO's Revised Kyoto Convention includes recommendations for a number of procedures that allow import duties and taxes to be suspended, deferred or claimed back under certain conditions. These procedures make sure that export-orientated manufacturers can compete effectively:

- without the burden of duties and taxes on their goods – especially when compared to countries with minimal or no tax requirements;
- without the risk of being taxed multiple times along the supply chain in operations that require goods to cross borders many times (eg export processing and assembly)
- by delaying the point at which duties and taxes are due and thus offering cashflow benefits.

One of the most common special customs procedures is customs warehousing, where goods may be stored free of duty and taxes. Many countries also operate dedicated export processing zones where goods may be stored or even processed without having to pay import duties. Duties only apply where goods leave the Customs-controlled area and are subsequently imported. Often, suitably trusted businesses are also permitted to pay duty and taxes on a periodic basis (eg monthly) instead of whenever the goods are declared. Transit procedures are important where goods move from the ports to Customs-approved inland locations or when in transit to countries without access to maritime ports (Box 2.5).

In addition to the above, special procedures may also exist for:

- travellers (including business travellers carrying merchandise and samples);
- postal traffic;
- the means of transport for commercial use (eg the vehicles carrying the goods;
- stores (eg on ships and aircraft);
- relief consignments (eg in the case of a humanitarian emergency) (see Chapter 10).

Depending on the country and procedures concerned, access to special customs procedures comes with conditions, such as:

- a financial security or bond upon which Customs can draw any applicable duties and taxes;

- the employment of qualified staff;
- a good compliance record;
- compliance with procedure-specific operational conditions (eg scale and physical infrastructure);
- compliance with procedure-specific administrative requirements (eg IT infrastructure and subscriptions to specialist software).

BOX 2.5

Summary of customs procedures with financial benefits as per the WCO's Revised Kyoto Convention (WCO, 2006)

- Deferment of duty and tax payments, for example, by allowing businesses to pay them on a monthly basis instead of for each and every declaration.
- Customs warehousing, where imported goods may be stored in a designated place (a customs warehouse) without payment of customs duties until goods are removed from that warehouse and released from customs control into free circulation. In some countries, such as those of the European Union, that warehouse may be of a virtual nature, such as in the form of an electronic inventory system.
- Entry into an approved Customs free zone, where goods in terms of taxes and duties are considered to be outside the customs territory. Subsequently, any taxes and duties upon goods do not apply while held or processed in the free zone.
- Customs transit without the need to pay duty and taxes, for example where the transport of the goods requires them to enter and leave a country en route to their final destination. Transit procedures also come into play where goods are moved from one customs facility to another (eg in the context of inland clearance facilities that permit customs clearance and inspections to take place away from the ports and borders).
- Inward processing relief, where goods may be brought into the country free from duties and taxes on the basis that such goods are intended for processing, manufacturing or repair and subsequent exportation.
- Outward processing relief where goods may be temporarily exported to another country for manufacturing, processing or repair and then

re-imported with total or partial exemption from import duties and taxes.

- Drawback, where goods are exported, and Customs refunds the import duties and taxes relating to the materials contained within those goods or consumed in their production.
- Processing for home use, where manufacturers import goods and materials and choose to pay duties and taxes on the finished goods in instances where the duties and taxes on the finished goods are lower than on their inputs.
- Temporary admission, where goods can be imported on a temporary basis with partial or full exemption from any customs duties and taxes. Temporary admission procedures are often used in the context of declaring: the means of transport (eg the truck carrying the cargo), personal effects of travellers, exhibition items, construction equipment that will leave the country upon completion of the project.
- Humanitarian relief, where an emergency has been declared and certain types of goods under strict conditions may be imported free from duty and taxes.

ACTIVITIES AND DISCUSSION POINTS

1. Seek to identify the main pieces of customs law applicable to the country in which you live. You might find them on the Customs website or within a public online 'trade information portal'. Keep a note of the main Regulations/Acts, Directives/Implementation Provisions and Guidelines that might apply.
2. Using your national trade tariff, try and find the correct HS heading (four digits) for cut flowers, a bicycle and a laptop computer.
3. Check the UK–EU Trade and Cooperation Agreement (available online at eurlex.europa.eu/legal-content/EN/TXT/?uri=OJ:L:2020:444:TOC) and see if you can find the origin rules for a motor car (HS heading 8703).

References

China and Peru (2009) China–Peru Free Trade Agreement: Annex 4 Product specific origin, Ministry of Commerce of the People's Republic of China; Ministerio de Comercio Exterior de Peru

Courts and Tribunals Judiciary (2020) Decisions, financeandtax.decisions.tribunals.gov.uk/Aspx/default.aspx (archived at https://perma.cc/2U5N-A37Z)

De Wulf, L (2005) Strategy for customs modernization, in *Customs Modernization Handbook*, eds L De Wulf and JB Sokol, pp 3–30, World Bank, Washington

EU and UK (2020) Trade and Cooperation Agreement between the European Union and the European Atomic Energy Community, of the one part, and the United Kingdom of Great Britain and Northern Ireland, on the other part, *Official Journal of the European Union*, **63** (L444), pp 14–1462, eur-lex.europa.eu/legal-content/EN/TXT/?uri=OJ:L:2020:444:TOC (archived at https://perma.cc/Y8N2-BA4T)

European Commission (2019) Explanatory notes to the Combined Nomenclature of the European Union *Official Journal of the European Union*, **62** (C119), eur-lex.europa.eu/legal-content/EN/TXT/?uri=OJ%3AC%3A2019%3A119%3ATOC (archived at https://perma.cc/S4VG-CX3A)

European Commission (2020) TARIC Consultation, ec.europa.eu/taxation_customs/dds2/taric/taric_consultation.jsp?Lang=en (archived at https://perma.cc/VJ8Z-HQ68)

European Union (2012) Consolidated Version of the Treaty on the Functioning of the European Union, *Official Journal of the European Union*, C326 (26.10.2012)

GATT (1947) The General Agreement on Tariffs and Trade.

GATT (1994a) Agreement on Implementation of Article VII (Customs Valuation), World Trade Organization, Geneva, www.wto.org/english/docs_e/legal_e/20-val_01_e.htm (archived at https://perma.cc/JN6Z-2LQC)

GATT (1994b) The General Agreement on Tariffs and Trade

George, C (2010) *The Truth About Trade: The real impact of liberalization*, Zed, London, New York

Grainger, A (2015) Customs Issues Falling under INTA's New Remit, European Parliament, Brussels, www.europarl.europa.eu/thinktank/en/document.html?reference=EXPO_STU(2015)534991 (archived at https://perma.cc/7JZF-64QN)

Homeland Security (2006) *What Every Member of the Trade Community Should Know About: Customs Value*, US Department of Homeland Security, Washington, DC, www.cbp.gov/sites/default/files/assets/documents/2016-Apr/icp001r2_3.pdf (archived at https://perma.cc/B2N7-FC6S)

Inama, S (2009) *Rules of Origin in International Trade*, Cambridge University Press, New York

League of Nations (1923) International Convention relating to the Simplification of Customs Formalities, League of Nations, Geneva, treaties.un.org/Pages/LONViewDetails.aspx?src=LON&id=565&chapter=30&clang=_en (archived at https://perma.cc/S2KV-XTFM)

MERCOSUR and SACU (2008) Preferential Trade Agreement between the Common Market of the South (MERCOSUR) and the Southern African Customs Union (SACU), Southern African Customs Union; Southern Common Market, www.sacu.int/docs/agreements/2016/mercosur-and-sacu-trade-agreement.pdf (archived at https://perma.cc/B53L-VNZ4)

OECD (2018) *Consumption Tax Trends 2018,* Organisation for Economic Co-operation and Development, Paris

OED (2019) *Oxford English Dictionary*, www.oed.com (archived at https://perma.cc/97XU-7WYG)

Politi, J and Williams, A (2020) Trump to suspend some tariffs for 90 days, *Financial Times*, www.ft.com/content/46add447-2048-4348-bd34-2088ad0e3bc8 (archived at https://perma.cc/RMN9-7K6S)

Sally, R (2008) *New Frontiers In Free Trade: Globalization's future and Asia's rising role,* Cato Institute, Washington, DC

Trebilcock, MJ, Howse, R and Eliason, A (2013) The most favoured nation principle, in *The Regulation of International Trade,* 4th edn, eds M Trebilcock, R Howse and A Eliason, pp 54–82, Routledge, London

UN (1950) Protocol amending the Convention signed at Brussels, on 5 July 1890, concerning the creation of an International Union for the Publication of Customs Tariffs as well as the Regulations for the execution of the Convention instituting an International Bureau for the publication of customs tariffs, and the Memorandum of signature, United Nations, Belgium, treaties.un.org/Pages/showDetails.aspx?objid=080000028015a1af (archived at https://perma.cc/P6MG-Y2SH)

UNCTAD (2021) GSP: Handbooks, unctad.org/publications-search?f%5B0%5D=product%3A498 (archived at https://perma.cc/9MP4-EBLD)

USA and Australia (2004) Free Trade Agreement: Annex 5-A Specific Rules of Origin, Office of the United States Trade Representation; Australian Government Department of Foreign Trade, ustr.gov/sites/default/files/ANNEX%205A%20AustraliaFTA.pdf (archived at https://perma.cc/E9WP-DUS3)

WCO (2006) Revised Kyoto Convention: International Convention on the Simplifications and Harmonization of Customs Procedures, World Customs Organization, Brussels, www.wcoomd.org/en/topics/facilitation/instrument-and-tools/conventions/pf_revised_kyoto_conv/kyoto_new.aspx (archived at https://perma.cc/N4SR-4437)

WCO (2017a) Explanatory Notes: HS 2017, World Customs Organization, Brussels

WCO (2017b) HS Nomenclature, 2017 edition, World Customs Organization, Brussels, www.wcoomd.org/en/topics/nomenclature/instrument-and-tools/hs-nomenclature-2017-edition/hs-nomenclature-2017-edition.aspx (archived at https://perma.cc/U6BT-TGZW)

WCO (2019a) List of the Contracting Parties to the Revised Kyoto Convention, 23 September, www.wcoomd.org/en/Topics/Facilitation/Instrument%20and%20Tools/Conventions/pf_revised_kyoto_conv/Instruments (archived at https://perma.cc/3XKB-RXDS)

WCO (2019b) *The WCO Annual Report 2018–19,* World Customs Organization, Brussels, www.wcoomd.org/-/media/wco/public/global/pdf/media/annual-reports/annual-report-2018_2019.pdf (archived at https://perma.cc/3XVZ-TPJ3)

Weerth, C (2008) Basic principles of customs classifications under the Harmonized System, *Global Trade and Customs Journal,* **3** (2), pp 61–67

Widdowson, D (2005) Managing risk in the customs context, in *Customs Modernization Handbook,* eds LD Wulf and JB Sokol, pp 91–99, World Bank, Washington, DC

WTO (2014) Agreement on Trade Facilitation (WT/L/931), World Trade Organization, Geneva, www.wto.org/english/tratop_e/tradfa_e/tradfa_e.htm (archived at https://perma.cc/AN85-M9NA)

WTO (2020a) Customs Valuation Agreement (Implementation of Article VII of the GATT), World Trade Organization, www.wto.org/english/res_e/publications_e/ai17_e/cusval_e.htm (archived at https://perma.cc/C2B4-KE7J)

WTO (2020b) Regional Trade Agreements Database, World Trade Organization, rtais.wto.org/UI/PublicMaintainRTAHome.aspx (archived at https://perma.cc/ZN87-C8FZ)

WTO (2020c) Rules of Origin, World Trade Organization, www.wto.org/english/tratop_e/roi_e/roi_e.htm (archived at https://perma.cc/9UQW-5WYM)

03

Customs declarations and control

This chapter, following on from Chapter 2, provides an overview of how goods are declared to Customs. Traditionally, the act of making a declaration formally places the goods under 'customs control'. While under the control of the customs administration, officers would assess the declarations and the goods. Assuming all is in order and subsequent to the payment of any applicable duties and taxes, goods would then be released from customs control – for example for release into 'free circulation' (in the case of imports), export or transit. However, there are many parties involved and usually the various border agencies need to be notified that the goods are coming. Moreover, declarations are now usually made in electronic form, often with direct or indirect integration into other transport and logistics processes. Let us take a closer look at the details.

The customs control system

Modern requirements for customs control are set out in the World Customs Organization's (WCO) Revised Kyoto Convention's General Annex, Chapter 6 (WCO, 2006). A key principle is that any good moved across a border must be declared to Customs. Failure to declare would be an offence, though simplified procedures are often available. For example, travellers at most international airports may declare their personal effects by walking through the red channel. Postal shipments benefit from simplified forms that can be attached to the parcel. Many countries also operate *de minimis* thresholds (eg US $800 for imports into the United States; USITA, 2021) below which any applicable customs formalities can be significantly reduced.

While under their control, the customs administration will normally:

- assess the declared information and goods;
- check that relevant obligations have been met – for example, that all the applicable import duties and taxes have been paid (Chapter 2);
- and inspect the goods if thought necessary.

Once the declaration has been approved, goods may be released from customs control and continue in their journey. Other, non-customs agencies, especially the quarantine services (Chapter 4), often have similar declaration and control requirements. Release from their control often needs to be coordinated with the customs administration (Chapter 7).

A common model for customs border control has six components (Figure 3.1):

1. Notification and/or advance declaration: to let Customs know that goods are coming.
2. Declaration: to give Customs the necessary information to correctly assess the goods.
3. Risk assessment: where Customs considers whether the goods need to be inspected.
4. Inspection: where Customs, if deemed necessary, will physically check the goods against what has been declared.
5. Payment: where the trader will arrange for the payment of any necessary import duties, taxes and fees.
6. Release: where Customs releases the good for onward transport.

The necessary compliance responsibilities fall upon: the trader or appointed customs representative (eg customs broker or agent; see Chapter 6); the transport carrier; those parties tasked with handling

FIGURE 3.1 Generic model for customs control at the border

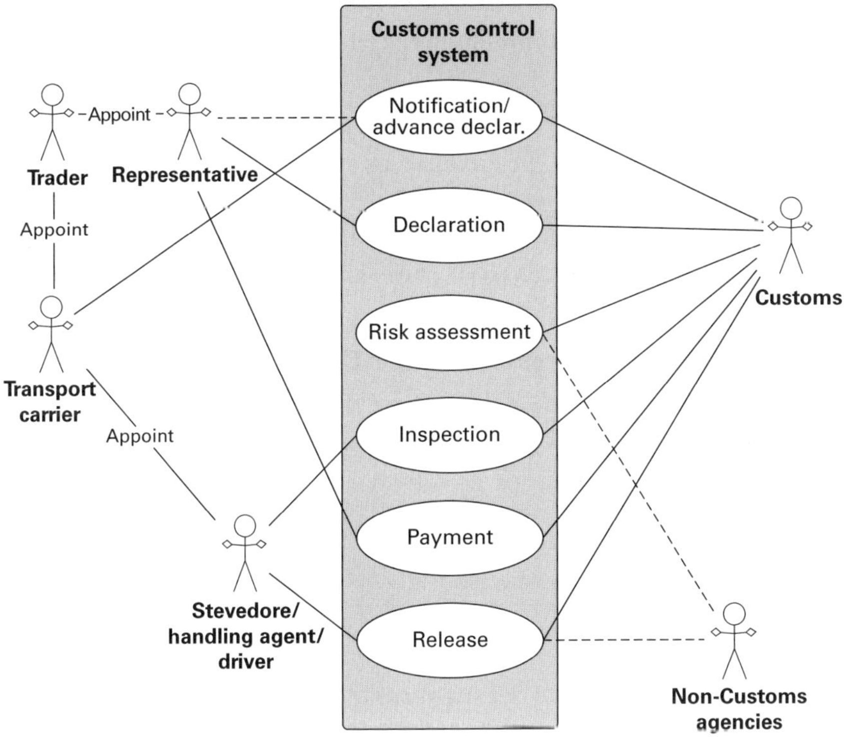

SOURCE © Trade Facilitation Consulting Ltd

the cargo at the port or border (eg to deliver goods to the inspection facility); and of course Customs, who may coordinate their work with other non-customs border agencies (Chapter 7). The subsequent subsections provide further detail.

Notifications and advance declarations

The information requirements for notifications and advance declarations normally tend to be significantly less onerous than the full declarations. Their purpose is to enable authorities to be on standby for when cargo arrives, assess relevant information in advance and, if need be, prepare for any inspection. In instances where notifications must be made prior to loading it also gives authorities the opportunity to deny boarding. Furthermore, advance notifications and declarations also enable border agencies to process aspects of the clearance formalities before the goods actually arrive, and can thereby help speed up the overall time it takes to clear goods at the ports and borders.

The principle of obligating maritime and air transport carriers to submit a cargo manifest in advance or immediately upon arrival to relevant authorities is long established (ICAO, 2017; IMO, 1998). Such notifications enable officers at the port or airport to prepare and be on standby. Since the events of 9/11 wider supply chain security considerations have also come into play (WCO, 2018a). These follow the original models developed in the United States and European Union (Widdowson *et al*, 2014). Advance declarations (or 'summary declarations') are now routinely relied upon by the customs administration around the world for an advance risk assessment – discussed later on in this chapter.

FOR BACKGROUND

Traditionally, the process of clearing goods through Customs started with the customs declarations – a document that is presented to Customs at that point in time when goods arrive at the border post or port. To help speed up processes at the border, the World Trade Organization's (WTO) Trade Facilitation Agreement's Article 7.1 (WTO, 2014b) is encouraging countries around the world to adopt customs procedures that allow import documentation and other relevant information to be submitted to the border agencies prior to the arrival of goods. This is to ensure that clearance processes can be arranged in a more efficient manner and initiated prior or immediately upon the arrival of the goods.

In many places where customs procedures are electronically enabled it is possible for importers to pre-lodge customs declarations. These are automatically submitted as soon as the transport carrier confirms that the goods have indeed arrived.

In most countries, especially for containerized shipments, separate pre-arrival or summary declaration must be submitted (usually by the transport carrier) so that Customs can conduct a risk assessment (see next section) in advance and decide whether to inspect and release the goods (Widdowson, 2016).

When managed well, decisions about inspection and clearance can be made before the actual shipment arrives. And, where information is submitted before loading in the country of export, it can also give border agencies and business operators an opportunity to stop goods before they are shipped.

Some countries may also allow, subject to authorization, advance declarations to be enhanced with the details normally declared in the import declaration. The two processes are thereby combined and can radically speed up the time it takes to clear goods. The Pre-arrival Processing Procedure that was implemented in 2019 by the Montenegro Customs Administration and the express parcel industry provides one such example (Grainger *et al*, 2021).

Depending on the country and its administrative arrangements, vessel manifest notifications and advance summary declarations are either made in the form of one single electronic transmission or as two distinct transmissions. Notification and advance declaration obligations usually fall upon the transport carrier – ie the party that actively brings the cargo in or out of the country. But in some countries, such as the United States, there are also notification obligations that fall upon the importer (Box 3.1).

BOX 3.1

United States Importer security filing (ISF 10+2)

In January 2009 the United States' SAFE Ports Act 2006 introduced the requirement for importers of cargo shipped in maritime containers to notify US authorities 24 hours before the loading of the vessel by filling an advance cargo declaration.

The **importer or appointed agent** must give following details:

1 manufacturer's (or supplier's) name and address;

2 seller's (or owner's) name and address;

3 buyer's (or owner's) name and address;

4 'ship-to' name and address;

5 container stuffing location;
6 consolidator's (container stuffer's) name and address;
7 'importer of record' number or foreign trade zone applicant identification number;
8 consignee number(s);
9 country of origin;
10 commodity number (at the WCO Harmonized System's six-digit level).

Moreover, the **shipping line** must declare the:

1 vessel stow plan;
2 container status messages.

Given the dual obligations falling upon the importer and carrier, these filing requirements are also referred to as the '10+2' programme.

Next to the cargo manifest, the Master of the vessel normally also has to notify relevant authorities about details concerning the vessel's stores (eg fuel, food), crew and any passengers. Reporting procedures are normally based on the International Maritime Organization's (IMO) Convention on the Facilitation of Maritime Traffic (FAL) (IMO, 1998). Similar requirements also apply to cargo landed by air where procedures follow the recommendations set out in the International Civil Aviation Organization's (ICAO) Annex 9 of the Chicago Convention (ICAO, 2017). Important to note is that as long as government agencies adopt standardize procedures and data formats (Chapter 9), established maritime and air transport carriers are usually able to automatically generate relevant manifest declarations by drawing on information provided by shippers when booking the shipment.

The time frames for advance declarations to customs administration are becoming more and more standardized, thanks, in part, to the work of the WCO and its 'SAFE Framework of Standards' (WCO,

2018a; Box 3.1). But time frame variances remain. For example, Widdowson (2016) finds that although the majority of countries with manifest reporting requirements for maritime container shipments demand that the submission is made 24 hours prior to loading (64 per cent), many countries (36 per cent) only require that cargo manifests be submitted prior to arrival. There are also instances where the recommended WCO time frames are not deemed practical. The European Union, to give one example, makes special allowance for transport on short sea-ferry routes (such as those operating in the North Sea, Irish Sea, Baltic Sea and the Mediterranean Sea). Operators only need to lodge the entry summary declarations two hours before arrival; for maritime bulk cargo shipments it is four hours before arrival (European Commission, 2020).

BOX 3.2

Recommended time limits for advance cargo and goods declarations, as per WCO SAFE Framework of Standards

- Maritime:
  - containerized cargo: 24 hours before loading at port of departure;
  - bulk/break bulk: 24 hours before arrival at first port in the country of destination.
- Air:
  - short haul: at time of 'wheels up' of aircraft;
  - long haul: four hours prior to arrival at the first port in the country of destination.
- Rail:
  - two hours prior to arrival at the first port in the country of destination.
- Road:
  - one hour prior to arrival at the first port in the country of destination.

The customs declaration

As already mentioned, a key principle for goods moved across borders is that they must be formally placed under customs control by declaring them to an appropriate customs procedure (WCO, 2006). These procedures might be import, export or transit – or any special customs procedures (Chapter 2; Box 2.5) that allow goods to be kept under customs control without having to pay duties and taxes, eg customs warehousing. Usually, the declaration is made by the trader or an appointed representative. That representative might be a licensed customs broker, a clearance agent or freight forwarder – practices and conditions governing customs representation can vary between countries (Chapter 7). However, it is routine in most countries for customs declarations to be lodged electronically. That said, requirements for also declaring supporting paper documents are common.

Customs declaration forms should follow a standard layout in line with United Nations (UN) document layout key (UN/CEFACT, 1981) and any relevant electronic document standards (WCO, 2020c). Many administrations around the world follow the example of the European Union's (EU) Single Administrative Document (SAD), which was designed to enable any type of customs declaration in any of the EU's official languages in one single document – whether for entry into an import, export, transit or other type of customs procedure. Though it needs to be noted that since 2016 it is only possible to make declarations to EU customs administration via electronic means.

SAD-type customs documents (paper or electronic) are now also used, for example, by member countries of the Association of Southeast Asian Nations (ASEAN), the Eurasian Economic Community (EAEC) and the Southern Common Market (MERCOSUR). SAD-type forms are also used for customs declarations in another 90 countries around the world that use the United Nations Conference on Trade and Development's (UNCTAD) ASYCUDA customs software (ASYCUDA, 2020) – an electronic software solution designed to enable customs administrations to automate customs processing in line with the requirements of standard customs procedures, including those stipulated in the WCO Revised Kyoto Convention.

Key details that need to be declared in a customs declaration include:

- the trader's identification number;
- a customs procedure code; and
- all the details necessary for assessing the correct amount of duties and taxes, along with operational details and supporting documents.

The trader's identification number (WCO, 2018b) is normally subject to application by the trader. It is usually issued by Customs and valid indefinitely, though in some countries it might have to be periodically renewed (eg every three years). Depending on the country concerned, this identification number can go by different names. In the European Union and the United Kingdom, for example, it is referred to as the Economic Operators Registration and Identification (EORI) number. In the United States traders need to reference their Inland Revenue Service's (IRS) Employer Identification Number (EIN) (CHP, 2020). In many countries, the trader's identification number may be similarly aligned with other official business or tax registration numbers. In some countries the identification number used by Customs is linked to wider e-government type services (eg Ireland or the United Kingdom) and can be obtained with minimal (if any) additional administrative effort.

The customs procedure code is a reference number (sometimes with letters) that enables electronic customs systems to correctly identify the procedure under which the declaration is to be processed. Procedure codes tend to be specific to the requirements of the country's electronic customs system. They can thus differ from one country to the next and the list of potential codes can be extensive (UK Government, 2020). Some countries may also use special tariff classifications numbers in order to declare goods to special customs arrangements. These will normally be within the WCO's Harmonized Systems (HS) chapters 98 and 99, which are reserved for any additional national requirements. In France, for example, humanitarian relief shipments can be declared by reference to the HS heading 9919 (Grainger *et al*, 2019).

Details that must be declared in order to work out the correct amount of customs duty, but also where to inspect the goods and who is responsible, concern the:

- **tariff** against which the goods have been declared, such as: the tariff classification number, country of origin, the customs value – all covered in Chapter 2;
- **commercial arrangements**, such as: the consignor (exporter), consignee, representative;
- **transport arrangements**, such as: point of entry or exit, place of loading or location of goods, details about the vehicle moving the goods, delivery terms (see Incoterms® 2020, Chapter 7);
- **goods,** such as: description, marks and numbers, weight (net and gross), volume, number of units and/or packages, value;
- **payment,** such as: person responsible for making payments, exchange rates, duty deferment accounts (if any), banking details.

In most countries the data used within a customs declaration is defined in line with the WCO's standard data model (WCO, 2020c) and limited to what is necessary for meeting the requirements of the declared procedure (WCO, 2006). However, customs administrations do often need additional supporting evidence to help confirm what has been declared. Thus, in many countries customs officers routinely ask for the commercial invoice along with sight of relevant transport documents. Depending on the country concerned, these might have to be provided only upon demand or submitted as an attachment (paper or electronic scan) to the customs declaration. Any importer wishing to take advantage of preferential tariff rates must usually also provide proof of eligibility in the form of a preferential origin certificate, invoice statement or movement document. For declarations above a certain value, it is common for the customs administration to also request details about how the customs value has been determined. This must often be made in a separate customs valuation declaration (WCO, 2020a). All goods subject to prohibitions and restrictions – such as, for example, goods subject to quarantine checks, most medicines and many chemicals (Chapter 4) – are normally subject to additional document requirements, including certificates, licences, permits and authorizations.

It is important to note that most countries allow for significantly less onerous customs declaration requirements when goods are shipped by parcel using the national postal services. The procedures here are governed by the Universal Postal Union and were first estab-

FIGURE 3.2 CN22 customs declarations for parcel shipment with national postal services

UL 000 000 014 CA

CUSTOMS DECLARATION May be opened officially **CN 22**

Designated operator

Important! See instructions on the back

☐	Gift	☐	Commercial sample
☐	Documents	☐	Returned goods
☐	Sale of goods	☐	Other (please specify):______

Quantity and detailed description of contents (1)	Net weight (2)	Value and currency (3)	H S tariff number* (4)	Country of origin* (5)
Total weight *(in kg)* (6)		Total value (7)		

I, the undersigned, whose name and address are given on the item, certify that the particulars given in this declaration are correct and that this item does not contain any dangerous article or articles prohibited by legislation or by postal or customs regulations

Date and sender's signature (8)

Size 74 x 105 mm, white or green

SOURCE UPU, 2018

lished under its Treaty of Bern in 1874. Subsequently, most countries allow for goods of less than SDR 300 (US $400/£270) in value to be declared with a simple CN22 label (Figure 3.2) that is attached to the parcel (UPU, 2018). Most countries also operate special procedures for goods accompanied by travellers, such as merchandise in baggage. Here it is often possible to make the declaration in person using the red 'Goods to declare' lane at airports and similar terminals (UK Government, 2019).

For trade with a few counties **Pre-shipment Inspection (PSI)** requirements also apply. These tend to be associated with governments in developing countries that: have additional control requirements for safeguarding national financial interests (eg to prevent capital flight, commercial fraud, and customs duty evasion); or have to compensate for inadequacies in administrative infrastructures (WTO, 2020). PSI procedures tend to be very onerous and require goods to be independently inspected by an inspection company before they are imported and declared to Customs. Before the goods are exported, the officially appointed PSI company must check the goods alongside relevant commercial documents. Providing all is satisfactory the inspection company then issues a report that the importer needs to attach to the customs import declaration. Where in force, PSI rules and requirements can be varied and subject to frequent change.

Risk assessment

In most parts of the world the sheer volume of goods traded far exceeds the capacity of the customs administration to inspect each and every shipment. Moreover, the associated costs, especially for importers and exports, would be prohibitive. Repeated exposure to inspection-related costs undermines business competitiveness and if sustained is a significant barrier to trade. The WCO's Revised Kyoto Convention (WCO, 2006) as well as the WTO Trade Facilitation Agreement (WTO, 2014a) thus stress the importance of applying risk management principles in the control and inspection of goods. Moreover, customs risk management is considered to be a sophisticated undertaking that requires skill and expertise (Geourjon and Laporte, 2005; Han and Ireland, 2014). It is defined by the careful consideration of:

- the likelihood of the goods and parties involved not being compliant with customs requirements; and
- the consequences resulting from failing to stop non-complaint goods (Widdowson and Holloway, 2011).

Such assessment is usually based on an underlying risk management framework (WCO, 2020b). Some aspects of customs risk management are public, and are communicated accordingly to help entice and reward good business compliance practices. Many aspects of risk management are strictly confidential, especially where they relate to day-to-day operational decisions and ongoing investigations. The need to intercept cargo and conduct an inspection is most urgent where the likelihood and consequence of a compliance breach is the greatest.

FOOD FOR THOUGHT

A physical inspection can represent a significant cost to business operators. Costs include (amongst others):

- additional cargo handling (such as arranging for transport to the inspection facility);
- labour costs associated with unpacking and repacking;
- delays and missed delivery deadlines;
- transport rearrangement costs;
- storage costs (during inspection); and
- inventory costs (where businesses keep hold buffer stock to soften the impact of border delays).

Moreover, over-zealous border inspection regimes tie up scarce inspection resources. Any time wasted by officers inspecting compliant shipments reduces the chances of intercepting non-compliant and illegal activities.

SOURCE Grainger *et al*, 2018

When evaluating the likelihood of a business operator not being compliant, customs administrations may distinguish between four broad categories (WCO, 2020b):

1. **Those who are voluntarily compliant** – these parties know what is required and always get compliance right; and if an occasional genuine error occurs (eg a minor declaration error) the appropriate procedures to make corrections and make amends are immediately initiated. Unless there is good reason, the need to inspect is minimal.
2. **Those that try to be compliant but do not necessarily always succeed** – there can be many reasons for operators falling into this category: they may have received poor advice, they may not always check the paperwork or their administrative and commercial practices might be sloppy. The threat of inspection can be used to coerce operators into adopting more compliant practices.
3. **Those that will avoid complying if possible** – for example, parties that if left unchecked might choose to cheat. Closer attention and active interventions, including occasional inspections, are necessary to ensure compliance.
4. **Those that deliberately do not comply** – ie parties that will break the law, including smugglers and other criminals. Active interventions along with border inspections are necessary to intercept and stop illegal activities.

Factors that might inform on the consequences of non-compliance when making a risk assessment can be broad, too. Often these factors are confidential. That said, certain goods can be particularly attractive to criminals, especially those where import duties and taxes are high – as is often the case with tobacco products. Customs officials might play closer attention to such goods, especially if the operators concerned are known to have compliance issues. Likewise, a common concern amongst those enforcing border controls is that dishonest operators may want to under-declare their goods, for example by deliberately mis-reporting the volumes, weight and quantities or deliberately using the wrong tariff classification codes. Thus, officers in instances of suspicion and where the risk is merited will conduct an inspection to check that what has been declared matches what has been shipped.

Usually, the risk assessment is automatically initiated upon the receipt of any advance declarations along with any subsequent information in the full declaration. Some administrations, such as those of the European Union (EU), may distinguish between a risk assessment for security proposes – which is based on the advance declaration – and another risk assessment for fiscal purposes – which is based on the full declaration (EU, 2013). Inspection selection criteria are often codified in the form of a 'risk profile'. Such a risk profile might be set to certain types of goods or types of operations that merit routine closer investigation.

Where the declared data matches those profiles, officers then take further steps, including, where necessary, a physical inspection. Some risk profiles might be confidential, others are widely known. For example, goods subject to additional control requirements by other regulatory agencies are routinely flagged automatically to customs officers so that they can check whether relevant conditions set by those agencies have been fulfilled (Chapter 4). Obvious errors in the declaration will also trigger a further investigation – for example,

FIGURE 3.3 Examples of data sources informing risk-based inspection decisions

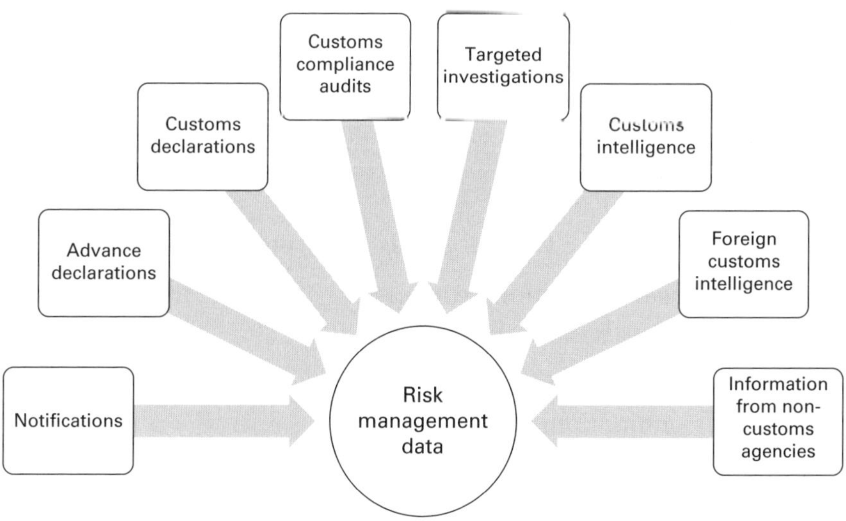

where goods are described as 'parts' and the required context is missing. Many risk profiles will draw on detailed intelligence collected by customs administrations at home, abroad and within the context of ongoing investigations by Customs and other law enforcement agencies (Figure 3.3). Businesses that trade regularly will want to play close attention to making sure that they are always compliant in order to mitigate any high-risk perception by Customs (Chapter 6). They may also participate in special customs partnership programmes that reward measures designed to emphasize their trustworthiness – so-called Trusted Trader or Authorized Economic Operator schemes (Chapter 7).

Inspection

Inspections will take place in instances where the border agencies decide to take a closer look at the goods. Usually, such decisions by customs officers should be based on robust risk analysis. However, in many countries non-customs agencies might be obliged to adhere to set inspection targets – as is, for example, the case for certain types of SPS controls (Chapter 4). The applied inspection methods and practices vary widely and often also have to accommodate the specific practicalities at the border crossing point, port or airport.

One key distinction is between inspection methods that are intrusive and those that are not. Intrusive methods require special handling facilities which inevitably require whoever is handling the cargo (eg stevedore, handling agent, truck driver) to deliver that cargo to the inspection facility. Such an intrusive inspection can take multiple formats, including:

- seal-checks, to make sure cargo has not been opened en route;
- a quick visual inspection (spot-check) to verify that the goods match what has been declared;
- sampling, where part of the consignment undergoes a more rigorous examination;
- a full inspection, where the entire consignment undergoes a rigorous examination.

During examination officers may need handling labour in order to move, open and unpack the selected consignments. Such handling at maritime ports is usually provided by stevedores and at airports by cargo handling agents. At road border crossing and ferry ports border staff usually direct the driver of the vehicle to the relevant inspection facility. Common examination practices, depending on the identified risk, include:

- counting, weighing and measuring, eg to make sure goods have not been over- or under-declared;
- scanning, to see if anything is hidden inside the goods;
- detailed analysis, for example by sending a sample to an official laboratory.

Non-intrusive inspection techniques should be less burdensome. For example, in many parts of the world border agencies routinely check for radioactive traces using relevant detectors. These can be installed at operationally efficient locations, such as along the road towards the border crossing or at a port gate controlling access to the port estate.

Images of what is inside containers, vehicles and goods can be made with gamma-ray and X-ray radiography systems. Such scanning systems normally require dedicated facilities, but unlike physical examinations, they have the advantage that containers and vehicles do not have to be opened. It also enables officers to view – with limitations – what is inside the vehicles and containers without having to break seals and other security devices. Many countries also allow for inspections to take place at locations away from the port or border. These tend to be less operationally constrained; in some cases the inspection might even take place at the trader's own premises, providing they are suitably authorized and equipped (Chapter 5).

Payment

A key purpose of customs control usually is to collect the applicable taxes and duties. The amount that traders need to pay is calculated by reference to the declared tariff classification, origin and customs value. The procedure code is also important since certain types of procedures provide for duty deferment or relief (see Chapter 2) and goods may move on without making payment at the border. Where payment is conditional for release, it can usually be made in multiple ways, such as: in cash; electronically; or on account, where relevant parties deposit sufficient funds for customs to draw upon.

In line with the WCO Revised Kyoto Convention many countries allow traders to defer payment. In the EU, for example, payment may be deferred for payment to the 16th day of the following month in question (EU, 2013). To take advantage of such a deferment account, the customs administration normally insists on a financial guarantee, which needs to be set up separately with a suitably authorized bank.

Independently from Customs, other types of payment may be due. Common are:

- electronic system charges and submission fees;
- processing fees for paper documents;
- customs inspections fees;
- inspection fees for non-customs border agencies;
- handling charges;
- storage and demurrage charges;
- infrastructure charges and tolls.

Each of the above might require their own payment arrangements. Often intermediaries add additional charges for making the payments on the trader's behalf. For example, at many ports it is customary for the shipping line to pay the stevedore's handling charges that arise within the context of a customs inspection. The shipping line may then choose to pass those charges on to their customers with an uplift to account for their incurred additional expenses. Ports and shipping lines do not normally permit cargo to leave the port estate until relevant fees and charges have been paid.

Release

'Release of goods means the action by Customs to permit goods undergoing clearance to be placed at the disposal of the persons concerned' (WCO, 2006). Release from the port or border is not necessarily dependent on the payment of taxes and duties. Goods may move under customs control to a customs-approved inland destination or a customs-approved facility where goods can be held under duty suspension. Goods are cleared by Customs once all formalities applicable to the declared procedures (eg import, export or transit) have been completed.

For some types of procedures this may necessitate traders or their representatives to submit supplementary customs declarations at some later point. For example, customs procedures where goods are released under customs control usually require traders to keep relevant records with details about handling and the goods' whereabouts. In the case where goods have been released for entry into a customs warehouse, the warehouse keeper is required to keep detailed inventory records which in turn are subject to customs scrutiny. That scrutiny of warehousing records might be via direct interfaces with the customs computer system or in the form of periodic audits (eg quarterly or annually) by customs officers.

Customs release is usually also dependent on presenting proof that any conditions set by other government agencies, such as those concerning quarantine inspections, have been met (Grainger, 2013). Figure 3.4 provides an illustrative summary of the many document requirements (paper or electronic) upon which release from customs control – as well as that of other agencies – may be dependent. Institutional arrangements, including the demarcation of responsibilities between Customs and non-customs agencies can vary significantly from country to country (Chapter 4).

Electronic infrastructure

At the heart of most customs control systems is an electronic IT system. It is able to take data – such as the cargo manifest, advance

FIGURE 3.4 Illustrative model of document requirements to effect release from border controls

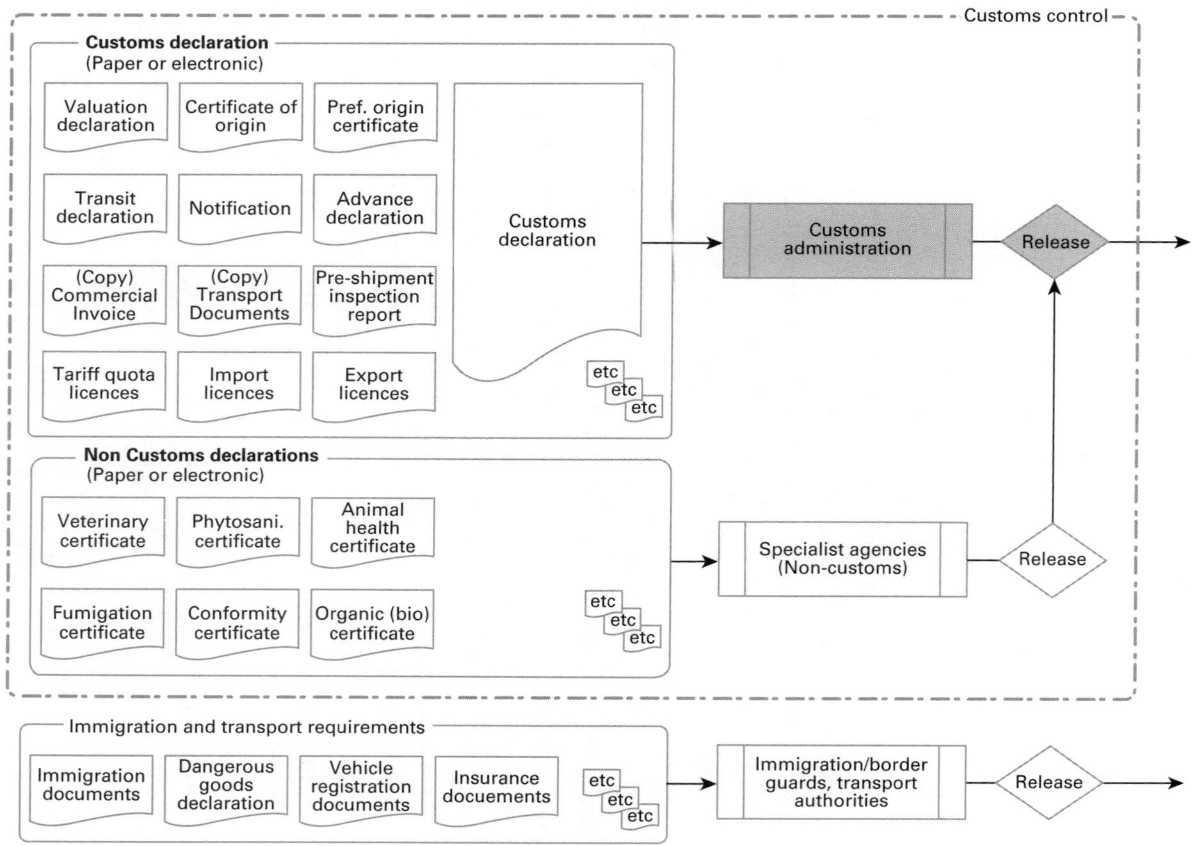

SOURCE © Trade Facilitation Consulting Ltd

declaration and full declaration – and process it in line with the applicable requirements. Depending on the country concerned, customs systems often have the following functionality:

- accept electronic notifications (eg cargo manifest), advance notifications and declarations;
- conduct an automatic risk assessment;
- process declarations in line with the requirements of the declared procedure;
- calculate and collect applicable duties and taxes;
- verify with other government agencies whether their controls have been completed;
- keep records by reference to the trader's reference number.

Customs systems can differ significantly in design and functionality. This might be the result of the fact that different customs administrations have embraced electronic solutions at different points in time or because they rely on bespoke software developed by their preferred provider. Depending on the prevailing e-government strategy there might also be considerable integration with other electronic government infrastructure. Operating models may differ, too. In some countries electronic customs solutions may be supplied as a contracted service while in others the customs system is run and developed in-house by the administration. Often the systems are a mix of in-house developments and contracted services. Amongst developing and emerging economies many use the ASYCUDA software developed by the United Nations Conference for Trade and Development (UNCTAD). Its first iteration was launched in the early 1980s with further updates in the mid-1980s (ASYCUDA V2), early 1990s (ASYCUDA++) and early 2000s (ASYCUDA World). Versions of the last two updates are used in over 90 countries (ASYCUDA, 2020).

As previously mentioned, much of the data used by Customs in the control of goods is derived from the commercial data arising between the seller and buyer and their respective transport arrangements. There is a considerable international effort to help standardize customs data requirements along with supporting document and electronic messaging formats (Chapter 9). Indeed, most countries, including those using ASYCUDA software, have aligned it with the specifications of the WCO Data Model (WCO, 2019) and the UN's recommendations for data simplification and standardization for international trade (UNECE, 2010).

Subsequently, many countries are served by specialist software companies who are able to support much of the information flow

FIGURE 3.5 Information flow between parties to effect customs release

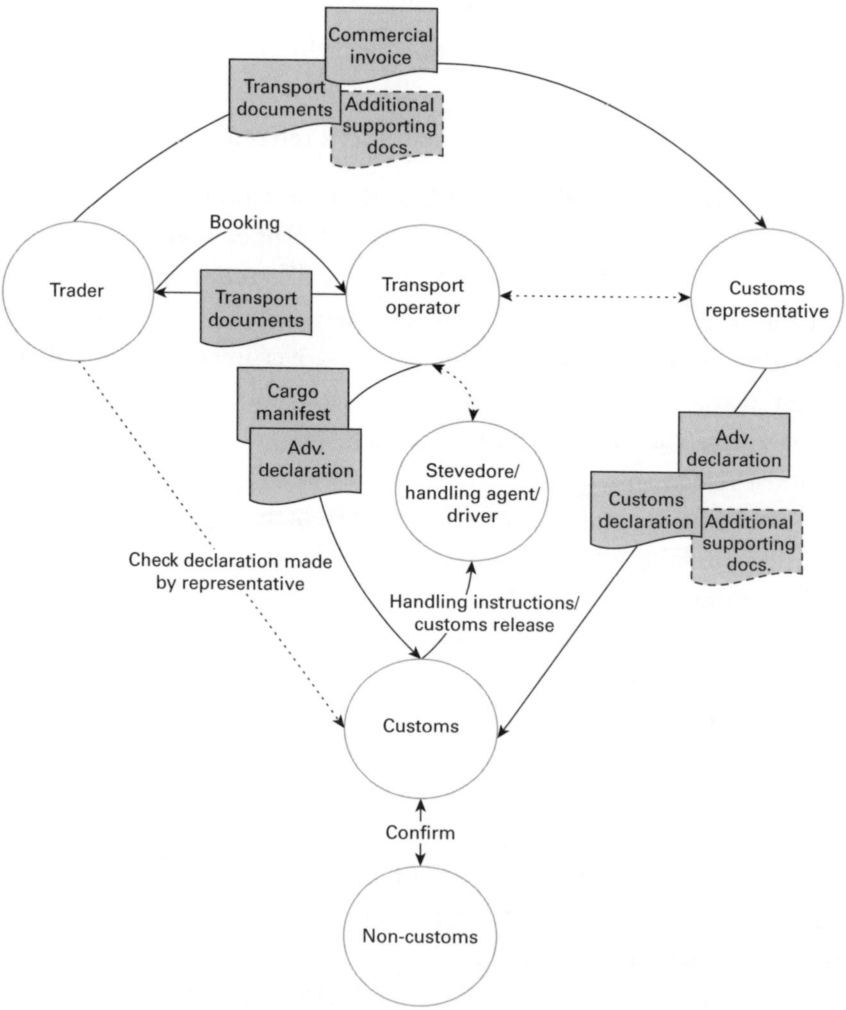

SOURCE Trade Facilitation Consulting Ltd

FIGURE 3.6 The exchange of information via a port community system to support the handling of maritime cargo

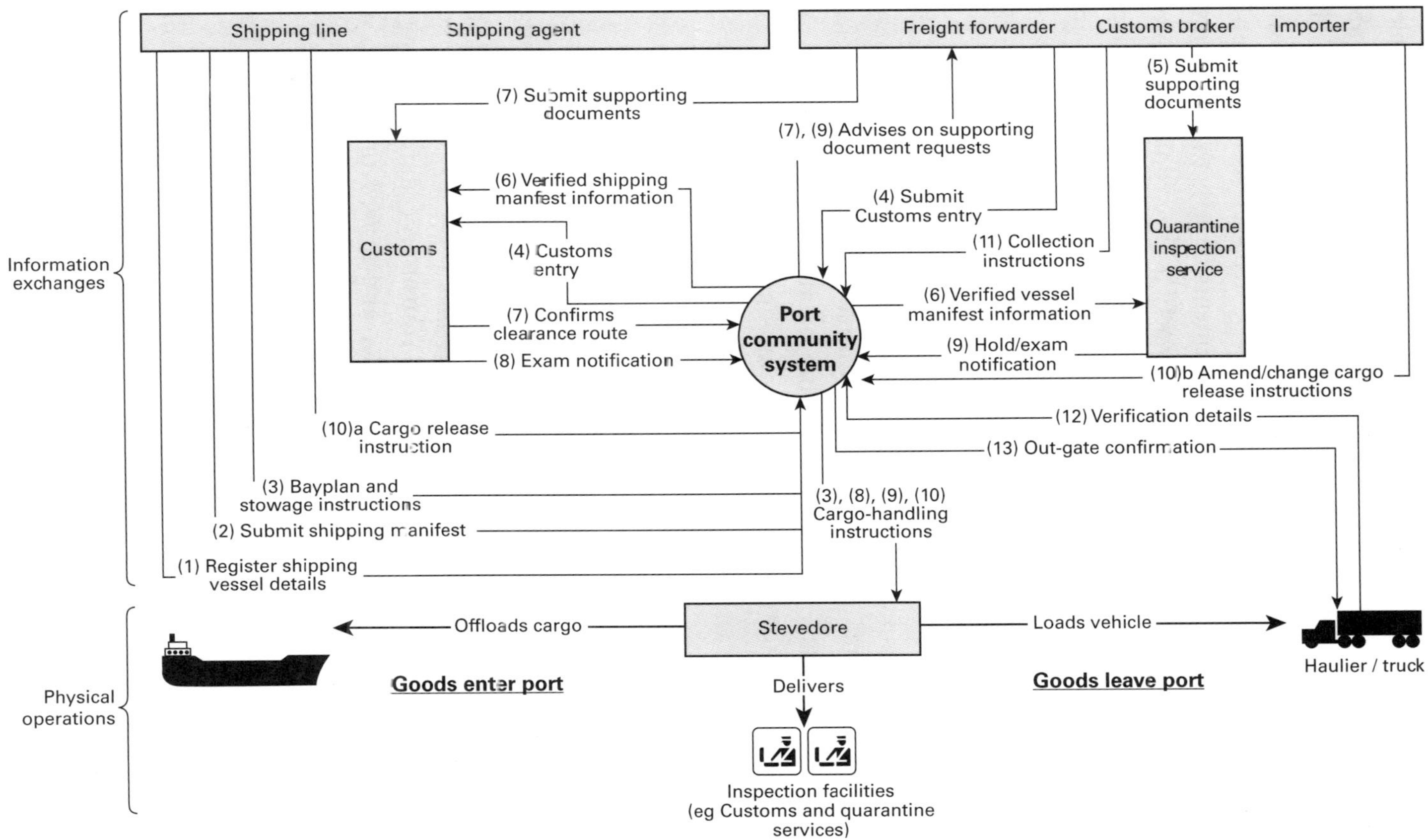

SOURCE Grainger, 2014

between the commercial parties and the border agencies via electronic means (Figure 3.5). Often these software solutions are also able to extract standard commercial and transport data from the trader's electronic systems and convert them into the relevant paper documents or their electronic equivalent. Often such software suppliers are also able to transmit those documents directly to the customs computer system in the right format via EDI (electronic data interchange) or web interface (Chapter 9). In the absence of such services, operators or Customs may have to take relevant documents and manually enter the data into the customs computer system. This can significantly add to the time it takes to clear goods – as well as to the cost of trading (Chapter 8).

At busy container ports and airports users may be served by specialist community systems. These take care of the exchange of all the operational and regulatory information necessary to effect customs release – be it to load a ship or aircraft for export, or to release cargo from the port estate for an import (Figure 3.6).

Customs transit

Customs transit procedures are very relevant for certain types of trade operations. They apply to transport operations where shipment between the country of export and the country of import goes via a third country, as will be the case for most trade with landlocked countries (unless made directly by air). Transit procedures also apply where goods are released at the border and moved onward to an inland destination whilst still under customs control – eg to an inland customs clearance station or dry port.

A key feature of transit procedures is a financial guarantee. This ensures that Customs can draw on applicable duties and taxes if goods do not leave the country as intended in the case of international transit or arrive at the designated inland destination in the case of national transit. Normally goods shipped under transit procedures also need to be sealed (eg inside a container or lorry trailer) with a customs seal. Release from the transit procedures at the exit border crossing or inland customs facility is usually conditional upon Customs checking that the seal has not been broken.

Transit procedures often require their own paperwork or electronic systems to capture when the goods are entered into transit and when they are released as well as to record the seal number and the financial guarantee details. Time limits and route constraints may also apply (WCO, 2000a). To help automate and speed up transit formalities, some trade partners have developed dedicated electronic solutions. These include, for example, ASEAN's Customs Transit System (ACTS) (ASEAN, 2020) and the European Union's New Computerized Transit System (NCTS) (European Commission, 2016).

More than 70 countries also subscribe to the *Transports Internationaux Routiers* (TIR) Convention. It first came into force in 1975 and provides for the international transport of goods under the cover of TIR carnets between contracting countries (UNECE, 2018). The TIR carnet is tied to a financial guarantee while goods are under transit. The goods must also be sealed in vehicles or containers. The TIR carnet arrangements are managed by the International Road Transport Union (IRU) and can be obtained from national road transport associations.

Transhipment procedures apply where transport and logistics arrangements are routed via hubs – as is often the case for containerized transport and shipments by air. Most countries with transhipment hubs offer significant simplifications in line with the WCO's Revised Customs Convention's transhipment guidelines (WCO, 2000b). A key characteristic of transhipment operations is that they take place within a relatively short time frame and usually within customs-controlled areas – such as a maritime port or airport. Transhipment declarations can thus normally be made by the transport operator using information that they have captured from shippers, their customers. At busy transhipment hubs (such as a container terminal or airport) it is often possible for carriers to lodge transhipment declarations in the form of aggregated lists. These tend to be generated automatically and processed electronically, matching inward movements with those going out.

Business support

Customs control goes hand-in-hand with business support. It is in the interest of customs administrations that businesses know how to be compliant. With a good risk management system in place customs administrations can reward businesses with a lighter touch as well as access to beneficial customs procedures. Customs administrations offer business support in a wider range of practical and procedural ways.

Much of the practical support focuses on advice and guidance. This often includes commitments to publishing all applicable procedures along with guidance in an easy-to-understand way. It often also includes the offer of formal training, eg online or in seminars (especially when Customs introduce new procedures and systems). Customs websites with details about customs procedures and requirements are now almost standard. It is also common for many administrations to set up business support groups where dedicated officers lend practical advice and guidance. And in some countries, such as those in the European Union, any person (including companies) 'may request information concerning the application of the customs legislation from the customs authorities' (Article 14 of the Union Customs Code (EU)).

Practical support can also be found in the form of service commitments. Often this includes commitments to process correctly declared declarations and effect release within a specific time period – eg no more than 24 hours – unless the risk assessment gives rise for further investigation. Similar service standards are common for customs' electronic infrastructure and interfaces, including commitments about reliability and responsible treatment of confidential data. Likewise, office and operating hours are often aligned with shipping and airline schedules.

Practical support may also include arrangements that allow transport operators carrying consolidated cargo (eg one vehicle with multiple consignments for different shippers) to offload any consignments selected for inspection (and later collection) and carry on their journey with the remaining consignments. Usually, it is also permissible for businesses to declare multiple shipments belonging to one consignment (eg where the consignment is too large to fit on one vehicle) to be declared on one declaration.

Procedural support can be equally varied and often follows in the commitments under the WTO Trade Facilitation Agreement (Chapters 8 and 9). Consistently compliant traders and those who have invested in making their supply chains secure, may, for example, apply for a trusted trader status. This, as discussed in Chapter 5, gives access to preferential customs treatment. In Chapter 2 reference has already been made to procedures that, subject to authorization, give additional operational or fiscal benefits.

Customs administrations usually offer advance binding tariff information (BTI). Businesses unsure about the correct tariff classification can apply to Customs for a binding decision. This is particularly useful for goods where the correct classification is ambiguous or has been subject to challenge. Where a BTI is used officers at the port or border are obliged to honour that decision. Similarly, fast-track appeal procedures (days or weeks rather than months or years) can quickly help resolve disputes arising within the clearance process. Most administrations also allow businesses to amend declarations (eg because the ship carrying the goods was diverted or delayed) as well as correct genuine administrative mistakes.

Increasingly, customs administrations are also bound to adhere to trade facilitation principles that seek to reduce the cost of compliance whilst still safeguarding control objectives (Chapters 8 and 9).

ACTIVITIES AND DISCUSSION POINTS

1. Discuss to what extent the assessment of customs risk should be influenced by the availability of customs officers to conduct inspections.
2. Reflecting on your TV viewing habits, give an account of how criminals might smuggle goods (or people) across a border. Discuss whether such criminal activity could be detected by scrutinizing the customs declaration.
3. Conduct a web search for your customs administration's website. Explore that website with particular focus on: a) the compliance requirements for importing goods; b) the type of business support services that the customs administration might offer.

References

ASEAN (2020) ASEAN Customs Transit System (ACTS), https://acts.asean.org/acts (archived at https://perma.cc/MY2Y-PZAS)

ASYCUDA (2020) About ASYCUDA, asycuda.org/en/about/ (archived at https://perma.cc/4ART-UKJF)

CHP (2020) Importers: Social security number/Tax Identification Number/IRS Number/Importer Number, help.cbp.gov/s/article/Article-314?language=en_US (archived at https://perma.cc/FV6M-FFHV)

EU (2013) Regulation (EU) No 952/2013 of the European Parliament and the Council of 9 October 2013 laying down the Union Customs Code (recast), *Official Journal of the European Union,* **56** (L269)

European Commission (2016) *Transit Manual* (TAXUD/A2/TRA/003/2016-EN), European Commission, Brussels

European Commission (2020) The Union Customs Code: A recast of the Modernised Customs Code, ec.europa.eu/taxation_customs/customs/customs_code/union_customs_code/index_en.htm (archived at https://perma.cc/HS7D-7VTZ)

European Union (1993) Commission Regulation (EEC) No 2454/93 of 2 July 1993 laying down provisions for the implementation of Council Regulation (EEC) No 2913/92 establishing the Community Customs Code, *Official Journal of the European Union,* **36** (L253), pp 1–177

Grainger, A (2013) *Trade and Customs Procedures: The compliance costs for UK meat imports,* Nottingham University, eprints.nottingham.ac.uk/2143/ (archived at https://perma.cc/5W84-QLM8)

Grainger, A (2014) Trade and customs compliance costs at ports, *Maritime Economics & Logistics,* **16** (4), pp 467–83, doi:10.1057/mel.2014.8

Grainger, A, Rundle, JM and Ahsen, SR (2019) Customs and humanitarian logistics. *Global Trade and Customs Journal,* (**4**), pp 154–68

Grainger, A, Bartels, K, Boskovic, T, Milosevic, S, Rackovic, M, Sowinski, Cand Pope, S (2021) What the example of Montenegro's new pre-arrival processing capabilities tell us about Customs performance measurement, *WCO News*

Grainger, A, Huiden, R, Rukanov, Band Tan, Y-H (2018) What is the cost of customs and borders across the supply chain? ... and how to mitigate the cost through better coordination and data sharing, *World Customs Journal,* **12** (1), pp 1–28

Han, C-R and Ireland, R (2014) Performance measurement of the KCS customs selectivity system, *Risk Management,* **16** (1), pp 1460–3799, dx.doi.org/10.1057/rm.2014.2 (archived at https://perma.cc/SBH3-HU3X)

ICAO (2017) Annex 9 to the Convention on International Civil Aviation: Facilitation (15th edn), International Civil Aviation Organization, Montreal

IMO (1998) Facilitation Convention (FAL), International Maritime Organization, London

UK Government (2019) Taking merchandise from GB in your baggage, www.gov.uk/guidance/taking-merchandise-from-the-uk-in-your-baggage (archived at https://perma.cc/4YTA-ZXGH)

UK Government (2020) Imports: customs procedure codes, www.gov.uk/government/publications/uk-trade-tariff-customs-procedure-codes/imports-customs-procedure-codes (archived at https://perma.cc/ZF6U-VQDD)

UN CEFACT (1981) Recommendation 1: United Nations Layout Key for Trade Documents, in Vol. ECE/TRADE/137, p 11, United Nations, Geneva

UNECE (2010) UNECE Recommendation 34: Data Simplification and Standardization for International Trade, United Nations, Geneva

UNECE (2018) *TIR Handbook: Customs Convention on the international transport of goods under cover of TIR carnets,* TIR Convention, 1975, United Nations, Geneva

UPU (2018) *Convention Manual*, Universal Postal Union, Bern

USITA (2021) De Minimis Value: Express shipment exemptions, www.trade.gov/de-minimis-value (archived at https://perma.cc/VF63-C9PB)

WCO (2000a) *Kyoto Convention – Specific Annex E – Chapter 1 Guidelines on Customs transit,* World Customs Organization, Brussels

WCO (2000b) *Kyoto Convention – Specific Annex E – Chapter 2 Guidelines on Transhipment,* World Customs Organization, Brussels

WCO (2006) *Revised Kyoto Convention; International Convention on the Simplifications and Harmonisation of Customs Procedures,* World Customs Organization, Brussels

WCO (2018a) *SAFE Framework of Standards (2018 edition),* World Customs Organization, Brussels, www.wcoomd.org/-/media/wco/public/global/pdf/topics/facilitation/instruments-and-tools/tools/safe-package/safe-framework-of-standards.PDF?la=en (archived at https://perma.cc/VLZ7-LYHL)

WCO (2018b) *WCO Guidelines on Trader Identification Number,* World Customs Organization, Brussels, www.wcoomd.org/-/media/wco/public/global/pdf/topics/facilitation/instruments-and-tools/tools/trader-identification-number/guidelines-on-trader-identification-number.pdf?db=web (archived at https://perma.cc/42Q8-V9S4)

WCO (2019) *Global Adoption of the WCO Data Model,* 1 July, World Customs Organization, Brussels, www.wcoomd.org/-/media/wco/public/global/pdf/topics/facilitation/instruments-and-tools/tools/data-model/global-adoption-of-the-wco-data-model_en.PDF?la=en (archived at https://perma.cc/8TPP-JMS7)

WCO (2020a) *Guide to the Exchange of Customs Valuation Information*, www.wcoomd.org/en/topics/valuation/instruments-and-tools/~/media/WCO/Public/Global/PDF/Topics/Valuation/Instruments%20and%20Tools/Guides/guide_exchange.ashx (archived at https://perma.cc/LAH8-YGK2)

WCO (2020b) *WCO Customs Risk Management Compendium,* www.wcoomd.org/en/Topics/Facilitation/Instrument%20and%20Tools/Tools/Risk%20Management%20Compendium (archived at https://perma.cc/A9NB-24EX)

WCO (2020c) *WCO Data Model: Tools and Instruments,* www.wcoomd.org/en/topics/facilitation/instrument-and-tools/~/link.aspx?_id=3BD324CD868948748147E210059706BC&_z=z (archived at https://perma.cc/TB6T-UU2R)

Widdowson, D (2016) Managing the border: A transformational shift to pre-export screening, *World Customs Journal,* **10** (2), pp 3–15, worldcustomsjournal.org/Archives/Volume%2010%2C%20Number%202%20(Sep%202016)/1806%2001%20WCJ%20v10n2%20Widdowson.pdf (archived at https://perma.cc/EAY2-8FV7)

Widdowson, D, Blegen, B, Kashubsky, M and Grainger, A (2014) *Review of Accredited Operator Schemes,* Centre for Customs and Excise Studies, Charles Sturt University, Bathurst, Australia

Widdowson, D and Holloway, S (2011) Core border management disciplines: Risk-based compliance management, in *Border Management Modernization,* eds G McLinden, E Fanta, D Widdowson and T Doyle, pp 95–113, World Bank, Washington, DC

WTO (2014a) Agreement on Trade Facilitation (WT/L/931), World Trade Organization, Geneva, www.wto.org/english/tratop_e/tradfa_e/tradfa_e.htm (archived at https://perma.cc/XSX4-488B)

WTO (2014b) Protocol amending the Marrakesh Agreement Establising the World Trade Organization, Decision of 27 November 2014: Agreement on Trade Facilitation (WT/L/940), World Trade Organization, Geneva

WTO (2020) Preshipment Inspection, www.wto.org/english/tratop_e/preship_e/preship_e.htm (archived at https://perma.cc/N6NB-CLD7)

04

Prohibitions, restrictions and other border procedures

Chapters 2 and 3 were largely about customs procedures that concern import duties and taxes, and the necessary declarations that have to be made to place goods under customs control and secure release. However, Customs, in concert with a long list of other regulatory agencies (Figure 4.1), is also responsible for the enforcement of controls for goods where their trade is restricted or prohibited. In addition, there are also procedures concerning vehicles carrying the traded goods and people who operate (drive) those vehicles. These all add to the challenge of cross-border logistics operations.

The practicalities associated with these additional procedures can be demanding for operators and government agencies alike and is the focus of this chapter. Many prohibited or restricted goods are subject to keen public scrutiny, especially where the measures seek to protect public health, national security, safety or the environment. Inevitably, where businesses trade in such goods additional documents are needed – usually in the form of certificates, licences, permits and authorizations that must be obtained by relevant authorities before export and/or before import (Box 4.1).

Documents might travel with the goods or need to be presented in advance by the trader or the trader's representative to the relevant agencies – as is commonly the case for most sanitary and phytosanitary procedures that apply to products of animal origin (eg meat and hides) and the soil (eg seeds and plants). Some procedures, such as for wood packaging and most foods, also have marking and labelling

FIGURE 4.1 Government organizations often involved in trade and border controls

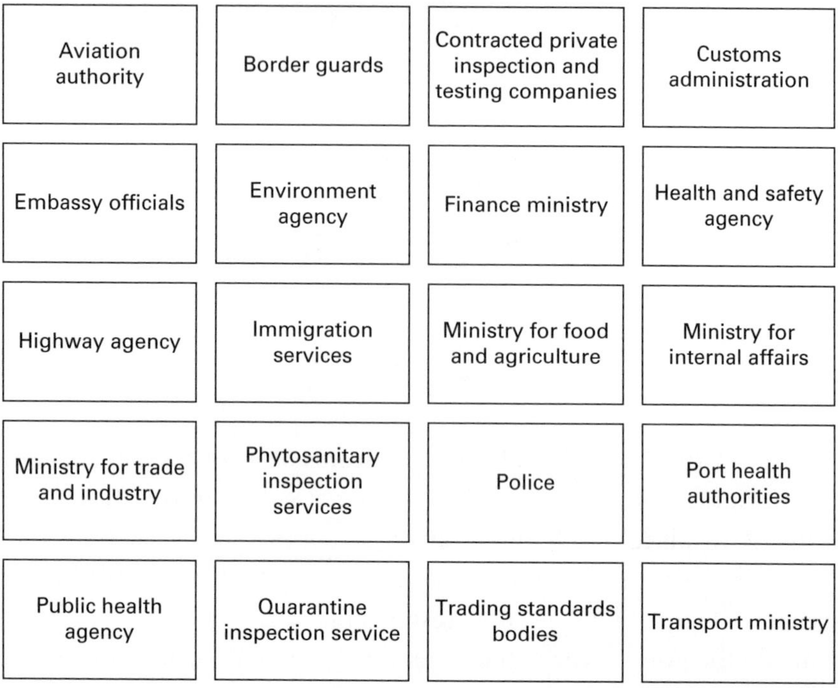

requirements. Customs officers are frequently tasked with assisting colleagues from other agencies (Figure 4.1). This often includes documentary checks to make sure they have completed their tasks before releasing the goods from customs control and onward transport. Those agencies, just like Customs, may also have their own pre-notification requirements.

BOX 4.1

Types of document commonly associated with non-customs procedures

- **Export licences or permits**, which are permissions to export – as is commonly the case for strategic export controls, such as those governing arms, dual-use items and the manufacture of weapons of mass destruction.

- **Import licences or permits**, which are permissions to import – as is commonly the requirement for importing regulated medicines.
- **Certificates**, which confirm compliance with regulatory specifications – as is commonly the requirement for the trade in products subject to veterinary and plant health checks.
- **Accompanying documents**, which move with the goods or vehicle – as is commonly required for special customs procedures like transit but also for cargo handling, dangerous goods and any requirements specific to the driver or vehicle (eg diving and operating licences).
- **Stamps and labels**, which have to be attached onto the goods or packaging – as is often the requirement for conformity with product safety and food labelling specifications.
- **Declarations/Notifications/Advance Notifications**, which are required for placing goods under the control of relevant authorities until they have completed all relevant checks – as is the requirement for customs control as well as quarantine controls, amongst others.
- **Supporting documents**, which are needed by the respective authorities where declared information needs to be substantiated – which in the case of non-customs checks often includes a copy of (or access to) the customs declaration as well as relevant transport and commercial documents.
- **Authorizations,** which grant business operators certain operational or fiscal privileges.

Prohibited and restricted goods

The list of goods that are subject to specific prohibitions and restriction – where trade is not permitted or only under strict conditions – can be long. World Trade Organization (WTO) rules permit these under Article XX of the GATT (GATT, 1994). Although the WTO list of permitted prohibitions and restrictions is extensive, they can be broadly attributed to grounds of:

- public morality, public policy or public security;
- the protection of health and life of humans, animals or plants;

FIGURE 4.2 Common prohibitions by reference to regulatory themes

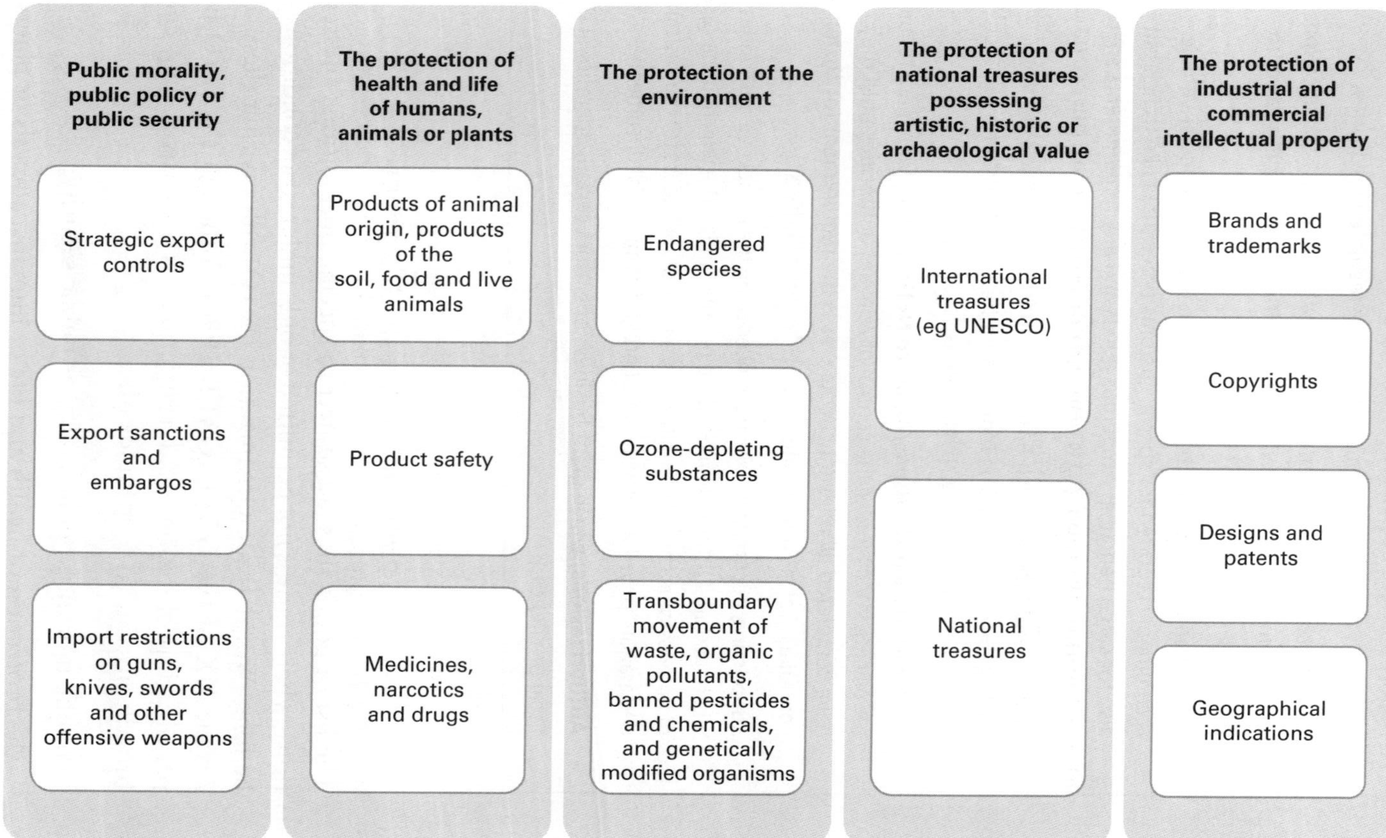

- the protection of the environment;
- the protection of national treasures possessing artistic, historic or archaeological value; and
- the protection of industrial and commercial intellectual property.

SOURCE European Commission, 2018

Often national prohibitions and restrictions are tied to wider international agreements or treaties between countries with shared concerns. Some prohibitions and restrictions might be driven by purely national sensitivities. Figure 4.2 offers an overview of common regulatory concerns that give rise to WTO permitted prohibitions and restrictions.

Public morality, public policy or public security

This is a broad category, but one big theme here is **export controls** born from security-related concerns at home or abroad.

Many goods are subject to **strategic export controls.** Typically, these encompass all goods that have been specifically designed or modified for military use, dual-use items (civilian goods that can also have military applications), associated technologies and torture instruments. Export controls normally also extend to radioactive substances, toxins and certain types of biological agents. To assist with compliance some countries publish lists that businesses must consult, with details about controlled goods and 'ratings'. 'Rating' systems differ from tariff classification and are specifically designed for export control purposes (DIT, 2019; BIS, 2020a). Many listed goods and ratings are the result of international treaty commitments and collaboration (see Box 4.2).

But procedures and practices do vary from one country to the next. Often export control obligations extend to goods that are seemingly benign, but have repugnant applications. For example, centrifuges used in medical research could also have applications in the development of biochemical weapons. IT and video equipment could be used for the surveillance of tortured prisoners. A pick-up truck could, with some refitting, be converted into a light armoured vehicle.

Where authorities decide that the trade is permitted, because it can be established that those goods do not violate underlying policy and treaty obligations, an export licence will be permitted. The licensing process can involve multiple specialist authorities with input from foreign policy officials, security specialists and intelligence agencies amongst others. Border agencies are usually tasked with checking those licences before export clearance. And they are also responsible for intercepting the export of any controlled goods where the licence was not obtained, and thus illegal.

BOX 4.2

International treaties, instruments and work programmes concerning export controls

- **Australia Group:** an informal global forum for countries that seeks to harmonize export controls.
- **Biological and Toxin Weapons Convention** (BTWC): in force since 1975 banning the development, production, stockpiling, acquisition and use of bacteriological and toxin weapons.
- **Chemical Weapons Convention** (CWC): in force since 1997 and bans the possession, development, stockpiling, transfer and use of chemical weapons.
- **Convention on the Prohibition of the Use, Stockpiling, Production and Transfer of Anti-Personnel Mines:** signed by 164 countries.
- **Hague Code of Conduct against Ballistic Missile Proliferation** (HCOC): signed by more than 140 countries.
- **Missile Technology Control Regime:** a grouping of 35 countries working together to restrict exports of missile and rocket systems.
- **Nuclear Supplier Group:** a group of countries that seeks to curb proliferation of nuclear weapons through the adoption of guidelines concerning nuclear exports and nuclear-related export.
- **The Wassenaar Arrangement on Export Controls for Conventional Arms and Dual-Use Goods and Technologies:** a group of 40 countries which, amongst other activities, drafts lists of arms and dual-use goods.

- **Treaty on the Non-Proliferation of Nuclear Weapons** (NPT) 1968: signed by over 180 countries.
- **UN Security Council Resolution 1540:** regarding the non-proliferation of weapons of mass destruction; unanimously adopted in 2004.
- **United Nation's Office for Disarmament Affairs:** a UN body that lends substantive and organizational support for norm-setting in disarmament-related policy areas.
- **United Nations Convention Against Torture and Other Cruel, Inhuman or Degrading Treatment or Punishment**, 1984.
- **United Nations Convention against Transnational Organized Crime** (UN Firearms Protocol) 2000: signed by 190 countries.
- **Zangger Committee:** an international committee with 39 members and includes all nuclear weapon states. It aims to assist the Treaty on the Non-Proliferation of Nuclear Weapons by harmonizing the interpretation of nuclear export control policies.

SOURCE Respective websites of all the listed organizations, 2021

Another export control theme is that of **trade sanctions and embargos.** These are driven by foreign policy concerns and prohibit or restrict trade with specific countries. Often, but not always, embargos and restrictions are applied after consultation with the United Nation's Security Council. Some sanction regimes are targeted against trade with listed named persons (individuals and companies). The UN's Security Council Consolidated List is one such example (UN Security Council, 2020), the United States' 'denied persons' list is another (BIS, 2020b). The trade in rough diamonds is restricted under the Kimberley Process Certification Scheme applied by more than 80 countries. The Kimberley Process aims to eliminate the trade in conflict diamonds, used by rebel movements or their allies to finance strife. Shipments of rough diamonds must be certified by the relevant authorities and those certificates must also be presented to Customs in order to maintain their conflict-free status (Kimberley Process, 2020).

Most countries also enforce strict national legislation that controls the **import of guns, knives, swords and other offensive weapons** (including parts and ammunition). The import of such goods is usually subject to a special import permit along with extensive conditions with regard to use, storage and ownership. These can differ from one country to the next and in part reflect public policy about weapon ownership. Border agencies are usually tasked with checking the licences of legal imports and intercepting any illegal imports (UK Government, 2018).

Many countries also ban the trade in **goods deemed to be immoral.** The range of goods that are deemed to be immoral can vary. In many places it includes indecent or obscene visual materials. The European Union bans the trade in dog and cat fur (European Union, 2007). Increasingly there is also worldwide concern about goods that are the result of production processes involving modern forms of slavery, forced labour and child labour (European Parliament, 2019) or prison labour (New Zealand, 2019). Many countries also enforce measures against organ trafficking and transplant tourism (Bos, 2015).

The protection of health and life of humans, animals or plants

This is a big subject area and can place a lot of demands on cross-border logistics operations. Resulting trade barriers are frequently the concern of dispute, and can make trade negotiations between countries difficult, especially where standards and procedures differ significantly – such as, for example, the differences in treating chicken meat between the United States and the European Union. The United States recommends that chicken should be treated with chlorine while the EU bans chlorine washing (Schraer and Edgington, 2019). There are three broad regulatory focal points: the trade in products of animal origin, products of the soil, food and live animals; product safety standards; and medicines and narcotics. Each of the controlled products within these groups comes with its own regulatory requirements.

PRODUCTS OF ANIMAL ORIGIN, PRODUCTS OF THE SOIL, FOOD AND LIVE ANIMALS

The trade in foods, live animals, products of animal origin and products of the soil is subject to sanitary, phytosanitary, animal welfare, veterinary and food safety measures. Amongst the member countries of the World Trade Organization (WTO) relevant requirements are addressed in its Agreement on the Application of Sanitary and Phytosanitary Measures (SPS Agreement) (WTO, 1995). But a key challenge is to reconcile the demands of individual countries that wish to keep their own SPS standards (in line with national requirements) and mitigating the resulting barriers to trade.

The SPS Agreement holds that all countries should maintain measures to make sure food is safe for consumers, and to prevent the spread of diseases or pests amongst plants and animals. Such SPS measures may:

- require products to come from disease-free areas;
- involve inspection (eg prior to loading in the country of export and/or at the border before release into the importing country);
- set requirements for specific treatment or processing (eg fumigation of plant products);
- maximum levels of pesticide residues (eg in fruit and vegetables);
- restrictions or limits on the use of certain food additives (eg sulphur in wine).

The SPS Agreement also encourages the adoption of international standards and harmonizing procedures, such as those of the:

- Codex Alimentarius Commission for international food standards, established by the United Nation's Food and Agriculture Organization (FAO) and the World Health Organization (WHO);
- World Organization for Animal Health (OIE);
- FAO's International Plant Protection Convention (IPPC).

However, the adoption and business compliance with such standards has a cost (Grainger, 2013). Those costs in turn have an adverse impact on trade. SPS requirements are frequently highlighted as a trade barrier, especially where they differ significantly between trade partners or are thought to be overly demanding – a point often made by developing countries (STDF, 2020).

The control and compliance system for **products of animal origin**, such as meat and hides, often involves checks by veterinarians accredited in the export market to which the goods are destined. That veterinarian must issue a health certificate in line with the export market's requirements and attach a seal to the shipped cargo. The importer then needs to notify relevant quarantine service at home, often in the form of an advance declaration with details about the health certificate. Upon arrival of the goods, quarantine officials are obliged to visually check the goods against the health certificate – in many countries this requirement applies to all (100 per cent) goods of animal origin. And, depending on governing control criteria, a more detailed physical inspection. The latter may involve sample taking and subsequent testing at an official or accredited laboratory. Fees apply and usually need to be paid in advance.

Checks must often be conducted at specialist facilities and goods selected for inspection must be presented at these; thus necessitating additional transport and handling. Providing all is in order, goods may be released by the veterinary health inspector and Customs (Figure 4.3), providing that all other import conditions, such as the payment of import duties, have also been met. However, special arrangements relating to inspection frequency, documents and associated procedures can help reduce compliance costs significantly. New Zealand, for example, enjoys advantageous treatment in many of its export markets by virtue of robust control measures at home and supporting trade agreements (Grainger, 2013).

The trade in **fish and fish products** can be subject to similar health certificate requirements. If required, these must usually be issued by approved authorities in the country of export and checked by officials in the country of import. In addition, many countries also apply controls to combat illegal, unreported and unregulated (IUU) fishing (FAO, 2020). These require the master of the fishing vessel to issue a Catch certificate. That certificate must then be validated by an authorized authority in the country where the fishing vessels is flagged (registered). The Catch certificate must then be passed on by the exporter to the importer (usually together with the health certificate). The importer in turn must present the Catch certificate to the relevant fishery or port health officials (Seafish, 2010).

FIGURE 4.3 Illustrative model of a veterinary checks control system

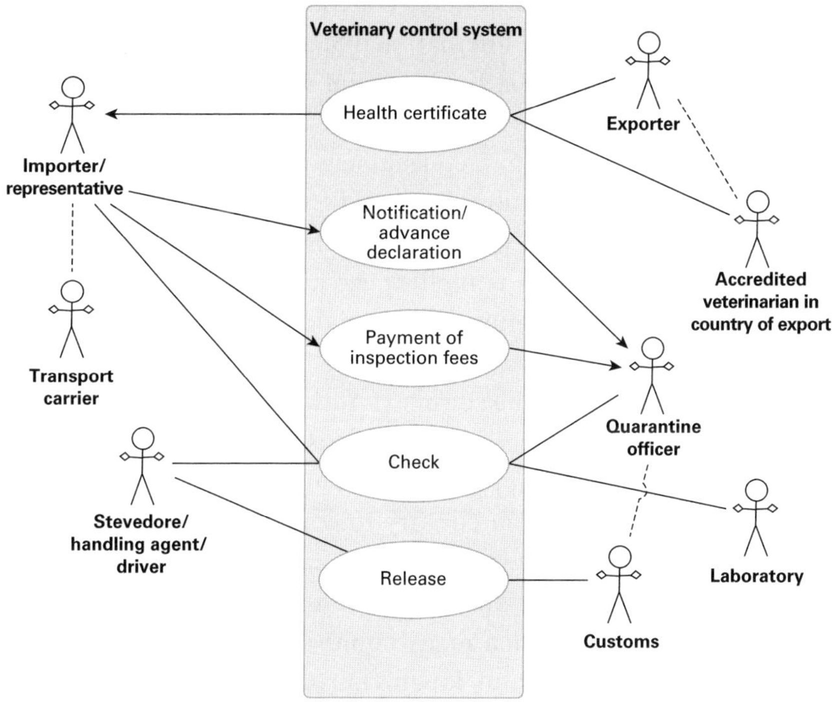

SOURCE © Trade Facilitation Consulting Ltd

Trade procedures for **phytosanitary controls** – to safeguard against pests and diseases in plants – are similar to those of veterinary checks. Usually exporters of plants, soils, products of the soil and used agricultural machinery need to arrange for a phytosanitary certificate (often also called Plant Health Certificate) that is issued by a competent authority recognized in the country where the goods are to be imported (IPPC, 2001). Once issued, the exporter must send that certificate to the importer. The importer in turn needs to pre-notify relevant phytosanitary officers (or quarantine officers) at the border or port. The officer there will then check relevant documents and might also conduct a physical inspection. The officer might also take samples for further laboratory analysis. There are of course many variants of this model and some countries, such as Kenya and the Netherlands, have adopted considerably less onerous electronic systems to help streamline and automate many of the procedures (Grainger *et al*, 2018).

The use of **wood packing** (eg crates and wooden pallets) and dunnage (to secure cargo inside ships or containers) is usually subject to the requirements of the International Standards for Phytosanitary Measures No 15 (IPPC, 2019). Compliant wood packaging material must either be heat-treated or fumigated and debarked. It can be identified by relevant manufacturing stamps and the International Plant Protection Convention logo (IPPC, 2020). Non-compliant wood packing found by Customs or other border officials must usually be: repacked into compliant packing; treated to ISPM 15 standards; destroyed; or returned – and if deemed necessary, returned with the cargo still inside.

Food controls can also be complex. At the ports and borders food is inevitably subject to veterinary or phytosanitary checks, but additional checks might also apply to certain high-risk foods. The list of high-risk foods differs from country to country. Food-related risks often also arise at very short notice, especially within the context of food contamination. One such example is the Fukushima nuclear disaster in 2016 after which many countries placed restrictions on animal feed and foods from Japan (European Union, 2016). Box 4.3, to give an example, lists high-risk foods that in 2018 were subject to additional import controls in the United Kingdom and in the European Union. One such control measure is the need for an aflatoxin certificate that is needed for the import of nuts (APHA, 2018).

Other types of checks apply, too. For example, before opening any temperature-controlled vehicles or containers it is good practice for importers to take a reading of the refrigerated container's temperature log and check that temperature controls were not breached during transport. Importers also need to make sure that food meets relevant national food labelling requirements (FSANZ, 2019) and quality standards, such as those governing wine and subject to additional document requirements (FSA, 2016).

BOX 4.3

Examples of high-risk foods subject to additional import controls in the United Kingdom and the European Union, 2018

- Brazil nuts from Brazil;
- fruits of the forest, genus *Vaccinium* (cranberries, bilberries, cowberries);
- hazelnuts from Azerbaijan;
- jelly sweets;
- nuts and dried fruit from Turkey;
- palm oil from Ghana;
- peanuts from China;
- peanuts from Egypt;
- pistachio nuts from Iran;
- spices from India;
- watermelon from Nigeria;
- wild mushrooms (uncultivated).

SOURCE APHA, 2018

Horticulture and marketing inspectorates are responsible for the administration and enforcement of applicable **marketing standards for fruit and vegetables** (UNECE, 2020a). These largely concern the quality and labelling of fruit and vegetables. A Certificate of Conformity with those standards must be presented before produce subject to those requirements can be imported. The horticulture and marketing inspector may also conduct a risk-based inspection to check that the produce matches the declared level of quality (OECD, 2006). Likewise, a number of countries – such as Canada, the European Union, Japan, Republic of Korea and Japan – enforce standards for goods marketed as **organic (or 'bio')**. Documentary proof of conformity is necessary, such as in the form of an organic Certificate of Conformity in the EU or the NOP Certificate in the United States. Applicable procedures at the border, depending on the country concerned, might be administered by the horticulture and marketing inspectors or Customs.

The trade in **live animals** in many countries is subject to strict animal welfare considerations. These tend to differ significantly from one country to the next. For Australia, to give one example, ships exporting live animals must comply with strict rules about ventilation, drainage and provision of water and food. During transport animals must also have on-demand access to food and water as well as enough space to lie down. Furthermore, ships must be fitted with special pens for sick animals to receive veterinary care. Mortality rates are investigated by the Australian Department of Agriculture, Water and Environment who formally report these every six months to the Australian Parliament (Australian Government, 2019).

In the European Union all imported animals must travel with a health certificate issued by an approved authority in the country of export. Upon arrival strict checks are conducted by official veterinarians at dedicated border control posts (European Commission, 2020b). Further checks may take place at the final destination. EU animal welfare rules and regulations also stipulate strict feeding and resting times. Applicable procedures are coordinated electronically using the European Commission's Trade Control and Expert System, TRACES (European Commission, 2020c). Some countries may offer simplified procedures for the movement of breeding animals, racing horses and pets. The EU's pet passport scheme is one such example (European Union, 2021).

PRODUCT SAFETY STANDARDS

Manufacturers, sellers and distributors are usually liable for the safety of their products. Product safety failures give rise to significant penalties and fines. Depending on the country concerned, product safety specifications are the result of public and private interaction, involving specialist government agencies, consumer bodies, distributors and manufacturers. Some of the safeguard measures might be self-imposed by, for example, manufacturers, industry bodies, or the expectations of buyers and end consumers. Some might be specified in the form of government regulations, or a mix of government and self-regulation (UNCTAD, 2017).

A common principle is the expectation that goods made available for sale are fit for purpose (UK Government, 1979). In some markets this also includes the requirement to comply with mandatory product standards. In the European Union, for example, mandatory product standards apply to most electronic equipment, civil explosives and medical devices (Box 4.4). When sold, compliance can be identified with the CE mark (*Conformité Européenne*). In some cases, the manufacturer has to conduct an independent conformity assessment before the CE mark can be affixed. Importers of goods subject to CE marking requirements need to verify that the manufacturer has made the necessary steps to allow the product to be placed on the EU market; that the necessary documentation is available upon request, including a Declaration of Conformity; and that contact with the manufacturer is possible any time (European Commission, 2020a). Other products, such as cosmetics or goods containing nickel (like zips and fashion jewellery) are also subject to mandatory standards, but do not need the CE mark.

TIP

The CE mark can be found on the back of most electronic devices. Take a look at the back of your mobile phone and see if you can find it.

Similar mandatory product standards exist elsewhere, too (OECD, 2020). For example, electronic products sold in the United States must be marked with the FCC mark which certifies that they are under the electromagnetic interference limits set by the Federal Communications Commission (FCC, 2020). Some export markets may require a Certificate of Free Sale, especially for cosmetics and medical devices. This is a document that is issued by the relevant authorities in the country where the goods have been manufactured and attests that the manufacturer meets the applicable product safety requirements at home.

BOX 4.4

Product categories subject to EU CE marking requirements

- active implantable medical devices;
- appliances burning gaseous fuels;
- cableway installations designed to carry persons;
- eco-design of energy-related products;
- electromagnetic compatibility;
- equipment and protective systems intended for use in potentially explosive atmospheres;
- explosives for civil uses;
- hot-water boilers;
- household refrigerators and freezers;
- in vitro diagnostic medical devices;
- lifts;
- low voltage;
- machinery;
- measuring instruments;
- medical devices;
- noise emission in the environment;
- non-automatic weighing instruments;
- personal protective equipment;
- pressure equipment;
- pyrotechnics;
- radio and telecommunications terminal equipment;
- recreational craft;
- safety of toys;
- simple pressure vessels.

SOURCE Adapted from Annex 1 of the European Commission's 'Blue Guide', 2016

TABLE 4.1 Policy and enforcement responsibilities for UK product safety and market surveillance, 2020

Focus	Market surveillance and enforcement responsibilities
Consumer product safety and weights and measures	Trading Standards
Construction products	Local Authorities
Safety of goods in the workplaces	Health and Safety Executive and Health and Safety Executive Northern Ireland
Medical devices	Medicines and Healthcare Products Regulatory Agency (MHRA)
Automotive products	Driver and Vehicle Standards Agency (DVSA)

Countries that enforce rigorous product safety regimes tend to focus their checks and controls at the point of sale (eg shops and supermarkets). Such practice is often referred to as 'market surveillance'. Market surveillance responsibilities may not necessarily fall under the umbrella of one single government agency. In the United Kingdom, to give one example, five different organizations share market surveillance enforcement responsibilities (Table 4.1). But border agencies, such as Customs, still play an important role in the enforcement of product standards, especially where the goods are shipped in from abroad and the market surveillance organizations have instructed Customs to stop and intercept suspicious shipments, or where the risk of non-compliance with applicable product standards is thought to be high.

MEDICINES, NARCOTICS AND DRUGS

Medicines tend to be highly regulated in most parts of the world. This is to protect humans and animals by making sure they are used responsibly, for example, under the supervision of medical practitioners (in the case of humans) or veterinarians (in the case of animals). However, there can be significant variances in the control arrangements of individual countries as well as for different types of medicines. Imports and exports into and out of the United Kingdom, for example, are subject to strict licensing conditions that apply to wholesalers and distributors, manufacturers and individual sellers. The customs declaration requires a reference to the licence (UK

Government, 2005). The border agencies are also tasked with intercepting unlicensed illegal trade.

Many medicines also contain narcotics that fall under the United Nations Convention against Illicit Traffic in Narcotic Drugs and Psychotropic Substances (UN, 1988). This convention contains comprehensive measures against drug trafficking, including provisions against money laundering and the diversion of precursor chemicals (substances that can be used in the illicit manufacture of narcotic drugs and psychotropic). Any legal trade in drugs, psychotropic substances and precursor chemicals is subject to strict export licensing conditions. Strict licensing requirements tend to apply, and Customs is usually the border agency tasked with checking those, along with responsibilities for intercepting any non-licensed illegal trades.

The protection of the environment

The fight against environmental crime is a significant enforcement theme for customs administrations and border agencies around the world, and is linked to a wide range of international conventions (WCO, 2020). They concern waste, dangerous chemicals, pesticides, pollutants, ozone-depleting substances and endangered wildlife (UNEP, 2018).

The Convention on International Trade in Endangered Species of Wild Fauna and Flora (**CITES Convention**) is enforced by more than 180 countries and controls the trade in endangered animals and plants as well as products derived from them (eg furniture, musical instruments, jewellery, powders) through a licensing system. Endangered species are listed in three appendices (CITES, 1973):

- Those listed in Appendix 1 are all those threatened with extinction. Trade in specimens of these species is permitted only in exceptional circumstances and is subject to an export permit (from the authorities where they originate) and an import permit (from the countries where they are destined).
- Species listed in Appendix 2 are not necessarily threatened with extinction, but export controls are deemed necessary to safeguard their continued survival.

- Species listed in Appendix 3 of the CITES Convention are protected in at least one of the CITES Convention's signatories and where that country has requested other signatories for assistance in controlling that species. An export permit is necessary if procured directly from the country with the control requirement; a certificate of origin is needed if exported from another country (CITES, 2020).

The UN's **Vienna Convention for the Protection of the Ozone Layer** (UNEP, 1985) and subsequent **Montreal Protocol on Substances that Deplete the Ozone Layer** (UNEP, 1987) seek to control and phase out the production of ozone-depleting substances. These instruments are universally endorsed by 198 countries (UNEP, 2020). Essential and exempted trade in substances falling under the agreement is subject to annual allotments and strict export and import licensing conditions.

The **Basel Convention on the Control of Transboundary Movements of Hazardous Wastes and their Disposal** entered into force in 1992 (UNEP, 1989). In 2020 the treaty had other 180 parties; although the United States signed the treaty it has not yet ratified it. Amongst its measures, the treaty requires that the trade in hazardous wastes and disposal of such is made subject to informed consent before an export may take place. Written consent must be provided by all countries involved (export, transit and import). For developed countries that are members of the OECD the treaty also bans any movement of hazardous waste for disposal in non-OECD countries (UNEP, 1994).

There are other international conventions with similar aims as the Basel Convention. The **Stockholm Convention** (UNEP, 2017), for example, includes provisions that prohibit or restrict the movement of persistent organic pollutants (harmful chemicals that remain intact in the environment for long periods). The **Rotterdam Convention** concerns itself with pesticides and industrial chemicals that have been banned or severely restricted for health or environmental reasons (UBNEP, 2017). The **Cartagena Protocol on Biosafety to the Convention on Biological Diversity** concerns the safe handling, transport and use of living modified organisms (where genes have been changed) that may have adverse effects on biological diversity with possible risk to human health (SCBD, 2000).

The protection of national treasures possessing artistic, historic or archaeological value

The international customs community is increasingly also concerned about the looting and destruction of cultural heritage sites in conflict zones and subsequent illicit trafficking of cultural objects (WCO, 2016). Such concern, to give one example of many, is also reflected in United Nations Security Council Resolutions 2199 and 2253 concerning cultural artefacts and the conflicts in Iraq and Syria. The **UNESCO Convention on the Means of Prohibiting and Preventing the Illicit Import, Export and Transfer of Ownership of Cultural Property** urges countries to adopt measures that prohibit and prevent the illicit trafficking of cultural property (UNESCO, 1970). National legislation designed to protect cultural heritage often makes the international shipment of such goods conditional on the issue of an export certificate. A common model for licensing places the burden on the exporter to apply for a licence. The issuing government agency may, depending on the nature of the artefact, consult with other specialist organizations (eg national museums and national libraries). If approved, the licence must then be declared along with the customs declaration (Arts Council, 2020).

The protection of industrial and commercial intellectual property

Intellectual property rights provide the basis upon which companies, creators and inventors secure a return on their investment in innovation and creativity (European Commission, 2014). Their protection has also become an integral part of the international trading system. Safeguards for the protection of intellectual property rights are a condition for WTO membership. The **WTO Trade-related Aspects of Intellectual Property Rights (TRIPS) Agreement** (WTO, 1994) sets requirements for the protection for brands and trademarks, copyrights, designs and patents, as well as the protection of geographical indications (eg protection of the term 'champagne' for sparkling wine from the Champagne region). Similar obligations also fall upon customs administrations from various regional and bilateral trade agreements (Pugatch, 2012). Customs administrations are usually responsible for intercepting infringing goods and preventing their circulation.

Procedures vary depending on the country concerned. Property rights owners that wish to have non-compliant goods intercepted at the border might be required to record their rights with the customs administration. If property rights owners have details about expected shipments that do not comply with property rights obligations, they may share these with the customs administration for their attention. Often, Customs charge fees to recover their costs when seizing such goods. One enforcement strategy for active property rights owners is, with careful legal guidance, to place orders with non-compliant organizations and then pass that information on to Customs for further action. Other law enforcement agencies may also work with Customs to stop illegal trade in counterfeit products. Public concerns about counterfeit medicines and counterfeit aviation parts, to give a few examples, can be particularly pressing (FDA, 2020).

Vehicles (means of transport)

The vehicles moving goods are themselves subject to a wide range of regulations. Most are mode-specific with a focus on:

- vehicle safety and standards;
- constraints on the supply of transport services;
- the environment;
- transport security.

Their impact on cross-border logistics operations is felt where procedures need to be complied with, and where authorities feel the need to check compliance at (or near) the border. In addition, the means of transport are also subject to customs controls – to make sure that any customs duties and other import taxes are correctly accounted for, in the event that the vehicle itself is subject to a trade transaction.

Road transport

Road vehicles are subject to a wide range of regulations. These concern the vehicles themselves as well as their use. Many of the regulations are driven by concerns for safety, though the impact on the environment in the form of noise and pollution can be a key theme as well. The work of the UN's World Forum for Harmonization of Vehicle Regulations, for example, addresses the regulatory requirements for the vehicle's lighting, instruments, controls, crashworthiness, environmental compatibility, tyres and wheels. Underlying UN Agreements provide for reciprocal acceptance of vehicle approvals in most of Europe, Central Asia, Australasia as well as Japan and a few African and Southeast Asian countries (UNECE, 2020b). The Regulatory framework in other countries can differ (FMVSS, 1999), and can also lack provisions for reciprocal acceptance of vehicle approvals.

National road safety regulations commonly concern obligations for driver training, driver and vehicle licensing, rest periods and motor insurance (Lowe and Pidgeon, 2020). They usually also include provisions for the enforcement of penalties and driving offences (eg speeding or driving under the influence of alcohol). At ports and borders there might be checks to confirm driving and licensing conditions along with appropriate insurance documents. Vehicle weight checks, using weighbridges, may be common in some places. In many European countries there are also strict weekend driving restrictions (FTA, 2017).

Transport operators usually also need an operating licence which makes the licence holder accountable for meeting relevant road safety and vehicle standards. Compliance with mandatory training requirements might apply. Just a few decades ago, many countries in the developed world would restrict the number of licences awarded and also set the tariffs that operators may charge (Bayliss, 1998). Although markets are increasingly deregulated, access to operating licences for foreign operated trucks is frequently subject to application, as is the case between Mexico and the United States (FMCSA, 2020), and restrictive quotas, as is the case between Turkey and the European Union (Servantie, 2017).

Air transport

Much of the regulation for air transport is coordinated internationally though the International Civil Aviation Organization (ICAO) and in adherence to its underpinning Convention on International Civil Aviation. The Convention's many requirements include:

- the certificate of registration;
- the certificate of airworthiness;
- crew licences;
- radio licences;
- reporting of cargo and crew (and passengers); and
- logbooks.

The Convention also asserts the principle that every state has complete and exclusive sovereignty over airspace above its territory. Routes, including their frequency and capacity, are subject to hundreds of mostly bilateral air transport agreements (ICAO, 2020). National aviation authorities are responsible for enforcing them. The International Air Transport Association (IATA) rules for dangerous goods apply to the handling of such, along with the requirement for the dangerous goods declaration (IATA, 2020).

Annex 17 of the International Civil Aviation Organization includes provisions to enhance security. One of its requirements is that cargo must undergo a security control before loading onto the aircraft. The Regulated Agent and Known Consignor (or shipper) programmes allow for scanning away from the airport, which is subject to authorization as well as reporting requirements (ICAO and WCO, 2013).

Maritime transport

Maritime transport is subject to a wide range of regulatory requirements embedded in international treaties and law as well as national legislation. Ships must be registered and comply with applicable maritime law. Amongst others, common subjects that place compliance requirements upon operators are: vessel safety, insurance, ships' waste and security. There are often also restrictions on cabotage, the permission for foreign ships to offer domestic services between coastal ports.

The IMO's International Convention for the Safety of Life at Sea (SOLAS) (IMO, 1974) provides for minimum standards for the construction, equipment and operation of ships. It also extends to the carriage of cargo along with conditions for the storage and handling of dangerous goods – including any necessary dangerous goods declarations (IMO, 2018b). The IMO's International Ship and Port Facility (ISPS) Code (IMO, 2003), which is linked to SOLAS, sets out a broad range of maritime and port-related security obligations. These include, amongst many others, the requirement for a Security Declaration between the ship and the port.

Ports normally also insist that vessels are suitably insured – in case, for example, of an accident and subsequent damage to the port infrastructure – for which evidence needs to be provided. That evidence might be provided in the form of a Lloyds Register number (Lloyd's Register, 2020). In addition, many maritime nations may, following risk criteria, initiate an inspection to check whether the calling ship is in line with the IMO's guidelines. Such inspection regimes include a general inspection upon boarding, a check of certificates and a more detailed walk-through. Identified deficiencies are marked on a checklist. If deficiencies are significant a more detailed inspection might follow. In severe cases the vessel might be detained (IMO, 2020). More and more countries around the world also require calling vessels to declare and account for any waste. This must then be disposed of at suitable ship reception facilities (IMO, 2018a).

Competition rules can also apply, restricting maritime operations to the vessel's flag. Although there has been significant liberalization (Stopford, 2009), restrictions can still apply, especially for domestic transport where national flag conditions might still apply (Pagel *et al*, 2019).

Customs

Customs administration's interest in the means of transport – land, sea or air – is to make sure that the vehicle is for commercial use and not for sale and thus subject (like any other import) to duties and taxes. The WCO Revised Customs Agreement holds that, where possible, vehicles used for commercial transport should be relieved from the payment of import duties and taxes. This is conditional upon the vehicle leaving (re-exported) within a specific period of time (Annex J/Chapter 3 in WCO, 2006). In certain circumstances some customs administrations may require a financial security or temporary admission document. The declaration of arrival should only require minimal information, and in the case of air and maritime transport is often notified along with cargo manifest information (ICAO, 2017; IMO, 1965). A declaration of departure may also be required (WCO, 2006).

The second customs concern relates to enforcement, to make sure the vehicle is not used for smuggling (eg undeclared goods added by the crew or driver). The means of transport may, just like any other good, be subject to risk management and inspection.

People

Cross-border logistics operations for goods can also have dependencies on procedures designed to control the movement of people. As a rule, most countries have strict visa and immigration rules. These may be relaxed or waived where countries agree to free-movement principles (as is the case between members of the European Union) or travel agreements (as is the case between the UK and Ireland). They may – but not necessarily – also be relaxed for transport workers, such as maritime and aviation crew. Aviation crew, for example, commonly benefit from special airport measures that expedite the inspection of crew and their baggage (ICAO, 2017). Transport operators are usually also obliged to record or register crew details – for example, by using the International Maritime Organization's Crew List form (IMO, 1965).

Transport operators may also have to be mindful of the risk of stowaways which in the case of maritime transport is subject to obligations ranging from prevention to reporting and disembarkation arrangements (IMO, 2018c). Additional challenges might also arise in environments where there is a high risk of people smuggling. Migrant smuggling is internationally condemned (UNODC, 2000) and in line with risk management principles (Chapter 5) additional inspections to vehicles and their cargo can be expected at locations where the risk of smuggling is known to be high. Those inspections might be led by immigration officers or by customs officers, depending on what specific powers are needed and the institutional arrangements in the country concerned.

ACTIVITIES AND DISCUSSION POINTS

1. How do economic concerns differ from those of public health, national security, safety or the environment? Is the collection of customs duties and taxes as important as the enforcement of prohibitions and restrictions? Discuss.
2. Research the requirements for importing restricted goods (eg industrial waste, medicines, protective personal body armour) into a country of your choice. Alternatively, consider the requirements for the export of such goods. Use internet resources, especially those offered by government agencies, to establish what non-customs documents are needed and how they may be obtained.
3. Following on from the previous exercise, draw a diagram that follows the template offered in Figure 4.1 (a so-called 'use-case diagram') and describe the arrows and lines between the stick people.

References

APHA (2018) *Handbook 2018/19*, Association of Port Health Authorities, Kent

Arts Council (2020) Export licensing, www.artscouncil.org.uk/export-controls/export-licensing#section-1 (archived at https://perma.cc/73AD-4EHT)

Australian Government (2019) Live animal export trade, www.agriculture.gov.au/animal/welfare/export-trade (archived at https://perma.cc/CDH8-626L)

Bayliss, B (1998) Regulation in the road freight transport sector, *Journal of Transport Economics and Policy*, **32** (1), pp 113–31, www.jstor.org/stable/20053758 (archived at https://perma.cc/5B7T-QR6X)

BIS (2020a) Export Administration Regulation (EAR), Bureau of Industry and Security, www.bis.doc.gov/index.php/regulations/export-administration-regulations-ear (archived at https://perma.cc/7YE3-6KDZ)

BIS (2020b) Denied Persons List, Bureau of Industry and Security, www.bis.doc.gov/index.php/policy-guidance/lists-of-parties-of-concern/denied-persons-list (archived at https://perma.cc/SDT6-DJF8)

Bos, M (2015) *Trafficking in human organs*, European Parliament, Brussels, www.europarl.europa.eu/RegData/etudes/STUD/2015/549055/EXPO_STU%282015%29549055_EN.pdf (archived at https://perma.cc/PEW8-SEHF)

CITES (1973) Convention on International Trade in Endangered Species of Wild Fauna and Flora (as amended)

CITES (2020) What is CITES? www.cites.org/eng/disc/what.php (archived at https://perma.cc/TTB5-NZTX)

DIT (2019) UK Strategic Export Control Lists, Department for International Trade, London

European Commission (2014) *Trade, growth and intellectual property*, European Commission, Brussels

European Commission (2016) The 'Blue Guide' on the implementation of EU products rules 2016, *Official Journal of the European Communities*, C 272/1

European Commission (2018) *P&R List: EU Prohibitions and Restrictions for Customs*, European Union, Brussels

European Commission (2020a) CE marking, ec.europa.eu/growth/single-market/ce-marking_en (archived at https://perma.cc/SFW8-V5WC)

European Commission (2020b) Live animals: Trade and Imports, ec.europa.eu/food/animals/live_animals_en (archived at https://perma.cc/362C-XZDP)

European Commission (2020c) TRACES: TRAde Control and Expert System, ec.europa.eu/food/animals/traces_en (archived at https://perma.cc/FPJ9-W6PK)

European Parliament (2019) Legislative Train Schedule: Ban on import of goods produced using modern forms of slavery and forced labour, incuding that of children, www.europarl.europa.eu/legislative-train/theme-europe-as-a-stronger-global actor/file-ban-on-import-of-goods-produced-using-modern-forms-of-slavery (archived at https://perma.cc/R89V-E69E)

European Union (2007) Regulation (EC) No 1523/2007 of the European Parliament and of the Council of 11 December 2007 banning the placing on the market and the import to, or export from, the Community of cat and dog fur, and products containing such fur (Text with EEA relevance), *Official Journal of the EU*, L 343, eur-lex.europa.eu/legal-content/EN/ALL/?uri=CELEX:32007R1523 (archived at https://perma.cc/FF8T-FDKP)

European Union (2016) Commission Implementing Regulation (EU) 2016/6 of 5 January 2016 imposing special conditions governing the import of feed and food originating in or consigned from Japan following the accident at the

Fukushima nuclear power station and repealing Implementing Regulation (EU) No 322/2014 (Text with EEA relevance), *Official Journal of the European Communities,* L 3, eur-lex.europa.eu/legal-content/EN/TXT/?uri=uriserv%3AOJ.L_.2016.003.01.0005.01.ENG (archived at https://perma.cc/GT49-G5YJ)

European Union (2021) Traveling with pets and other animals in the EU, https://europa.eu/youreurope/citizens/travel/carry/animal-plant/index_en.htm (archived at https://perma.cc/B7NW-DAEQ)

FAO (2020) Illegal, Unreported and Unregulated (IUU) fishing, www.fao.org/iuu-fishing/en/ (archived at https://perma.cc/9S4Z-R364)

FCC (2020) Equipment Authorization: Approval Guide, www.fcc.gov/engineering-technology/laboratory-division/general/equipment-authorization (archived at https://perma.cc/3CRR-Y4DQ)

FDA (2020) Counterfeit Medicine, www.fda.gov/drugs/buying-using-medicine-safely/counterfeit-medicine (archived at https://perma.cc/GBY2-BQVN)

FMCSA (2020) Cross-Border Operating Requirements for Mexico-domiciled Motor Carriers, www.fmcsa.dot.gov/international-programs/cross-border-operating-requirements-mexico-domiciled-motor-carriers (archived at https://perma.cc/2SA2-BK46)

FMUSS (1999) Federal Motor Vehicle Safety Standards (FMVSS) and Regulations

FSA (2016) *Importation and movement of wine products,* Food Standards Agency, London, www.food.gov.uk/sites/default/files/media/document/FSA-Importation-and-Movement-of-Wine-Products-May-2016.pdf (archived at https://perma.cc/88K4-C4QV)

FSANZ (2019) Food Standards Code (Australia New Zealand), www.foodstandards.gov.au/code/Pages/default.aspx (archived at https://perma.cc/8KQQ-7U4M)

FTA (2017) *European Road Freight Guide,* Freight Transport Association, Tunbridge Wells

GATT (1994) The General Agreement on Tariffs and Trade

Grainger, A (2013) *Trade and Customs Procedures: The compliance costs for UK meat imports*, Nottingham University, eprints.nottingham.ac.uk/2143/ (archived at https://perma.cc/3DVZ-SABA)

Grainger, A, Huiden, R, Rukanov, B and Tan, Y-H (2018) What is the cost of customs and borders across the supply chain? … and how to mitigate the cost through better coordination and data sharing, *World Customs Journal,* **12** (1), pp 1–28

IATA (2020) *Dangerous Goods Regulations (DGR) (61st Edition),* International Air Transport Association, Geneva

ICAO (2017) Annex 9 to the Convention on International Civil Aviation: Facilitation (15th edition)

ICAO (2020) ICAO's Database of Aeronautical Agreements and Arrangements, cfapp.icao.int/dagmar/main.cfm (archived at https://perma.cc/3FJX-UMF7)

ICAO and WCO (2013) *Moving Air Cargo Globally: Air Cargo and Mail Secure Supply Chain and Facilitation Guidelines,* International Cival Aviation Organization, Montréal, cfapp.icao.int/tools/38thAssyiKit/story_content/external_files/ICAO-WCO_Moving-Air-Cargo-Globally.pdf (archived at https://perma.cc/2GG4-FPXC)

IMO (1965) Convention on Facilitation of International Maritime Traffic (FAL) (as amended)

IMO (1974) International Convention for the Safety of Life at Sea (as amended)

IMO (2003) *ISPS (The International Ship and Port Facility Security) Code, 2003 Edition,* International Maritime Organization, London

IMO (2018a) *Consolidated Guidelines for Port Reception Facility Providers and Users*, International Maritime Organization, London

IMO (2018b) *IMDG Code – 2018 Edition,* International Maritime Organization, London

IMO (2018c) Resolution FAL.13 (42) Revised guidelines on the prevention of access by stowaways and the allocation of responsibilities to seek the successful resolution of stowaway cases

IMO (2020) Port State Control, www.imo.org/en/OurWork/MSAS/Pages/PortStateControl.aspx (archived at https://perma.cc/Y3MT-AQ6J)

IPPC (2001) International Standards for Phytosanitary Measures Number 12: Guidelines for Phytosanitary Certificates

IPPC (2019) ISPM 15: Regulation of wood packaging material in international trade (2018)

IPPC (2020) Logos, www.ippc.int/en/logos/ (archived at https://perma.cc/Q6SV-5TRS)

Kimberley Process (2020) What is the Kimberley Process? www.kimberleyprocess.com/en/what-kp (archived at https://perma.cc/76TE-KZ67)

Lloyd's Register (2020) LR Ships in Class, www.lr.org/en/lrofships/ (archived at https://perma.cc/SA82-4PTZ)

Lowe, D and Pidgeon, C (2020) *Lowe's Transport Manager's and Operator's Handbook 2020*, Kogan Page, London

New Zealand (2019) Customs Import Prohibition (Goods Produced by Prison Labour) Order 2019, *New Zealand Gazette,* (2019/211), www.legislation.govt.nz/regulation/public/2019/0211/latest/whole.html (archived at https://perma.cc/RJ4L-3F8D)

OECD (2006) Decision of the Council revising the OECD Scheme for the Application of International Standards for Fruit and Vegetables (as amended)

OECD (2020) Consumer Product Safety, www.oecd.org/sti/consumer/consumer-product-safety.htm (archived at https://perma.cc/2YHR-JPQJ)

Pagel, J, Brannon, I and Kashian, R (2019) Jones Act: Protectionist policy in the twenty-first century, *Maritime Economics and Logistics,* **21** (4), pp 439–63, doi: dx.doi.org/10.1057/s41278-019-00123-9

Pugatch, MP (2012) Intellectual property rights and trade,in *International Trade Policy,* eds K Heydon and S Woolcock, Ashgate, Farnham

SCBD (2000) The Cartagena Protocol on Biosafety to the Convention on Biological Diversity

Schraer, R and Edgington, T (2019) BBC Reality Check: Chlorinated chicken, how safe is it? www.bbc.co.uk/news/uk-47440562 (archived at https://perma.cc/J3B4-ZBU2)

Seafish (2010) *IUU: Guide for exporters,* Seafish, Edinburgh

Servantie, D (2017) *The Quota Issue of the Turkish Road Transport Sector in the EU,* Economic Development Foundation, Istanbul

STDF (2020) Standards and Trade Development Facility, www.standardsfacility.org (archived at https://perma.cc/E6KW-L6RS)

Stopford, M (2009) *Maritime Economics,* 3rd edn, Routledge, London

UBNEP (2017) Rotterdam Convention on the Prior Informed Consent Procedure for Certain Hazardous Chemicals and Pesticides in International Trade (revised)

UK Government (1979) Sale of Goods Act 1979

UK Government (2005) Import a human medicine, www.gov.uk/guidance/import-a-human-medicine (archived at https://perma.cc/F4MQ-DFPV)

UK Government (2018) Guidance: Guns, knives, swords and other offensive weapons: UK border control, www.gov.uk/guidance/import-controls-on-offensive-weapons (archived at https://perma.cc/9ZQR-QSU2)

UN (1988) United Nations Convention against Illicit Traffic in Narcotic Drugs and Psychotropic Substances

UN Security Council (2020) *United Nations Security Council Consolidated List,* United Nations, New York, scsanctions.un.org/fop/fop?xml=htdocs/resources/xml/en/consolidated.xml&xslt=htdocs/resources/xsl/en/consolidated.xsl (archived at https://perma.cc/SVR8-597N)

UNCTAD (2017) *Manual on Consumer Protection* (UNCTAD/DITC/CPLP/2017/1), United Nations, Geneva

UNECE (2020a) Fresh Fruit and Vegetables: Standards, www.unece.org/trade/agr/standard/fresh/ffv-standardse.html (archived at https://perma.cc/KBP3-UPKJ)

UNECE (2020b) Working Party 29: Introductions, www.unece.org/trans/main/wp29/introduction.html (archived at https://perma.cc/S8SN-MM92)

UNEP (1985) The Vienna Convention for the Protection of the Ozone Layer

UNEP (1987) The Montreal Protocol on Substances that Deplete the Ozone Layer

UNEP (1989) Basel Convention on the Control of Transboundary Movements of Hazardous Wastes and their Disposal

UNEP (1994) The Basel Convention Ban Amendment

UNEP (2017) The Stockholm Convention on Persistent Organic Pollutants (revised)

UNEP (2018) *Green Customs Guide to Multilateral Environmental Agreements,* United Nations Environment Programme, Nairobi

UNEP (2020) Treaties, ozone.unep.org/treaties/montreal-protocol (archived at https://perma.cc/TU9N-UE2P)

UNESCO (1970) Convention on the Means of Prohibiting and Preventing the Illicit Import, Export and Transfer of Ownership of Cultural Property

UNODC (2000) United Nations Convention against Transnational Organized Crime

WCO (2006) *Revised Kyoto Convention; International Convention on the Simplifications and Harmonisation of Customs Procedures*, World Customs Organization, Brussels, www.wcoomd.org/en/topics/facilitation/instrument-and-tools/conventions/pf_revised_kyoto_conv/kyoto_new.aspx (archived at https://perma.cc/PS3T-22M7)

WCO (2016) Council Resolution on the Role of Customs in Preventing Illicit Trafficking of Cultural Objects

WCO (2020) Environment Programme, www.wcoomd.org/en/topics/enforcement-and-compliance/activities-and-programmes/environment-programme.aspx (archived at https://perma.cc/P28S-B87B)

WTO (1994) Annex 1C of the Marrakesh Agreement Establishing the World Trade Organization: The Trade-Related Aspects of Intellectual Property Rights (TRIPS) Agreement

WTO (1995) The WTO Agreement on the Application of Sanitary and Phytosanitary Measures (SPS Agreement)

05

Border facilities

Operations and design

Although, as highlighted in Chapter 3, it is increasingly common in many parts of the world to clear goods electronically, paper documents can still form part of the wider inspection and control regime. Thus, officers at gateway locations often still need facilities to collect paper documents from relevant parties, be it from those parties accompanying the goods (eg truck drivers or business travellers with commercial baggage) or any other type of representative (eg brokers and agents). Moreover, border facilities are frequently the location where inspections take place. And from a logistics point of view, many might view the border as a bottleneck at which the flow of goods stops.

Indeed, as touched upon in Chapter 1, it is the image of the boom barrier that is all too often invoked when visualizing a national border. The United Nation's Convention on Road Signs and Signals (UN, 1968) provides one such example. It recommends that the road traffic sign for a border contains a black horizontal line framed within a red circle, notifying any driver that the border may not be passed without stopping at the customs boom barrier.

Stopping goods for inspection has a significant impact on commercial logistics operations. Goods no longer move, which inevitably adds to costs that are in addition to the costs of all the paperwork or their electronic equivalent as outlined in Chapter 3. Poorly designed borders and inspection practices also undermine the officers' ability to do their job well. Worst case: poor inspection practices provide a strong incentive for less honest operators to seek clandestine routes across the border without giving officers the opportunity to stop, assess or inspect.

To ensure efficient border operations suitable border facilities are necessary. The requirements for those facilities are dependent upon many factors, which is the subject of this chapter. Considerations that impact upon border design inevitably are embedded in operational requirements by both the border agencies and business operators that seek to clear the border expediently and without undue delay. Many of those requirements will be unique to the mode of transport and subsequent cargo-handling practices, others will be linked to wider inspection and control policies – especially with regard to the adopted risk management practices and the overall levels of compliance, but also with regard to service expectations.

Other factors also come into play, and are largely spatial in nature. They concern the location, including the geography of that location, along with the available space (footprint of the facility) and the flow of goods through that facility. Inevitably, resources are constrained. Where facilities are over-specified with insufficient levels of throughput, it may prove difficult to recover the development and operating costs of those facilities. And where fees are thought to be prohibitive, they will, just like tariffs, have a detrimental impact on trade. Should such fees in part be absorbed by the government (ie tax payers) instead, it raises questions about whether public money had been put to best use. Under-specified inspection facilities, or facilities unfit for their purposes, are similarly detrimental to trade. Bottlenecks are likely to arise, creating queues, adding to delay and cost which undermine business competitiveness.

Operations

Most border crossings with border stations, including ports and airports, serve two types of operations. The first is to support administrative controls, for example by processing paper documents and confirming that goods can be released. Often the control systems used require declared goods to be placed into channels. A colour is normally attributed to these channels, such as 'red' for stop and 'green' for go (as is the case at most international airports) and 'yellow' where further information, including additional documents, is needed before a decision can be made. At border crossings where the control processes are electronic and automated, or allow for alternative control arrangements, such as at the importer's own premisses (with a default 'green' at the border), the impact of control requirements on border design requirements might be minimal. However, border facilities usually also need to accommodate the various border agencies' need to inspect goods along with the vehicles carrying those goods and the people responsible.

Inevitably all inspection decisions are derived from the applicable regulatory control requirements. These concern Customs as well as the many other regulatory agencies that have an interest in the control of goods across borders – including the vehicles that move those goods and the people that operate those vehicles. The long list of common prohibitions and restrictions which place control and inspection demands in addition to those of Customs have already been outlined in Chapter 4.

The decision to inspect or not is the outcome of applied risk management practices (Chapter 3). Sophisticated risk management frameworks can often quickly identify those business operators who are routinely compliant. Inspection, thus, is not normally necessary. Subsequently, amongst many trading nations with sophisticated risk management practices, intrusive border inspections by Customs are the exception and not the norm. But, amongst goods subject to prohibitions and restrictions inspections can frequently still be routine, but the level of intrusiveness and subsequent activities may differ. For example, quarantine checks in many places are performed on all goods subject to those controls (100 per cent). At their most basic the inspection will entail a check to make sure the declared sanitary or phytosanitary health certificates are correct. However, there is also a high likelihood that the veterinary or phytosanitary inspector will also want to check the seals on the vehicle or container to make sure they have not been broken. They may also open the consignment to check whether the goods inside match what has been declared. The latter can be operationally intensive, necessitating specialist facilities along with additional handling and the resealing of the cargo before being released by Customs. They may also decide to take a sample and send it to a laboratory for further analysis (Grainger, 2013).

Also worth highlighting is that not all borders are equal; there is considerable diversity in practice. For example, many countries collaborate with their neighbours and trade partners and seek to coordinate their control and inspection activities (Chapter 7). This helps reduce requirements for border control and inspection facilities, for example by sharing the control and inspection facilities. The results are lower operating costs and impact upon traders and their competitiveness. More and more countries are also members of customs unions with a significantly reduced need for border control and subsequent inspection requirements (Chapter 8). In the European Union the borders amongst its 27 Member States have for most intents and purposes been removed. There is no need for border control stations at all.

Inspections

Inspection practices are dependent on the relevant border agency's regulatory objectives and mandate. For Customs, usually the most visible agency at the border, inspection regimes are linked, as highlighted in Chapter 2, to the collection of duties and taxes and to the enforcement of prohibitions and restrictions. The inspection of goods may thus serve customs' administrative or executive functions. Administration-motivated customs inspections aim to check that declared information is indeed correct, and that applicable duties and taxes have been correctly assessed (Box 5.1).

Enforcement-motivated customs inspections are about intercepting clandestine cross-border movements that are hidden within regular shipments or vehicles. Quite separately, customs administrations often commit significant enforcement resources to the detection of illegal shipments smuggled via unofficial routes, away from regular border crossing facilities. But it is important to note that in many countries this might be an activity performed by the border guards, perhaps working alongside customs officials or independently.

BOX 5.1

Compliance-motivated inspections: examples

In the European Union the import duties for orange juice depend on whether the juice is frozen (HS subheadings 2009.11) or not (HS subheading 2009.12) and if the Bix value (which is a measure of sugar content within an aqueous solution) is greater or less than 67 (European Commission, 2020). A customs officer concerned about the correct tariff classification of orange juice and subsequent duty rate might want to check whether the orange juice is frozen or not, and the officer may also want to check that the Bix value is above or below 67.

Many countries offer preferential tariff quotas that are awarded by reference to quantity, eg 10 tonnes per quota licence. If the awarded quantity is exceeded (ie more than 10 tonnes), regular import duties must be paid on the excess. Since regular import duties are many times greater than the preferential duties, the risk of under-declaring weight might be perceived to be high. Given the risk and amount of duties involved, there may be a higher than normal frequency of inspection decisions aimed at confirming the declared weight in line with the quota licence (Grainger, 2013).

The Irish Times on 9 March 2012 reported that a large Irish fruit and vegetable importer declared more than 1,000 tonnes of garlic from China (with an applicable duty rate of €120 per 100kg) as apples, and thus avoided paying a total of €1.6 million in duty. The full inspection of one of the containers at Dublin port and subsequent investigation revealed that the imported goods were not as declared (*The Irish Times*, 2012).

As touched upon in Chapter 3, when conducting inspections at border crossing facilities, officers may apply non-intrusive techniques, such as a quick visual check of the outside packaging along with marks and numbers, or the taking of an X-ray image to see what is inside. Such non-intrusive approaches are usually significantly less time-consuming than intrusive approaches and allow officers to inspect a greater number of shipments within a given time period.

Intrusive inspection approaches often require goods to be unloaded and unpacked, too. This might be followed by further time-consuming activities, such as counting, weighing and measuring, for example, to verify declared quantities. It might also involve the taking of samples for further investigation. It might involve a thorough turnout where the entire shipment is examined in detail. Depending on the inspection objectives, it might also involve the taking of samples for further testing at official laboratories. If laboratory testing is necessary, it can take several days for the results to come back, depending on the type of test, the speed at which samples are sent to the laboratory, and the capacity of the laboratory. Standard inspection practices, as already touched upon in Chapter 3, include:

- seal checks, to make sure cargo has not been opened en route;
- a quick visual inspection (spot-check) to verify that the goods match what has been declared;
- sampling, where part of the consignment undergoes a more rigorous examination;
- a full inspection, where the entire consignment undergoes a rigorous examination;
- counting, weighing and measuring, eg to make sure goods have not been over- or under-declared;
- scanning, to see if anything is hidden inside the goods;
- detailed analysis, eg by sending a sample to an official laboratory.

For certain types of checks and goods it is most practical to perform the inspection at or on the vehicle. This might be the case for bulk shipments with cargo volumes in excess of hundreds or thousands of tonnes, where samples are taken on the vessel and if necessary, sent for further analysis elsewhere. Likewise, certain types of checks can be incorporated into the port or border infrastructure, such as routine radiation scanning that may be automatically conducted at the port gates. Many checks can be conducted before goods are loaded and sealed. This means that any additional checks, for example when entering the port or border facility, may limit themselves to checking documents and verifying the seal. However, any further analysis, especially where containers and goods need to be unpacked, normally requires specialist inspection facilities.

Inspection facilities

Dedicated inspection facilities are ideally designed to accommodate efficient inspection practices, including the right equipment along with supporting tools and infrastructure. They also help protect the cargo from unnecessary damage, especially where inspection practices require shelter from the elements or where the integrity of the goods must be maintained – as is the case for most temperature-controlled goods, but also those subject to sanitary conditions, especially foods. Dedicated facilities are also needed for container and vehicle scanners. These might be fixed installations, though it is not uncommon to see border agencies also make use of mobile scanning equipment that can be moved from one border location to the next with relative ease – though suitable land and space for operating the mobile equipment still needs to be in place.

Routine scans for gamma radiation do not normally require any additional cargo handling. Readings are taken automatically whenever a vehicle carrying passes the scanner. And those scanners are normally allocated at strategic locations, such as the entrance or access road to the port gate. Should the fixed installation of gamma radiation scanners not be possible, officers may rely on smaller handled scanners, such as a standard Geiger meter.

It is common for border agencies to stipulate that certain categories of goods can only be entered into the country at specialist inspection facilities where qualified specialist officers have a presence. Such stipulations frequently apply to the trade in animals, products of animal origin, plants and plant products. And where the inspection demands equipment that is not routinely available at the border, it is common for officers to send a sample to a specialist laboratory and hold the goods until the test results have been returned. This can frequently happen in the course of sanitary and phytosanitary checks, for example, where inspectors are concerned about parasites, pesticide residuals in plants, disease or food contaminations – such as toxins (eg aflatoxins in nuts) or veterinary medicine residuals (such as antibiotic traces in meats or farmed fish).

Inevitably, when conducting an inspection, officers require access to the declared information that is held within the electronic customs system or relevant paper documents. Mobile tablets along with supporting IT systems make it increasingly easy for officers to access and process this information during the inspection, rather than having to go back to the office. Within inspection sheds officers or handling agents working with them are equipped with relevant handling equipment to lift and unpack goods. Inspection buildings must also be suitable for the types of goods handled, especially if they are temperature controlled. Officers usually also rely on a wide range of specialist scanners and tools, including sniffer dogs.

Physical movement and handling

Inevitably, the degree of handling and movement depends on the outcome of control decisions. Where there are no or minimal control or inspection requirements goods might be placed in the 'green' channel for onward transport. They may be placed on hold until necessary additional information has been obtained (ie placed in the 'yellow' channel). Or they may be placed into the 'red' channel for movement to the relevant inspection facilities. These might be the customs shed, a container or lorry scanning facility, or an inspection facility dedicated to specialist types of inspections, such as those needed by the quarantine services.

Practices differ between border locations and to a large extent depend on whether the goods are accompanied or not. Cargo on a truck, for example, would normally be accompanied by a driver. Merchandise baggage is normally transported within the luggage or vehicle of a business traveller. In these instances, officers need to instruct the individual carrying the goods to take them to the appropriate inspection facilities. In the case of unaccompanied cargo (eg shipping container, airfreight, unaccompanied truck trailer on a ferry), relevant handling needs to be arranged. At maritime ports such services are often performed by stevedores. At airports they tend to be performed by the airline's handling agent. At the inspection facility further handling is normally necessary. These relate to unpacking and presenting the goods. Inevitably this requires specialist equipment and labour. This, too, needs to be arranged and tends to form part of the service provided by stevedores and handling agents.

Inevitably, where goods are subject to inspection, relevant fees can be high. In many countries, inspectors will charge an inspection fee. Likewise, handling agents and stevedores will also charge the transport operator for their services. Within some operating models, fees are charged on a flat-rate basis and apply to all who use the facility – independent of whether goods are subject to inspection or not. Often, they are levied at full cost upon those operators responsible for the inspected goods. In many places, there may also be special arrangements for trusted operators. The United States, for example, offers trusted travellers and business operators access to its Free And Secure Trade programme (Box 5.1). The programme provides for expedited processing at the borders with Canada and Mexico. Membership for truck drivers is subject to background checks. To gain full benefits, the goods carried must also relate to trade between trusted business partners participating in the Customs and Trade Partnership Against Terrorism (C-TPAT) programme (USPB, 2014). Brazil's 'Blue Line' programme is a similar initiative that rewards low-risk operators with preferential fast-track treatment at ports and borders (Morini *et al*, 2015), as are most trusted trader and supply chain security programmes discussed in Chapter 7.

BOX 5.1

Free And Secure Trade programme (FAST) benefits for participating drivers and their eligible cargo at the border

- access to dedicated lanes for greater speed and efficiency in processing transborder shipments;
- reduced number of inspections, resulting in reduced delays at the border;
- priority, front-of-the-line processing for CBP inspections.

SOURCE USPB, 2014

Service considerations

A key service consideration within the management of inspections is scheduling and queue management. Good border officials commonly draw on advance information, such as customs notifications and transport manifests. This allows them to plan ahead and make sure that shifts and resources match traffic flows. Perishable goods may have to be given priority to ensure that goods do not deteriorate unduly. The same principle applies to shipments of live animals. Where goods are accompanied, for example by truck drivers, appropriate rest facilities (including parking and amenities) need to be in place. Text messaging systems and information boards are needed to alert drivers about waiting periods and inspection slots. Where it is known that inspections are mandatory – as is often the case with products of animal origin and products of animal origin – good practice might also include advance booking provisions so that operators can plan around the allocated slot.

Most government agencies commit themselves to service agreements that promise shippers to conduct inspections within a specific time frame. However, where inspection is dependent on third parties – such as for cargo handling – delays can arise outside the control of the agency. A common complaint at ports where cargo-handling operators do not operate on a 24/7 basis is that if inspection decisions are made at the end of the day or just before the weekend, release is delayed until the next working day – which in the case of a weekend can be several days away (Grainger, 2013). Thus, good practice – in line with the WTO Trade Facilitation Agreement (WTO, 2014) – is for customs administrations to process relevant information prior to the goods' arrival. This enables the administration to allocate sufficient inspection resources for when the cargo arrives and coordinate more effectively with cargo handlers to conduct inspection in an expedited manner.

In line with the WTO Trade Facilitation Agreement (WTO, 2014) more and more countries are also committing themselves to joint inspection principles, which include the requirement for the various border agencies (eg Customs and quarantine services) to align working hours and develop shared inspection facilities. In the case of land borders that level of coordination should ideally also extend to officials on the other side of the border (Polner, 2011). This includes single 'one-stop border post' facilities where official controls and inspections are conducted by officials from both sides of the border. In the case of Sweden, Norway and Finland border guards from the respective countries may even conduct controls and inspections on behalf of one other (Poutiainen, 2015).

Location

The location of border stations where goods can be made subject to inspection is inevitably linked to the world's transport networks. Commonly, they are located at gateway locations, such as a road or rail crossing, maritime port or airport. As such they are the first or last point at which national government agencies can enforce sovereign authority. Though under special arrangements goods may, within the confines of applicable control procedures, move to other inspection locations that may be adjacent to gateway locations or further inland. In some countries, such as those in the Western Balkans, many border clearance facilities are based inland. A large proportion of traffic arriving at the land borders is shipped under transit arrangements, including a customs seal, to those facilities (ITC and GIZ, 2020).

Gateway facilities must usually be authorized by Customs and other relevant border agencies to receive (land) or dispatch (load) cargo. Those authorization conditions, as is the practice in the United Kingdom (HMRC, 1979), are likely to include requirements for the provision of suitable border inspection infrastructure and facilities (including buildings and office facilities) along with the implementation of systems that ensure that goods on the port estate are not released without giving Customs the opportunity to inspect and formally release them.

Space at gateway locations such as a port or airport can be severely restricted. For port and airport operators dedicating land to border control-type operations also has an opportunity cost – especially if the facilities use up more space than is needed (eg because they were over-specified). It is common for border agencies to routinely release goods in line with the shipper's declaration for onward transport and conduct relevant inspections elsewhere – for example, at an inland customs facility. A financial security in the form of a bond or guarantee is usually required (Chapter 3). Airport and port operators may also have agreed special transit arrangements, where goods may leave one part of their estate for an inspection in another part of the port estate.

Figure 5.1 presents one such illustrative (completely fictional) example in which the port estate consists of three terminals that each provide for customs control but certain specialist checks can only be accommodated in Terminal A. Subsequently, any goods landed in Terminal B or C that need to be inspected in Terminal A require transit arrangements to be put in place.

Larger shippers and transport operators may own their own terminals that are located away from the port or border. In many countries, for example, the national postal services operate dedicated facilities where the handling of international postal shipments goes hand-in-hand with customs control. Any resulting inspection decisions take

FIGURE 5.1 Multiterminal port estate with one single inspection facility

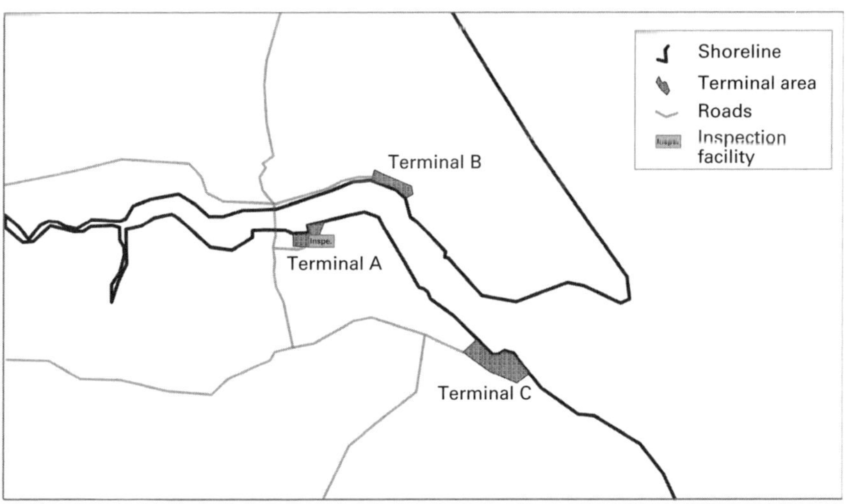

SOURCE © Trade Facilitation Consulting Ltd

place in the same building (Koch, 2015). Similar joint commercial and regulatory operations can also be found with non-customs agencies. For example, FloraHolland – one of the world's largest flower traders – has a facility within the Netherlands that is located away from the airport; authorities permit shipments to be shipped to that facility under customs transit arrangements and phytosanitary inspections are routinely conducted at that facility instead of at the airport (Grainger *et al*, 2018).

Design

The design of operations facilities and systems has a rich literature, though with few exceptions (OSCE and UNECE, 2012; Zarnowiecki, 2010) very little has been published about the specific design requirements for border and inspection facilities. Standard design principles for any type of facility (Tompkins, 2010) hold that they should:

- provide a return on assets;
- improve customer satisfaction;
- reduce costs;
- integrate into the supply chain.

In the case of border facilities this means that they have to meet the expectations of the various government agencies as well as those that present cargo to them. Cross-border traffic flows are shaped by trade policy and subsequent global supply chain configurations. Efficient border design helps reduce their impact on logistics operations and can also help enhance control and inspection outcomes. Inevitably, design considerations for efficient inspection facilities – like any other facility – are dependent on factors such as location, flow and operating practices, many of which have already been discussed in this chapter.

However, there are many more factors, and observation, when crossing borders, that can frequently reveal poor border designs. Many land border crossings, for example, are plagued by long queues which are the result of not being able to segregate traffic. Everyone is stuck in the same traffic jam and low-risk vehicles cannot be fast-tracked or prioritized. At maritime ports a big operational challenge can be frequent changes in dominant traffic directions – for example, when ships arrive there might be a rush to collect cargo, and likewise, just before ships depart there might be a last-minute run for loading. This can often also be observed at busy airports. Most air cargo is carried on passenger flights, which tend to have a preference for landing slots in the morning or evening.

Further flow factors that impact upon design considerations include:

- sudden changes in inspection requirements, for example in response to product contaminations, as might be the case with sudden food scares, or new public health measures, such as the testing of drivers for Covid-19;
- changes in trade policy which can lead to an increase or reduction in cross-border business activity, or a shift in logistics and transport arrangements;
- economic growth or decline with impact on trade flows;
- changes to global production systems that impact on the location of production facilities or the types of goods traded;
- the type, range and diversity of goods handled at the inspection facility.

When it comes to developing or improving existing border facilities, building in scope for flexibility can be a good idea. That said, the available footprint and service demands can be a limiting factor. Inevitably, it may be necessary to consider shifting many aspects of the operation away from the border to less operationally constrained locations, such as inland. Even better might be to encourage compliance behaviours that reduce the need for enforcement-type activities, including inspections, at the border.

In this context it might be worth highlighting that the pareto principle applies to border operations, too. In most countries the bulk of trade and customs declarations can usually be attributed to a small number of business operators. Thus, regulatory control arrangements that foster good compliance practices (for example, through risk management or blue lane/FAST type arrangements) help make the need for border infrastructure less urgent.

ACTIVITIES AND DISCUSSION POINTS

1. This chapter provides a broad overview about the operations and design of border facilities. Inevitably practices are likely to differ significantly from one location to the next. Choose a border crossing location of your choice and consider what the most important factors for operation and design might be for business operators and officials.
2. Become a 'virtual' inspector. Use Google Maps to explore a border facility of your own choice.
3. Discuss the pros and cons for conducting physical inspections at a border location as opposed to an inland location.

References

European Commission (2020) TARIC Consultation, ec.europa.eu/taxation_customs/dds2/taric/taric_consultation.jsp?Lang=en (archived at https://perma.cc/5B48-72S2)

Grainger, A (2013) *Trade and Customs Procedures: The compliance costs for UK meat imports,* Nottingham University, eprints.nottingham.ac.uk/2143/ (archived at https://perma.cc/WQR7-5GLW)

Grainger, A, Huiden, R, Rukanov, Band Tan, Y-H (2018) What is the cost of customs and borders across the supply chain? … and how to mitigate the cost through better coordination and data sharing, *World Customs Journal,* **12** (1), pp 1–28

HMRC (1979) Customs and Excise Management Act 1979

ITC and GIZ (2020) *Support to the Facilitation of Trade between CEFTA Parties,* Deutsche Gesellschaft für Internationale Zusammenarbeit (GIZ), International Trade Centre (ITC), Bonn

Koch, D (2015) Customs and Post, a new era of cooperation, *WCO news,* (76), pp 28–30

Morini, C, Machado, LHT, Porto, PCdS, Fernandes, RM and Trevisan, R (2015) An applied case of customs compliance and trade facilitation in Brazil: 'Blue Line' diagnosis and challenges, *Customs Scientific Journal,* **5** (1)

OSCE and UNECE (2012) *Handbook of Best Practices at Border Crossings: A trade and transport facilitation perspective,* Organization for Security and Co-operation in Europe, United Nations Economic Commission for Europe, Vienna, www.osce.org/eea/88238 (archived at https://perma.cc/7ZMA-JW4A)

Polner, M (2011) Coordinated border management: From theory to practice, *World Customs Journal,* 5 (2), pp 49–64, worldcustomsjournal.org/archive/volume-5-number-2-september-2011/ (archived at https://perma.cc/3B5Q-ML4K)

Poutiainen, M (2015) Managing land borders, the innovative Finnish model, *WCO news,* February (76), pp 12–16, www.wcoomd.org/~/media/wco/public/global/pdf/media/wco-news-magazines/wco_news_76.pdf (archived at https://perma.cc/K28Y-EP3J)

The Irish Times (2012) Man jailed over garlic tax scam, *The Irish Times,* 9 March, www.irishtimes.com/news/man-jailed-over-garlic-tax-scam-1.702973 (archived at https://perma.cc/ZD3U-ATHC)

Tompkins, J A (2010) *Facilities Planning,* 4th edn, Wiley, Chichester

UN (1968) Convention on Road Signs and Signals (2006 consolidated version), United Nations

USPB (2014) FAST Lane Requirements at Land Border, US Customs and Border Protection, www.cbp.gov/document/guidance/fast-lane-requirements-land-border-poe (archived at https://perma.cc/V2B8-C7DZ)

WTO (2014) Protocol amending the Marrakesh Agreement Establishing the World Trade Organization, Decision of 27 November 2014: Agreement on Trade Facilitation (WT/L/940), World Trade Organization, Geneva

Zarnowiecki, M (2010) Borders, their design, and their operations, in *Border Management Modernization,* eds G McLinden, E Fanta, D Widdowson and T Doyle, pp 37–78, World Bank, Washington, DC

06

Trade and customs compliance management

Trade and customs compliance operations go hand-in-hand with the control demands of Customs (Chapter 3) and other regulatory agencies (Chapter 4). This entails the need for business operators to provide an advance notification (or summary declaration) to let authorities know, in part, that goods are coming. It also entails a full declaration along with any supporting documents that are frequently needed. The release from customs control and that of other authorities is usually subject to conditions, such as the payment of import duties and taxes and any additional requirements that might arise within the context of prohibitions and restrictions. As was the focus in previous chapters (and summarized in Box 6.1) there can be many regulatory requirements with which businesses must comply.

BOX 6.1

Examples of common regulatory requirements in international trade

- Tax revenue collection:
  - collection of customs duties, excise duties and other indirect taxes;
  - payment of duties and fees;
  - management of bonds and other financial securities.

- Safety and security:
  - security and anti-smuggling controls;
  - dangerous goods;
  - vehicle checks;
  - immigration and visa formalities;
  - export licences.
- Environment and health:
  - phytosanitary, veterinary and hygiene controls;
  - health and safety measures;
  - CITES controls;
  - ships' waste.
- Consumer protection:
  - product testing;
  - labelling;
  - conformity checks with marketing standards (eg fruit and vegetables).
- Trade policy:
  - administration of quota restrictions.

SOURCE Grainger, 2011

Most declarations to the border authorities are likely to require supporting details and documents, too. For Customs, as outlined in Chapter 3, this might be the commercial invoice and relevant transport documents. Further documents that must be obtained before the goods arrive are often needed, too – such as documents confirming eligibility to preferential tariffs, but also documents specific to the control requirements of non-customs agencies, for example health certificates where goods are of animal origin and phytosanitary certificates for products of the soil (Chapter 4). Common steps necessary for business operators to comply with the various export and import arrangements between one and the next are outlined in

Box 6.1. These inevitably start with preparing the relevant commercial documents that provide the context within which the trade takes place. It is important to note, though, that the steps outlined in Box 6.1 are seldom performed by one party alone, and responsibility is derived from the specific commercial arrangements between the buyer and seller, and the enlistment of any specialist services, such as those of customs brokers, freight forwarders and agents.

BOX 6.1

An illustrative model of common steps necessary to clear goods through customs between neighbouring countries

Steps necessary to clear goods across a border between two neighbouring countries normally involve the following:

1 **Prepare commercial documents** that are required to support customs declarations (eg commercial invoice, transport documents).

2 **Apply and obtain any applicable licences permits and certificates in line with any restrictions** (Chapter 4). These might be documents that:

  a are needed to support the export declaration, for example where export controls apply;

  b must be obtained in the country of export to help meet conditions in the importing country (eg preferential origin certifications in order to take advantage of lower preferential tariff rates, health certificates in the case of quarantine controls);

  c any conditional documents that must be secured in the importing country and take time to obtain (eg import licences for controlled and restricted goods or for goods subject to import tariff quotas).

3 **Customs export declaration**: where an export declaration along with supporting documentation is made to Customs in the country of export.

4 **Customs export clearance**: where Customs approve the export declaration and releases the goods for export. Release may be dependent on a physical inspection (though these tend to be more frequent for imports). Release may be also dependent on presenting any applicable export licence (eg for strategic goods, trade in waste) and the payment of any export duties – though it is important to note that very few countries choose to tax exports.

5 **Pre-notification to Customs** in the importing country: this usually has to be made by the transport carrier. The information provided is used by Customs to conduct an initial risk assessment about whether the cargo needs to be inspected upon arrival – or deny permission to load where the pre-notification regime requires the notification to be made before loading.

6 **Full declaration of goods to Customs**: where goods are formally placed under customs control until all applicable conditions [including those of any other border agencies] have been met (eg payment of duties).

7 **Present the means of transport**: where the vehicle transporting the goods is declared to Customs.

8 **Immigration checks**: where operators of the transport vehicle (eg truck driver) needs to submit and present relevant documents, such as their passports and visas.

9 **Customs examination**: where goods, in the event of a customs examination, need to be moved to relevant inspection facilities.

10 **Customs release and onward transport**: where all customs requirements as well as those of non-customs agencies have been suitably met (eg by paying applicable import duties and taxes). Where duties and taxes are suspended or deferred, goods remain under formal customs control and conditions apply (eg attachment of a transit seal to the vehicle of container, and the arrangement of a financial guarantee or bond).

11 **Archiving and storing relevant information**: many countries require operators to keep records of the declarations to enable audits by Customs, especially where they have been used to take advantage of special or preferential customs procedures. Countries with VAT regimes that allow exports to be 'zero-rated' usually also require business operators to hold on to any evidence confirming that goods have indeed been exported.

NOTE *Additional pre-notification, declaration and inspection requirements apply where goods are subject to the control of non-Customs border agencies – eg those responsible for SPS goods.*

Despite the fragmented nature of most compliance operations between exporters, importers and intermediaries, getting trade and customs compliance right is important. Compliance failures can have serious implications. In extreme cases, where compliance breaches are found to be deliberately criminal, custodial sentences apply (BBC, 2012). Fines and penalties are common for unintended, honest mistakes. Though the scale of the fine or penalty is usually dependent on the gravity of the mistakes and any efforts in correcting them. A poor compliance record with Customs and other border agencies is also likely to have a bearing on risk scores, which in turn will translate into more frequent inspections at the border. The business competitiveness is weakened.

Inevitably, incomplete or erroneous declarations delay the clearance of goods. This in turn will undermine delivery schedules, JIT-type business models, transport planning and logistics performance. Where delays arise regularly, it also increases the need for additional warehousing to offset the impact of delay with buffer stock. Business competitiveness is undermined. Conversely, good trade and customs compliance capabilities can go a long way towards minimizing border-related delays. A good compliance record is also conditional for access to standard special customs procedures – such as customs warehousing or duty drawback (Box 2.5) – and also for participation in special customs regimes, such as those concerning supply chain security (Chapter 7), and for utilizing their associated operational benefits.

But the requirements of trade and customs procedures are not just operational in nature. They are also relevant to wider supply chain management considerations, especially where they give access to preferential duty rates and reduce the cost of supply. Modelling eligibility to preferential duty rates within the applicable preferential origin rules (Box 2.4) and production arrangements across the supply chain requires extensive expertise – especially where origin rules make stipulations about national content requirements. A detailed understanding of trade and customs procedures is also conditional for taking advantage of export market opportunities. Without knowing the applicable rules for placing goods on those markets in line with their governing regulatory requirements access (if at all) will be tricky.

The wider business objectives for good trade and customs compliance management can thus be summarized as follows:

1. Safeguard compliance to ensure that border-related risks, including fines and exposure to custodial sentences, are minimized along with any border-related risks to the company's logistics operations.
2. Reduce costs by taking advantage of lower tariffs and advantageous customs arrangements.
3. Develop sustained competitive advantages by safeguarding compliance and reducing associated costs.

Compliance practices

In every international freight movement, goods are exposed to trade and customs controls at least twice – once in the country of export and once in the country of import (Figure 6.1). Further procedures and controls may also apply along the way when in transit. Without appropriate clearance from authorities, those goods will not reach their final destination. Trade logistics is conditional on clearance from the authorities in each of the countries through which the goods move. Thus, successful compliance with applicable formalities is a key operational requirement in global supply chains – irrespective of whether those goods are supplies in the form of raw materials, pre-assembled goods or products for sale in line with end customer expectations.

FIGURE 6.1 Trade logistics operations between a seller and buyer

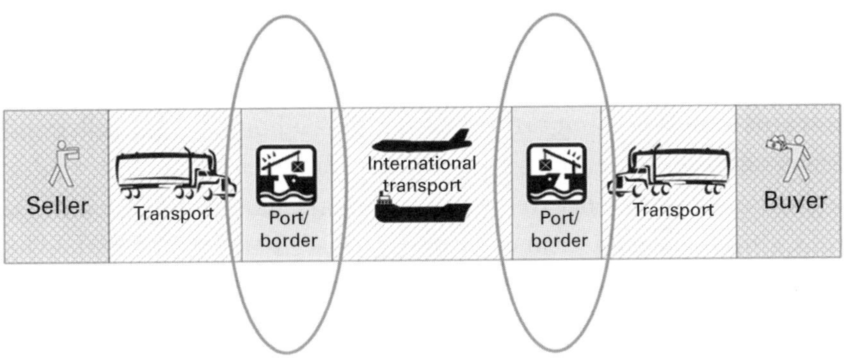

SOURCE Grainger, 2017

The movement of goods from the seller to the buyer normally requires goods to be:

- transported to the port or border in the country of export;
- cleared for export;
- shipped (eg by sea or air);
- cleared for import; and
- transported on from the port or border to the buyer or the buyer's customer.

The challenge of trying to work out which party is responsible for what, including port and customs clearance, is nothing new. The International Chamber of Commerce, with a history dating back to the 1920s, has developed a set of standard trading terms that buyers and sellers may choose to follow. These Incoterms® are now well established and widely used to lend clarity about the respective parities obligations (ICC, 2019). The majority of operations, such as transport and customs clearance, are likely to be subcontracted to specialists, such as freight forwarders, transport and logistics companies, insurance companies, banks and customs clearance agents or brokers. A clear understanding of the obligations with regard to trade and customs procedures by reference to the Incoterms® and the activities of intermediaries is integral to good trade and customs compliance management. It is also relevant for border agencies when seeking to understand who is responsible for what in typical cross-border business operations.

The Incoterms®

When making arrangements for the sale of goods, the obligations towards export and import formalities depend on what the seller and buyer agree. Experienced businesses commonly choose to agree those obligations by reference to the International Chamber of Commerce's (ICC) International Commercial Terms (ICC, 2019). Trademarked by the ICC as 'Incoterms®' the first edition was published in 1936. Periodic updates have been made to accommodate developments in contemporary trading practices, such as carriage by air, use of containerized units, multimodal operations and reliance on electronic information. The latest edition, the 8th, is Incoterms® 2020 (ICC, 2020).

The Incoterms® 2020 describe the seller's and buyer's respective obligations, risks and costs within sales and purchasing contracts. The main benefit from using the ICC's standardized Incoterms® is that they are well established in international trade practice and law (Murray *et al,* 2012). And next to clarity about the obligations for import and export formalities, they also provide the seller and buyer with clarity about:

- who is responsible for organizing carriage, insurance and obtaining shipping documents, and obtaining applicable import or export licences;
- the point at which the seller is deemed to have delivered the goods and the burden of risk – if things go wrong – is transferred over to the buyer; and
- who has to bear applicable costs, such as those relating to transport, packaging, loading, unloading, checking and security.

SOURCE ICC, 2019

The Incoterms® 2020 edition offers 11 standardized rules upon which the buyer and seller may draw (Figures 6.2a and 6.2b) four of which are exclusive to transport by sea and inland waterways. The ex-works rule (EXW) places the least amount of burden on the seller. Where goods are sold on an EXW basis the delivery point, the point at which the goods (but not necessary the title) transfer from the seller to buyer, is at a mutually agreed collection point – which will often be at the seller's warehouse or manufacturing facility. Any subsequent transport along with insurance and the customs' export, transit and import formalities fall upon the buyer. The DDP (delivered duty paid) rule, by contrast, places the majority of obligations and responsibilities – including those for the export, transit and import formalities – upon the seller. The DAP (delivered at place) and DPU (delivered at place unloaded) rules also place much of the burden on the seller, although the obligations for import formalities fall upon the buyer. In between the EXW rule and the three 'D' rules, sellers and buyers may set their respective obligations by reference to where the goods are:

- placed onboard the vessel at the port of loading (CFR, CIF and FOB);
- handed over to the carrier (CPT and CIP);
- loaded onto the means of transport provided by the buyer or placing them at the disposal of the buyer's carrier (FCA);
- placed on the port's quay or a barge, alongside the ship (FAS);
- placed onboard the vessel nominated by the buyer (FOB).

> INCOTERMS®: THEIR USE WITHIN THE CONTEXT OF STANDARD SHIPPING CONTAINERS
>
> The Incoterms® for the maritime modes (FAS, FOB, CFR, CIF) all require goods to be delivered alongside or on a vessel. Although standard shipping containers are carried by maritime vessels, containers are commonly delivered to the terminal or container yard – not alongside or on a vessel. Thus, multimodal terms like FCA, CTP and CIP are generally more suitable for containerized cargo shipments.

Each of the 11 Incoterms® 2020 rules contains 10 articles that describe the obligations of the seller on the left page of the Incoterms® publication (ICC, 2019) and the corresponding obligations of the buyer on the right page. It is prudent, whenever agreeing to an Incoterms® rule, to consult the details for each of the 10 Articles (A1-10/B1-10) along with relevant guidance (ICC, 2019).

Articles A7 and B7 specify the respective obligations for the export and import formalities (Table 6.1). The exact details are specified in the rules' respective articles (ICC, 2019). The way for the seller and buyer to correctly adopt the Incoterms® 2020 is by referencing them in their sales contract by stating the chosen Incoterms® 2020 rule followed by the named place and edition; for example: 'FCA 33

FIGURE 6.2 Incoterms®: maritime modes of transport

■ Export Formalities
□ Import Formalities

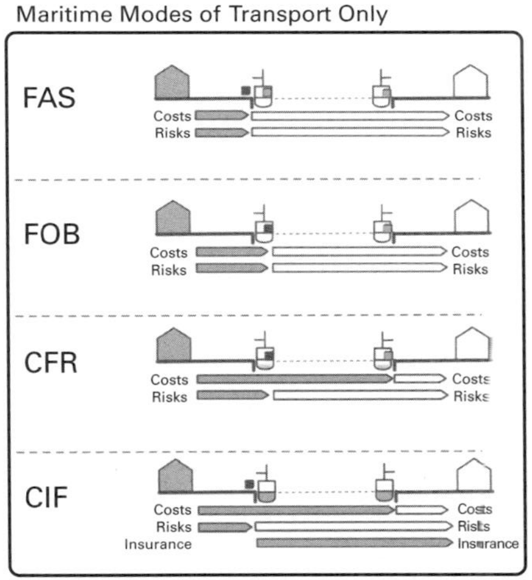

FAS	Free Alongside Ship
FOB	Free on Board
CFR	Cost and Freight
CIF	Cost, Insurance and Freight

SOURCE Figures 6.2 and 6.3 have been prepared by Trade Facilitation Consulting Ltd for illustrative purposes only. Incoterms® is a trademark of the International Chamber of Commerce. These charts have not been produced or endorsed by ICC. Official ICC products can be found at 2go.iccwbo.org

FIGURE 6.3 Incoterms®: all modes of transport

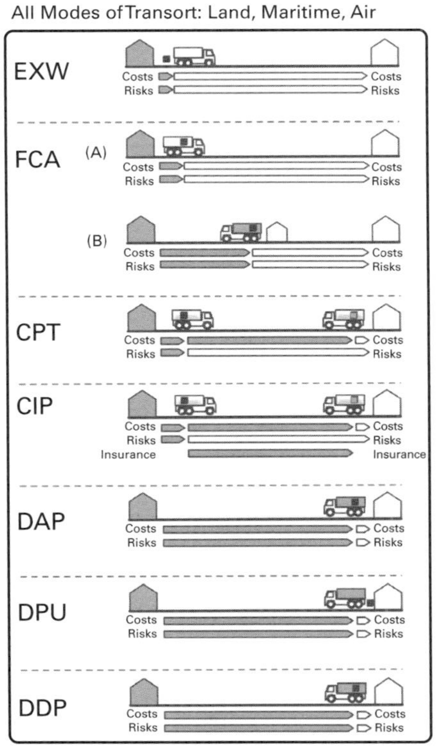

EXW	Ex-Works
FCA	Free Carrier
CPT	Carriage Paid to
CIP	Carrier and Insurance Paid
DAP	Delivered at Place
DPU	Delivered at Place Unloaded
DDP	Delivered Duty Paid

TABLE 6.1 Article titles for each of 11 Incoterms® 2020 rules

A1/B1: General obligations
A2/B2: Delivery/taking delivery
A3/B3: Transfer of risk
A4/B4: Carriage
A5/B5: Insurance
A6/B6: Delivery/transport documents
A7/B7: Export/import clearance
A8/B8: Checking/packaging/marking
A9/B9: Allocation of costs
A10/B10: Notices

avenue Président Wilson, Paris, France, Incoterms® 2020'. Standard commercial invoice templates along with the customs declaration commonly also require reference to the adopted Incoterm®, in order to provide clarity about responsibilities and the wider commercial context, which amongst other issues is also important for the determination of the declared customs value (Box 6.3).

BOX 6.2

The significance of the Incoterms® 2020 for compliance with customs procedures

It is usually necessary to make reference to the selected Incoterms® rule in the relevant commercial documentation, especially the commercial invoice and in transport documents. This clarifies the wider commercial context, which amongst other issues, is particularly relevant in the assessment of the correct customs value (Chapter 2, Box 2.3)

For example, in Chapter 2 it was explained that in many countries the customs value is based on the so-called transaction value and includes the cost of international transport and insurance. Such transport and insurance costs are inclusive in a sale where the goods are sold on a CIF basis. However, they are not inclusive when sold on an FOB basis – and thus would need to be added to the declared customs value. Yet, for countries such as the United States, where international carriage and insurance does not form part of the transaction value, they would not need to be added.

Incoterms® rule references can also be significant when trying to work out the eligibility for preferential (lower) tariff treatment for goods where the origin rules specify product specific national content conditions (Chapter 2, Box 2.4). That national content often has to be calculated by reference to EXW price – see, for example, in the EU–Korea Free Trade Agreement (European Union and Republic of Korea, 2011). Yet, in other trade agreements, such as those negotiated by ASEAN, calculations might be based on the FOB price – as is the case for the Agreement between ASEAN and Korea (see Annex 3, Appendix 1 in ASEAN and Republic of Korea, 2006).

The ASEAN–Korea Agreement also refers to the FOB price when granting duty-free treatment for low value goods (ie imports of less than US $200; see Annex 1, Appendix 1 in ASEAN and Republic of Korea, 2006) – the so-called *de minimis* rules.

Occasionally, some countries might also make reference to Incoterms® in their national additions to the HS systems. Panama offers one such example where the tariff classification for whisky includes reference to the CIF price:

> **2208.30.10** Alcohol etílico sin desnaturalizar con grado alcohólico volumétrico inferior al 80 % vol; aguardientes, licores y demás bebidas espirituosas: Whisky: Con valor **CIF** inferior a B/.70.00 cada caja (12 unidades).

For additional examples, see ITC, 2021

Customs brokers and agents

Sellers and buyers frequently delegate a significant part of their respective compliance obligations to specialists, such as freight forwarders, customs brokers and agents. The range of services that they can offer is quite broad and often tied into wider transport service packages that range from door-to-door shipments (eg DDP or DAP) to more select operations, such as those from the seller's premises to the port. Trade and customs services may also be tied into other third-party logistics services, such as customs warehousing.

The advantage of using customs brokers or agents is that they tend to be very experienced, tend to have access to ready-made networks and infrastructure (especially where declarations must be made electronically using specialist software) and also benefit from significant economies of scale (Verwaal and Donkers, 2003). Economies of scale result from being able to spread fixed costs, such as the employment of specialists and investments in electronic systems, over larger volumes of customs declarations. As a result, the cost per declaration for an agent can be significantly less when compared to what it would be if lodged by the trader without specialist third-party support.

Brokers may also be able to offer relatively quick and unbureaucratic access to special customs arrangements, such as customs warehousing and the deferred payment of import duties and taxes. They are usually also able to make sure that relevant declarations are made on time with minimal effort, especially when the service offering is tied in with transport and logistics responsibilities and customs-relevant transport details are available at their fingertips. However, for traders the use of third parties has its own costs, that include the cost of putting appropriate contracts in place, providing them with all the relevant information necessary to complete declarations, and supervising their performance (Grainger, 2016). Larger operators may also develop bespoke electronic interfaces with their appointed agents to help automate much of the necessary data needed for trade and customs compliance operations (Hausman *et al*, 2010).

The list of services offered by brokers can range from preparing import, export and transit documents right up to implementing sophisticated compliance systems (Box 6.4). Much of the service offering depends on the size of the firm. They may be small scale with focus on the trade and customs formalities in one specific country. They may specialize in a specific sector that has unique requirements (eg food and vegetables) or focus on a specific port or border crossing. Others may be bigger in scale, with a regional or global footprint. Very often customs clearance services are also offered by freight forwarders and international logistics companies. Border and customs clearance services might be priced separately, or as part of a wider service bundle that includes transport, insurance, handling and other logistics requirements.

BOX 6.3

List of typical services provided by customs brokers and clearance agents

- prepare import, export, transit documents;
- complete and submit customs import, export and transit declarations;
- check supporting documents and information;
- prepare and submit information relating to special customs procedures (eg duty deferment and customs warehousing);
- pay duties and taxes as well as any other regulatory fees that might apply;
- arrange or assist in the presentation of goods to customs inspectors;
- process duty and tax refund applications;
- make amendments and corrections to declarations made;
- maintain document records (in paper or electronically) as required by law;
- provide advice on classification, valuation and origin rules;
- assist clients in setting up a compliance system (eg instructions about best practices, responsibilities, use of appropriate software).

SOURCE Adapted from Grainger, 2016; WCO, 2018

In some countries – especially in the Americas, the Caribbean and in some African countries – sellers and buyers may not have the choice of making the declarations themselves. Only licensed customs brokers or agents are permitted to make customs declarations (WCO, 2018). However, the trend, in line with the recommendations of the Revised Kyoto Convention (WCO, 2006), is not to make the use of customs brokers mandatory and to give businesses the choice of whether they wish to appoint a third party or make the declarations themselves. Where applicable, professional licensing requirements are either defined by the customs administrations or an independent professional body. Common criteria for becoming a licensed broker or agent include:

- a sound knowledge of applicable rules and regulations;
- good knowledge of international trade and logistics practices;
- a good compliance record and suitable financial capacity;
- capabilities to interact with the administrations via electronic means;
- financial securities (such as in the form of a customs bond);
- evidence of suitable work experience and training;
- compliance with applicable establishment criteria, such as a registered office and citizenship;
- adherence to a professional code of conduct.

SOURCE WCO, 2018

In some countries, aspiring customs brokers may also need to sit for a professional exam. In some places that exam will be followed by a formal interview which seeks to establish the moral and ethical character of the aspiring agent (WCO, 2018). But licensing requirements for customs brokerage services are not without controversy. Especially when demand for brokerage services exceeds supply and the number of licensed brokers is capped or restricted by overly restrictive examination practices. This is one of the reasons why in many countries – including much of Northern Europe – the use of licensed customs brokers or agents has not been made mandatory. However, companies (or persons) wishing to make a customs declaration, even if it is submitted by an agent, must usually apply for an authorization number. Processes for such authorization are often very straightforward. In the UK and EU, for example, it can usually be obtained in a matter of a few clicks using the relevant online government services (Irish Revenue, 2021; UK Government, 2021).

A key point to be mindful of is that the declarant (the person who makes the declaration or in whose name such declaration is made) is normally fully liable for the customs declaration (WCO, 2006). However, where the declaration is made by a representative – such as an agent or broker – it is prudent for businesses to check who exactly is liable. Most countries allow for both direct and indirect representation

(Box 6.4). A direct representative acts in the name of and on behalf of another person. A direct representative is thus not necessarily liable for the declaration made. Whereas an indirect representative, who acts in his or her own name but on behalf of another person, is liable. And where representation to Customs is made by an agent in a direct capacity, it is prudent for traders to periodically check that what was declared has indeed been correctly declared in line with given instructions. In many larger firms customs and trade compliance managers can spend much of their time checking and supervising appointed customs agents (Grainger, 2016).

BOX 6.4

Customs representation in the European Union

Article 18

Customs representative

1. Any person may appoint a customs representative.

Such representation may be either direct, in which case the customs representative shall act in the name of and on behalf of another person, or indirect, in which case the customs representative shall act in his or her own name but on behalf of another person.

SOURCE Union Customs Code, EU Regulation No 952/2013, European Union, 2013

TRANSPORT CARRIERS

The transport carrier's main function is to carry the cargo for the shipper. This might be a commercial shipping line, airline, trucking company or railway operator. While the seller and buyer (or appointed agents) in line with their selected Incoterm® are responsible for many of the border formalities, some also fall upon the transport carrier moving the goods. Procedural obligations for carriers include the need to pre-notify relevant authorities about the cargo that is to arrive (eg in the form of a shipping manifest) and related advance information to enable a security risk assessment (eg in the form of a summary declaration). Usually, transport carriers are also made responsible for presenting the cargo to Customs in the event of a physical inspection – which in the case of air cargo and maritime cargo may necessitate close cooperation with relevant cargo-handling companies or stevedores (Chapter 5).

The requirement for the carrier to notify Customs in many parts of the world was discussed in Chapter 3. However, from a compliance management point of view it is important that traders always provide the transport operator with the correct information. This ensures that the advance declarations made by the transport company match up with the customs declarations made by or on behalf of the trader.

> TIP
>
> Often international transport is booked weeks if not months in advance. By the time goods are ready for shipment facts relating to those goods may have changed. Shippers may, to give a few examples, decide at the last minute to: change the goods; ship to a different end customer at the same port; change the quantities; or switch shipping containers. Thus, good practice for shippers is always to check that the most recent data about the shipment has also been passed on to the transport operators. Ensuring that information is accurate avoids the liabilities and problems that will result from inconsistencies between advance notifications to Customs made by the carrier and customs declarations made by or on behalf of the trader.

CARGO HANDLERS AND STEVEDORES

When cargo is selected for a physical inspection it is the carrier who is normally responsible for presenting the consignment to the relevant authorities. However, at most ports and airports this responsibility is delegated to cargo handlers or stevedores. These are companies responsible for the loading and unloading of aircraft and ships, including any tasks relating to moving the cargo to the inspection facilities. Charges by cargo handlers or stevedores to the carrier are usually then passed on, sometimes with an uplift, to the importer. The costs of cargo handling specific to inspections can be even greater at locations where the inspection facilities are some distance away from the border or terminal. Likewise, multiple inspection requirements further inflate costs – eg a customs X-ray followed by a physical customs inspection and then a further inspection by the quarantine authority at a different facility.

It is worth noting that some traders will want to be able to have control over who ships the goods, especially if the carrier's uplift for inspection-related handling services is thought to be too high. In such instances Incoterms® where the carrier is nominated by the importer (eg CIF) might be preferable to those where the carrier is nominated by the exporter (eg FOB).

PORT AND TERMINAL OPERATORS

Customs and border management obligations also fall upon port and terminal operators. National customs legislation often requires them to ensure that the cargo handled at their facilities can be easily located and that goods are only loaded for export or onward inward transport once cleared by Customs. This requires the maintenance of a robust record-keeping system that can track goods while on the estate as well as the customs status for those goods. Such systems require many interfaces; with the transport carriers, the importers and exporters or their nominated agents, stevedores or cargo handlers, Customs, and other border agencies (eg the quarantine services). At busy ports and airports electronic systems – so-called port community systems (Figure 3.6, Chapter 3) – are often put in place (Long, 2009).

National customs legislation usually also requires ports to be secure. This is to prevent cargo being removed clandestinely without customs' permission, for example, by controlling access to the port estate via gates and through the installation of fencing and surveillance equipment. Overlapping transport legislation also demands that the port estate is secure, especially against threats from terrorist and organized criminals (Widdowson *et al*, 2014). Thus, port and terminal operators also need to control who enters the port estate along with additional mode-specific security demands governing cargo and vehicles.

In some countries (such as the United Kingdom), as part of their authorization conditions, ports also have to furnish customs officers with appropriate office facilities and inspection facilities (Grainger, 2010). If handling products of animal or plant origin, similar obligations for office and inspection facilitates also apply towards the quarantine services. Subsequently, port operators will charge carriers for the use of inspection facilities. Depending on the policies and practices at the port concerned, the associated costs might be billed: a) as a flat fee levied on each and every consignment, irrespective of whether an inspection takes place or not; or b) on a use basis, where inspection fees are only levied on those consignments that have been selected by the relevant authorities (Grainger, 2013).

BANKS

Banks play a big role in international trade. They are often relied upon as a source of finance, helping sellers and buyers bridge the gap between when orders are placed and when orders are delivered. But there is another role that financial institutions play. They facilitate the payment of fees and charges (UNECE, 2012b), including the payment of: customs duties and taxes; inspection fees; the charges levied by carriers, stevedores and handling agents. Depending on the country and border concerned, such payments may be made: a) on account, where the relevant party can draw on a credit facility; or b) upon request, where payment needs to be actively initiated. The latter is often a delaying factor for customs and borders clearance. Banks are also relied upon for financial guarantees and bonds, which are conditional for access to most special and simplified customs procedures (UNECE, 2012a).

Customs and trade compliance management in practice

For customs and trade compliance managers tasked with getting businesses' compliance right, the job can have an operational focus, a strategic focus or both. Inevitably it is intertwined with wider logistics and supply chain management considerations (Grainger, 2017). Successful logistics operations are dependent on making sure that the correct amount of duty is paid, and where applicable, that the required proof of export has also been obtained – so that, for example, VAT may be zero-rated (see Chapter 2).

Linked to logistics operations, the job is also about making sure that the necessary information for import and export declarations has been collated accurately and on time from relevant parties so that goods can be cleared through Customs without delay (Chapter 3). When things do not work out as planned, customs and trade compliance managers often spend much of their day firefighting, liaising with authorities to ensure that delays are minimized (eg by correcting mistakes or by obtaining missing documents). Prudent customs and trade compliance managers, as mentioned earlier in this chapter, may also choose to actively audit and check the performance of appointed customs representatives, for example, by double-checking declarations made in the company's name. Last but not least, it is also about identifying and implementing available beneficial customs procedures (see Chapter 3) that can help speed up clearance or reduce duty liabilities.

From a supply chain point of view the job of a customs and trade compliance manager is also about supporting procurement decisions by informing colleagues about the scale of import duties and taxes as well as giving advice on any risks that might be associated with wider trade policy developments – such as sanctions, restrictions or trade wars. Customs knowledge is also relevant for production location decisions where the construction or use of alternate facilities can reduce duty liabilities. Often the customs and trade compliance manager is also the designated contact person for customs-led supply chain security programmes that require companies to vet suppliers and customers for compliance with specific security obligations (see Chapter 7).

At the corporate level customs and trade compliance managers often also need to ensure that systems put in place to manage compliance are suitably robust. This is particularly important in countries where the company's senior accounting officer is liable for making sure that taxes are correctly accounted for – as is, for example, the case in the UK under its Finance Act 2009. Issues surrounding corruption – where agents or staff feel tempted to bribe border officials – may be of a similar concern. In many countries, such as the United States under its Corrupt Practice Act enacted in 1977, such payments are strictly illegal even if made abroad. It thus often falls upon customs and trade compliance managers to make sure that no such illegal payments are made to corrupt border officials abroad.

The customs function within international businesses

A traditional model for customs and trade compliance managers, especially if the job takes a wider strategic or compliance-type role, is to work at the company's headquarters – often reporting directly to the finance or legal manager – in an in-house advisory facility. This 'go-to person' then becomes the designated contact person for all things customs, whether it is logistics, supply chain or otherwise compliance-related. Often such a role also demands direct input into the company's administrative system, for example, by ensuring that functional standard operating procedures (SOPs) such as those governing logistics and procurement decisions adequately reflect the needs of customs compliance. It is also not uncommon for customs and trade compliance managers to work in teams with IT professionals to help ensure that the data necessary for customs declarations is always correct and to assist with automating compliance operations.

Another model for customs and trade compliance managers is to sit alongside logistics colleagues offering immediate support as and when needed – especially in operational environments where border-related demands can be technically demanding. This might be the case, for example, where businesses declare a wider range of goods (such as retailers) or where compliance operations demand a high level of personal involvement – as can be the case where documents are still paper-based or where declarations can only be lodged by suitably qualified individuals. Inevitably, the job of a customs and trade compliance manager can vary from one company to the next (Grainger, 2016) though in line with the company's requirements focus will be on ensuring that compliance is managed in a way that non-compliance risks are minimized. Often it is also about making sure that the compliance burden does not unnecessarily add to the cost of moving goods across the border, for example, by taking advantage of special procedures that confer preferential treatment. The latter may also confer competitive advantages, especially if the compliance capabilities of competitors are not as well managed.

Safeguarding compliance

Senior customs managers usually have many years of experience, often gained as customs officers or clearance agents. In their career development they may also have worked for extended periods as independent customs consultants or with specialist law and accountancy firms. It is not uncommon for senior customs managers at the world's largest companies to also hold multiple professional qualifications that, next to those relevant for customs, also extend to logistics, supply chain management, information technology, tax or law (Grainger, 2016).

Typically, senior customs managers within larger multinational firms have three mechanisms at their disposal to ensure that customs issues receive due consideration within their company. The first is in person as the in-house expert or 'go-to person'. The second mechanism is of an indirect nature by relying on the company's administrative systems. The third mechanism is to contract out to third parties. Smaller companies often struggle to find all expertise in-house, which some would argue makes it particularly important for policy makers to ensure that good business support is available (Chapter 3).

The number of employed in-house customs professionals, when compared to other compliance-type activities (such as tax or accounting) tends to be small. A key part of the job can be to develop a good relationship with the relevant authorities in order to help build trust, lend input into how trade and customs procedures should be best designed and participate in partnership programmes – such as those concerning supply chain security (Chapter 7). However, much of their time is spent on making sure that the company is indeed compliant. In that effort, senior customs managers may avail themselves of the services provided by third parties. They may also provide extensive input into the company's management and operations systems.

Drawing on third-party services

As already mentioned in this chapter, reliance on third-party services to submit customs (and other) declarations has many benefits. However, it is very common for customs agents to operate as a direct representative, only. Subsequently, the company is still liable for customs declarations. A significant part of the customs manager's responsibility thus is to ensure that the appointed third parties are issued with the necessary customs instructions and to monitor their performance, for example, by setting contractually pre-agreed key performance indicators (KPIs) and to conduct occasional audits of the services provided. In some countries it is possible for registered businesses to access the customs computer and view the declarations that have been lodged by their agents. Good practice is to review these regularly, and if errors are identified, to ask the agent to make relevant corrections and amend immediately – and thus reduce the risk and impact of any resulting fines and penalties.

Businesses may also reach out to third-party trade and customs experts for specialist advice. This is common for more complex questions about preferential origin rules, customs valuation and tariff classification-type questions. Experts may also be relied upon to implement any special customs procedures that confer operational or fiscal advantages – including, amongst others, customs warehousing and duty drawback (Chapter 2, Box 2.5). Third parties are often also relied upon in the implementation of specialist software, including systems that can automatically generate much of the required customs data by drawing on information held in other electronic systems – such as those used for invoicing, logistics, accounting and procurement.

Utilization of the company's management system

Many larger companies have developed sophisticated management systems with defined standard operating procedures (SOPs) for most of their activities. Often SOPs are tied to the company's quality management system (which might also be independently certified, eg under ISO 9000). Company employees are expected to follow the SOPs and when necessary, review and update them. Senior customs managers may set (or help define) SOPs that apply to all processes that might touch upon customs, such as:

- **procurement** and decisions about the preferred Incoterms® and resulting obligations for suppliers;

- **logistics** with regard to the performance of appointed customs agents, but also to safeguard that the data they use for customs declarations is correct;
- **finance and accounting** to make sure that details concerning customs, especially the commercial invoice, are correct;
- **sales and marketing** to support customers' trade and customs requirements;
- **human resources** to make sure that appointments comply with any stipulations set by the border agencies, including professional qualifications and criminal record checks.

In addition to SOPs, senior customs managers may also implement electronic solutions that can automate many of the compliance processes – especially those relating to making electronic customs declarations. To enable automation, it is necessary to make sure that customs-relevant information (eg the commercial invoice, tariff classification, origin, consignor and consignee, shipping details) are captured correctly. Thus, a significant task for some senior customs managers is always to make sure that staff know what data to enter into the electronic systems and ensure that it is always up-to-date and not shoddy. The delivery of training can be a significant aspect of the customs manager's portfolio of activities.

ACTIVITIES AND DISCUSSION POINTS

1. Research what requirements apply if a person (individual or company) wishes to make a customs declaration in a country of your choice.
2. What are the pros and cons for tasking a customs agent or broker with making a customs declaration? Make a list and discuss.
3. Some customs practitioners argue that if they were to report to the logistics manager, there would be a conflict of interest – the need to move goods quickly trumps wider compliance considerations. This is best avoided by ensuring that the customs function is standalone or is part of the company's wider tax and legal compliance team. Discuss!

References

ASEAN & Republic of Korea (2006) Agreement on Trade in Goods Under the Framework Agreement on Comprehensive Economic Cooperation Among the Governments of the Member Countries of the Association of Southeast Asian Nations and the Republic of Korea, Kuala Lumpur, Malaysia, 24 August 2006, ASEAN Secretariat, https://asean.org/?static_post=asean-republic-of-korea-free-trade-area-2 (archived at https://perma.cc/K4PF-5FVE)

BBC (2012) Ireland garlic scam: Paul Begley jailed for six years, www.bbc.co.uk/news/world-europe-17320460 (archived at https://perma.cc/B566-NK7R)

European Union (2013) Regulation (EU) No 952/2013 of the European Parliament and the Council of 9 October 2013, laying down the Union Customs Code (recast), *Official Journal of the European Union,* **56** (L269)

European Union and Republic of Korea (2011) Council Decision of 16 September 2010 on the signing, on behalf of the European Union, and provisional application of the Free Trade Agreement between the European Union and its Member States, of the one part, and the Republic of Korea, of the other part, *Official Journal of the European Union*, L127 (14.5.2011), https://eur-lex.europa.eu/legal-content/en/ALL/?uri=OJ:L:2011:127:TOC (archived at https://perma.cc/3R74-XPQC)

Grainger, A (2010) The role of the private sector in border management reform, in *Border Management Modernization,* eds G McLinden, E Fanta, D Widdowson and T Doyle, pp 157–74, World Bank, Washington, DC

Grainger, A (2011) Trade facilitation: A conceptual review, *Journal of World Trade*, **45** (1), pp 39–62

Grainger, A (2013) *Trade and customs procedures: The compliance costs for UK meat imports*, Nottingham University, eprints.nottingham.ac.uk/2143/ (archived at https://perma.cc/TK33-R4LN)

Grainger, A (2016) Customs management in multinational companies, *World Customs Journal*, **10** (2), worldcustomsjournal.org/Archives/Volume%2010%2C%20Number%202%20(Sep%202016)/1806%2001%20WCJ%20v10n2%20Grainger.pdf (archived at https://perma.cc/78HV-KNS4)

Grainger, A (2017) Trade and customs procedures in international transport: Requirements, issues and trends, in *International Freight Transport: Cases, structures and prospects,* eds A. Beresford and S Pettit, pp 57–75, Kogan Page, London

Hausman, WH, Lee, HL, Napier, GRF, Thompson, A and Zheng, Y (2010) A process analysis of global trade management: An inductive approach, *Journal of Supply Chain Management*, **46** (2), pp 5–29, doi:10.1111/j.1745-493X.2010.03187.x

ICC (2019) Incoterms® 2020, International Chamber of Commerce, Paris

ICC (2020) Incoterms® rules history, iccwbo.org/resources-for-business/incoterms-rules/incoterms-rules-history/ (archived at https://perma.cc/Y5GS-MDDE)

Irish Revenue (2021) Register for an economic operators' registration and identification (EORI) number, www.revenue.ie/en/online-services/services/common/register-for-an-eori-number.aspx (archived at https://perma.cc/J8UT-SXDY)

ITC (2021) Incoterms® in Market Access Map, www.macmap.org/en/resources/incoterms (archived at https://perma.cc/S95Q-SMQU)

Long, A (2009) Port community systems, *World Customs Journal*, **3** (1), worldcustomsjournal.org/archive/volume-3-number-1-april-2009/ (archived at https://perma.cc/5KR2-CZGC)

Murray, C, Holloway, D, Timson-Hunt, D, Dixon, G and Schmitthoff, CM (2012) *Schmitthoff: The Law and Practice of International Trade*, 12th edn, Sweet & Maxwell, London

UK Government (2021) Get an EORI number, Gov.uk, www.gov.uk/eori (archived at https://perma.cc/23YA-5FDD)

UNECE (2012a) Guarantee and Security, tfig.unece.org/contents/guarantee-and-security.htm (archived at https://perma.cc/A9JP-SMUA)

UNECE (2012b) Payment, tfig.unece.org/contents/intro-domain-payment.htm (archived at https://perma.cc/66RW-89ZU)

Verwaal, E and Donkers, B (2003) Customs-related transaction costs, firm size and international trade intensity, *Small Business Economics*, **21** (3), pp 257–71

WCO (2006) Revised Kyoto Convention: International Convention on the Simplifications and Harmonization of Customs Procedures, World Customs Organization, Brussels, www.wcoomd.org/en/topics/facilitation/instrument-and-tools/conventions/pf_revised_kyoto_conv/kyoto_new.aspx (archived at https://perma.cc/KVA9-32YK)

WCO (2018) WCO Customs Brokers Guidelines, World Customs Organization, Brussels

Widdowson, D, Blegen, B, Kashubsky, M and Grainger, A (2014) Review of accredited operator schemes: an Australian study, *World Customs Journal*, 8 (1), pp 17–34

07

Coordinated border management and supply chain security

When crossing borders, as outlined in Chapter 3, businesses are obliged to place goods under the control of relevant authorities (by making a declaration) and seeking their release. And, as has been outlined throughout this book (see Figure 4.1), there are many regulatory authorities, of which Customs is usually the most visible one. The respective regulations that they enforce relate to trade and tax policy (Chapter 2) as well as the enforcement of prohibitions and restrictions along with controls on people and the vehicles that move goods across borders (Chapter 4). Failure to administer and enforce border controls effectively undermines the authority of the state and gives rise to threats that range from the failure to collect taxes effectively to the undermining of market performance, public health and national security, amongst others (Figure 7.1). Businesses that fail to comply expose themselves to criminal and civil penalties. Consistent compliance failures jeopardize any access to favourable treatment by the border authorities; competitiveness is diminished (Chapter 6).

In addressing the enforcement of regulatory requirements, border agencies, especially Customs, have taken considerable inspiration from the supply chain metaphor where cooperation and coordination between the relevant parties provides for improved outcomes. Coordinated border management practices focus on enhancing the links within and between agencies at and across the border (G2G). Related ideas in supply chain security extend the focus from the

FIGURE 7.1 Threats to society resulting from poor border performance

Threats to national income

- Uncollected taxes and duties
- Failure to meet budget commitments
- Adverse trade investment climate

Threats to the market

- Unfair competition by non-compliant businesses
- High compliance costs and barriers to trade

Threats to public policy

- Illegal imports of narcotics and drugs
- Illegal trade in repugnant goods
- Increased levels of crime

Threats to public security

- Illegal exports of arms and weapons
- Uncontrolled imports of arms and weapons

Threats to the health and life of humans

- Illegal import of unlicensed medicines
- Unsafe goods
- Non-compliance with product standards

Threats to the health of animals and plants

- Illegal importation of diseased and high-risk goods

Threats to the environment

- Illegal trade in endangered species
- Illegal trade in regulated pollutants and substances

Threats to national and international treasures

- Illegal trade in antiques, artefacts and other cultural items
- Loss of national heritage

Threats to industrial and commercial property

- Loss of intellectual property
- Undermined public confidence in brands resulting from counterfeit goods

SOURCE © Trade Facilitation Consulting Ltd

border to the entire supply chain by cooperating with relevant authorities (G2G) and with trusted business operators (G2B). Both concepts play a central theme in the evolving trade and customs policy – especially within the context of trade facilitation which seeks to reduce friction in cross-border operations (Chapter 9) – but also have a literature in their own right.

Coordinated border management

As touched upon in previous chapters, there are many government agencies with an interest in border management (Chapter 4, Figure 4.1). Their interests concern the administration and enforcement of controls specific to the cross-border movement of goods, the vehicles that transport those goods and the people operating and handling those goods. Coordinated border management is about improving the performance of those border agencies by encouraging them to work together. This idea is not new and goes by several almost synonymous labels. The term 'coordinated border management' is used in much of the work of the World Customs Organization, who have produced a detailed compendium on the subject (WCO, 2015). The WTO has adopted the term 'border agency cooperation' along with binding commitments under the Trade Facilitation Agreement (WTO, 2014). Detailed guidelines drafted by the European Commission use the term 'integrated border management' (European Commission, 2010).

Irrespective of the label, coordinated border management has one or more of the following objectives:

- improved enforcement capabilities by taking coordinated efforts to stopping illegal trades;
- smoothened operations within and between agencies that translate into cost savings and performance enhancements;
- improved utilization of scarce resources (eg finance, staff, equipment, facilities) through shared use;
- the effective day-to-day operations of shared facilities and systems;

- the reduction of trade compliance costs and streamlined interfaces with business operators;
- clear command lines along with a clear demarcation of responsibilities;
- the sharing of skills and expertise.

Examples of coordinated border management are plentiful. These range from agreements about recognizing official documents and certificates to the implementation of shared electronic infrastructure (Box 7.1). At land borders coordinated border management is also about the development and use of shared border facilities. For example, at the borders between Switzerland and Germany as well as the borders between Switzerland and France so-called 'One-Stop Border Posts' (or 'juxtaposed' borders) have been in place since the 1960s. And at these shared facilities the respective administrations work side-by-side at one single location – as opposed to operating two separate facilities, one at each side of the border (Polner, 2011). Within an international context, coordinated border management is also about sharing operational information and intelligence between customs administrations – ie 'customs-to-customs' as specified in the WCO's SAFE Framework of Standards (WCO, 2018).

BOX 7.1

Examples of coordinated border management

1 Mutual recognition of documents and certificates – for example, where a document issued by an agency in one country is recognized by the authorities elsewhere without the need for further validation.

2 Joint company audits and inspection visits where control objectives overlap – for example, in the context of customs, VAT and tax audits.

3 Harmonized data standards, where the various government agencies agree on standardized datasets to enable more streamlined data-sharing.

4 Synchronized border inspections, where relevant authorities conduct their controls jointly and thus reduce the need for repeated handling operations.

5 Harmonized operating hours in line with the requirements of business operators.

6 Sharing of intelligence, information and data about business operators to enable more informed risk profiling and targeted investigations.

7 Pooled facilities and equipment to enable better utilization and save costs, eg in the form of shared office building, inspection facilities, staff transport.

8 Collaborative criminal investigation and prosecution. The United States' Border Enforcement Security Task Force (BEST), for example, targets cross-border crime and is organized in teams that operate across 16 federal states and draws on members from more than 100 different US law enforcement agencies.

9 Joint international investigations into cross-border crimes (which are often coordinated via INTERPOL or the WCO).

10 The operation of one-stop border infrastructure.

11 Cross-training of officers. In Finland, for example, customs officers are trained by the Border Guard to be able to inspect identification documents and visas. Border guards in turn are trained by Customs to search vehicles and recognize prohibited and restricted goods.

12 Single window-type solutions that are in line with UN CEFACT Recommendation 33 (UN CEFACT, 2004) provide for a single interface between business and government (as opposed to one with each agency).

SOURCE Adapted from Grainger and Hintsa, 2017

Coordinated border management practices are also strongly encouraged under the WCO's Revised Kyoto Convention (Table 7.1), and the WTO Trade Facilitation Agreement (WTO, 2014) makes some of those requirements for border agency cooperation binding upon WTO member countries (Article 8, Box 7.2). Furthermore, the WTO Trade Facilitation Agreement also encourages the adoption of the single window concept (Chapter 9) where countries implement systems (preferably electronic) that enable all government agencies to interact with the business community via one single interface (UN CEFACT, 2004).

TABLE 7.1 WCO Revised Kyoto Convention standards with relevance to coordinated border management

Standard	Synopsis and commentary
Standard 3.1	The location of customs facilities is to be determined by factors that take the needs of business operators into account. It is reasonable for operators to expect a streamlined service that also meets the border control needs of other agencies.
Standard 3.11	Paper documents shall be in accordance with the UN Layout Key; electronically lodged declarations shall be compliant with international standards agreed by WCO members. Information sharing between different agencies (and the business community) is made easier; thanks to international data standards much of this can be done automatically.
Transitional Standard 3.35	If goods must be inspected by Customs and other (non-customs) authorities then such inspections should, as far as possible, be carried out at the same time.
Standard 3.3	Office hours at common border crossings are to be aligned.
Transitional Standards 3.4 and 3.5	Controls by the respective customs agencies at common border crossings should, where possible, be operated jointly and share the same facility.
Standards 6.3–6.4	Risk management is to be used for customs control purposes. The decision to inspect goods, including the means of transport, is to be based on risk analysis. Information and data provided by non-customs agencies can significantly enhance customs risk management capabilities
Standard 6.7	Mutual administrative assistance agreements are to be sought to enhance control. This provides the legal basis for one customs administration to assist another.
Standard 6.8	The Customs shall seek to cooperate with the trade and seek to conclude Memoranda of Understanding (MoUs) to enhance customs control. Such MoUs can serve multiple purposes. For example, MoUs can be used: to negotiate access to sensitive information; reward businesses for compliant behaviour; encourage operational practices that support customs control (eg vetting of suppliers and customers).

(continued)

TABLE 7.1 (Continued)

Standard	Synopsis and commentary
Standard 6.9	The Customs shall use information technology and electronic commerce to the greatest possible extent to enhance customs control. Control capabilities, especially where they relate to non-customs agencies, are significantly enhanced where the respective electronic systems are integrated.
Standards 7.2–7.4	Computer applications shall use internally accepted standards. The development of computer applications shall consider the needs of all parties (necessitating extensive consultation with those parties). These standards concern the interfaces with the business community as well as the interfaces with all the non-customs agencies.

SOURCE Adapted from WCO, 2006, 2015

BOX 7.2

Border agency cooperation obligations specified in the WTO Trade Facilitation Agreement, Article 8

1. Each Member shall ensure that its authorities and agencies responsible for border controls and procedures dealing with the importation, exportation and transit of goods cooperate with one another and coordinate their activities in order to facilitate trade.
2. Each Member shall, to the extent possible and practicable, cooperate on mutually agreed terms with other Members with whom they share a common border with a view to coordinating procedures at border crossings to facilitate cross-border trade. Such cooperation and coordination may include:
   - **a** alignment of working days and hours;
   - **b** alignment of procedures and formalities;
   - **c** development and sharing of common facilities;
   - **d** joint controls;
   - **e** establishment of one-stop border post control.

SOURCE WTO Trade Facilitation Agreement, 2014

As the examples and the WCO and WTO obligations show, coordinated border management has both domestic and international dimensions (Aniszewski, 2009). Domestic coordination takes place within the respective government agencies and between the respective agencies. Some also refer to this as inter-service and intra-service cooperation (European Commission, 2010). International coordination happens where the respective border agencies reach across the border to work together with their counterparts.

Intra-agency coordination is important to ensure that controls and administrative practices are applied consistently, but still allow for a degree of flexibility to accommodate local operational requirements – such as those of an airport as opposed to those of a container terminal, or those of an urban region with lots of international trade activity and large ports as opposed to those of remote regions that are less inhabited and have long land borders. Good coordination of control and administrative practices can also significantly reduce friction and help improve performance (Grainger, 2008), cutting out, for example, the scope for duplication or mitigating the risk of businesses having to accommodate inconsistent interpretations of the applicable rules and procedures.

A common administrative model for government agencies is to operate in tiers that consist of the local level, the district (or regional) level, and the national level (European Commission, 2010) (Figure 7.2). The local level is primarily focused on the day-to-day operations of a specific border facility; be it a land border, port or airport, inland clearance facility or other type of border (eg free zone border) or facility (eg specialist international postal facility). The district level is characterized by offering shared services within a wider administrative district or municipality with multiple border facilities (eg port, airport and inland facilities). The district level may also include devolved or federal units and provide shared services for multiple locations, including mobile units. The national level is frequently located within the capital at the centre of the political and administrative power. Many officers working at the national level will be involved in policy-type considerations. Within the national headquarters coordination between functional units or departments is necessary, too. Some functions at this level might be general, such as IT services, training, procurement and human resources, others might be more

FIGURE 7.2 Administrative tiers found within common border management models

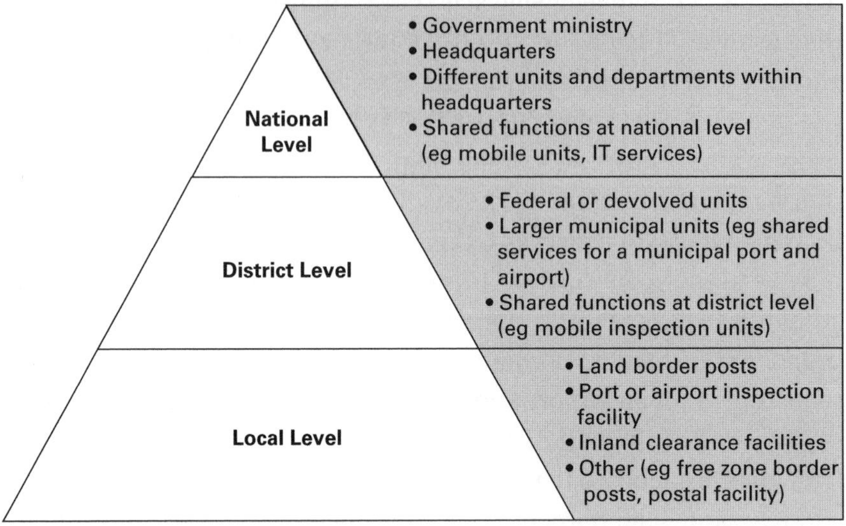

SOURCE © Trade Facilitation Consulting Ltd

specific, such as the provision of advanced specialist expertise (eg concerning tariff classification, valuation and origin) to colleagues located at the local or district level.

Good coordination practice between the administrative levels takes place along vertical and horizontal lines (Figure 7.3). For example, Chapter 2 highlighted some of the technical complexities relating to customs valuation, origin and classification. Officers may disagree on their correct interpretation. Technical support from the district and national level can help ensure a higher level of consistency in the interpretation of such rules and requirements. Likewise, policy agreed at the national level should be informed by the practicalities experienced at the local level. Much of contemporary trade and customs policy is about reducing the impact of compliance costs, which requires a detailed understanding of operational practices at the local level (Grainger, 2008).

Coordination between agencies also has vertical and horizontal components. At the local level, coordination allows for smoother operations between agencies and business operators by enabling joint inspections. It also enables agencies without executive powers to draw on the immediate assistance of those who do (usually Customs) to stop goods on their behalf. A high level of coordination can also provide for shared use of inspection facilities and minimize any cargo-handling operations associated with presenting goods to officials. This can have significant cost benefits for the business community.

At busy ports inspectors from different agencies may also share facilities as well as interfaces with the local electronic port system. At some ports officers also carpool when moving around the port estate. At the district and national level, coordination also provides scope for the development of aligned procedures and shared systems. This includes, for example, the adherence to single window principles, that allows the business community to submit all documents necessary to clear goods (in paper or electronic form) via one single interface, and usually in a streamlined manner so that information required by multiple agencies does not have to be declared more than once (Chapter 9).

International cooperation can take place at the local level between officers on both sides of the border (UNCTAD, 2011); for example, when operating shared inspection facilities or along trade lanes between officials in the country of departure and the country of arrival (as is often the case when authorities work together to weed out cross-border crimes) or in the control of transit goods. Usually such cooperation is governed by bilateral or multinational cooperation agreements (Aniszewski, 2009). These might be linked to wider trade agreements or more specific standalone agreements, such as customs cooperation agreements and mutual assistance agreements

FIGURE 7.3 Intra- and international cooperation between administrative levels

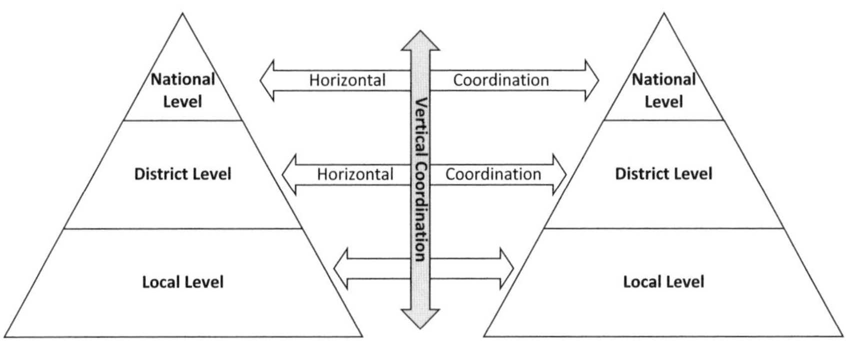

between customs authorities, or veterinary and phytosanitary agreements between relevant inspection services (Grainger, 2015).

Customs cooperation and mutual assistance agreements are increasingly common (see box below). Some customs administrations, like that of the United States, are able to draw on an extensive network of agreements. Typically, such agreements cover issues such as the sharing of information relating to the enforcement of customs law, the assessment of customs duties, offences and advance data (such as that relating to pre-notification). Customs agreements usually also cover formal assistance which might be spontaneous in the course of an investigation or specific to the recovery of customs claims, surveillance and information, controlled delivery, experts and witnesses. They also often address issues such as hot pursuits when officers need to cross the border in pursuit of their duties, surveillance activities, covert investigations and the joint control of investigation teams (WCO, 2004). Customs administrations by reference to the WTO Trade Facilitation Agreement, Article 12 (WTO, 2014), may also draw on measures concerning the sharing of business compliance data, such as customs declarations and supporting documents. The WTO Trade Facilitation Agreement also encourages customs administrations to share information about best practices in managing customs compliance along with technical guidance and support for capacity building purposes.

EXAMPLES OF CUSTOMS COOPERATION AND MUTUAL ASSISTANCE AGREEMENTS

United States of America

ASIA: China, Hong Kong, India, Indonesia, Japan, Korea, Malaysia, Maldives, Mongolia, Philippines, Singapore, American Institute in Taiwan, Taipei Economic and Agricultural Representative Office (TECRO), Vietnam

AUSTRALIA: Australia and New Zealand

AFRICA: Algeria, Gabon, Ghana, Kenya, Mauritius, Morocco, Nigeria, Senegal, South Africa, Tunisia

EUROPE: Austria, Azerbaijan, Belarus, Belgium, Bulgaria, Cyprus, Czech Republic, Denmark, European Community, Finland, France, Germany,

Greece, Hungary, Ireland, Italy, Latvia, Lithuania, Malta, Montenegro, Netherlands, Norway, Poland, Portugal, Romania, Russian Federation, Serbia, Slovakia, Spain, Sweden, Turkey, Ukraine, United Kingdom

NORTH AMERICA: Canada and Mexico

SOUTH AMERICA: Argentina, Brazil, Chile, Colombia, Costa Rica, Dominican Republic, Ecuador, Honduras, Panama, Paraguay, Peru, Trinidad & Tobago, Uruguay, Venezuela

MIDDLE EAST: Bahrain, Israel, Jordan, Kazakhstan, Pakistan

SOURCE CBP, 2020

European Union

Association of Southeast Asian Nations (ASEAN), Pan-Euro-Mediterranean countries, Canada, China, Georgia, Hong Kong, India, Japan, Korea, Republic of Moldova and Ukraine, New Zealand, United States of America, Norway

SOURCE European Commission, 2020

Japan

Australia, Austria, Belgium, Brazil, Canada, China, European Union, France, Germany, Hong Kong, Italy, Macao, Mexico, Netherlands, New Zealand, Norway, Republic of Korea, Russia, South Africa, Spain, Taiwan, United Kingdom, United States, Uzbekistan

SOURCE Japan Customs, 2020

South Africa

Algeria, Argentina, Brazil, Canada, China, Czech Republic, Democratic Republic of Congo, France, India, Iran, Japan, Mozambique, Netherlands, Norway, Sudan, Turkey, United Kingdom, United States of America, Uruguay, Zambia, Zimbabwe

SOURCE SARS, 2020

Case study: Finland's land borders

Finland borders Sweden, Norway and Russia. Finland, Sweden and Norway are members of the Schengen Area and passport-type border controls amongst these three countries is not normally required.

Finland, like Sweden, is a member of the European Union and goods may move freely between the two countries. Customs border controls for trade between Finland and Sweden are not normally necessary either.

Norway and Russia are not part of the European Union and customs controls do apply here. However, Norway is a member of the European Free Trade Area (EFTA) and as such has access to the European Unions' Internal Market. Furthermore, an agreement between Norway and the European Union permits Norwegian customs authorities to perform a wide range of customs checks and formalities (including the collection of duties and taxes) on behalf of the Finnish or Swedish customs authorities (European Union, 1997). This shared approach provides for extensive resource savings between Norway and Finland; a border that is located in a relatively remote part of the world with comparatively little economic activity. The shared approach to customs also ensures that business operators only need to stop at one single border post as opposed to two (WTO, 2005).

Given the close relationships with Sweden and Norway, most of Finland's border control demands focus on the border with Russia. The main agencies responsible for border management are Finnish Customs and the Finnish Border Guards along with the Police. These three agencies work together closely under various cooperation agreements at the national and regional (district) level. The agreements bind the respective agencies to:

- ensuring that resources are deployed in accordance with risk analysis;
- enhancing the effectiveness of crime prevention control; and
- avoiding duplicating and overlapping functions.

The agreements also provide for:

- intelligence sharing between the three agencies;
- cooperation in the drafting of new legislation;
- common approaches to international cooperation;
- joint use of equipment and technology; and
- clear command structures and demarcation of responsibilities.

The level of cooperation also extends to joint training and teams. At some locations the respective agencies may, when the situation demands, step in for each other (Poutiainen, 2015). Customs officers are trained by the Border Guard to be able to inspect identification documents and visas. Border guards are trained by Customs to search vehicles and recognize prohibited and restricted items.

Like most customs agencies, Finnish customs is responsible for the collection of duties and taxes and is relied upon by other government agencies to check compliance with any applicable prohibitions and restrictions (Chapter 4). And in Finland, Customs also play a part in the control of vehicles and people moving goods. Subsequently, Finnish customs also need to work closely with a wide range of different government agencies (Table 7.2).

TABLE 7.2 List of government agencies with which the Finnish customs administration routinely collaborates

Ministry	Government agencies
FINANCE	Tax administration
INTERIOR	Police
	Border Guard
TRANSPORT AND COMMUNICATIONS	Transport Safety Agency
AGRICULTURE AND FORESTRY	Food Safety Authority
	Agency for Rural Affairs
FOREIGN AFFAIRS	Department for External Economic Relations, Political Department
SOCIAL AFFAIRS AND HEALTH	Medicines Agency
	Supervisory Authority for Welfare Health
	Radiation and Nuclear Safety Authority
EDUCATION	Copyright organizations
	Board of Antiques
ENVIRONMENT	Environment Institute
	Oil Pollution Compensation Fund
EMPLOYMENT AND THE ECONOMY	Safety and Chemicals Authority
	Board of Patents and Registration
DEFENCE	Ministry of Defence

SOURCE Adapted from Poutiainen, 2015

CASE-SPECIFIC ACTIVITIES AND DISCUSSION POINTS

1 By reference to the Finnish case create a list of examples that can be categorized as: a) national; and b) international cooperation. Discuss whether the Finnish example provides lessons for application at borders elsewhere, eg those of the country within which you live.

2 Discuss to what extent border coordination efforts may differ at remote border posts (such as those between Finland and Norway) as opposed to busy border posts with lots of traffic.

3 Discuss the impact that trade agreements may have on the demands for border control.

Supply chain security

This is a relatively new addition to the workload of customs administration and is born from political fears about the misuse of globally operating supply chains for criminal and terrorist purposes.

Relevant policy took shape subsequent to the terrorist attacks on 11 September 2001 in New York and Washington. After the US government took immediate measures that stopped all inbound air traffic and drastically slowed down movements across land borders and through seaports, commercial trade came almost to a standstill. It only resumed upon strong political pressures to greatly increase inbound security into the United States. And risks to national security stemming from the perceived limits to controlling international supply chains were already a concern.

But it was also recognized that modern supply chains and their ability to move goods efficiently underpin much of the wealth generated through global trade. Thus, as highlighted by Flynn (2000, 2002), creative thinking on the part of the private sector, states and international bodies to explore how to best improve border controls was required. What resulted was a customs policy aimed at identifying security threats within cargo before the cargo is shipped and extending the customs control beyond the border to encompass the entire supply chain (Widdowson *et al*, 2014a, 2014b). And importantly, also make best use of finite enforcement resources whilst enhancing border control capabilities without jeopardizing global trade flows (Grainger, 2007).

One of the United States' first initiatives was to require shippers to pre-notify US Customs and Border Protection (USCBP) by submitting an 'Advance Manifest' containing cargo details to enable risk analysis and, if need be, to stop cargo before it arrives at the border – a requirement that has now become the norm in most countries (Chapter 3). Another initiative introduced in the United States was its voluntary Customs Partnership Against Terrorism (CTPAT). CTPAT rewards businesses that subscribe to strict standards designed to prevent tampering of US-bound supply chains in exchange for expedited customs clearance and fewer customs examinations. Similar customs initiatives were also developed elsewhere – including Sweden, Canada, Australia and New Zealand (Grainger, 2007). For many countries the desire to give US authorities assurance about the integrity of US-bound cargo and thereby safeguarding continued US market access without undue delays at the ports and borders was a driving force for developing those procedures (Widdowson *et al*, 2014a, 2014b).

The European Union introduced similar requirements through its Security Amendment to the Customs Code (European Union, 2005). Like the initiatives in the United States, this introduced the requirement to pre-notify Customs (by the carrier) in the form of an Entry Summary Declaration (Chapter 3). It also set out the framework for a voluntary Authorized Operator Programme (AEO) with compliance and security components. The compliance components give suitably authorized businesses easier access to advantageous customs procedures (eg customs warehousing, duty deferment, etc) while the security components aim to reduce the operator's risk score and thereby reduce the likelihood of inspections at the ports and border.

WCO Safe Framework of Standards

The global customs community – spurred on by the rapidly unfolding programmes in the United States, Europe and elsewhere – developed the WCO SAFE Framework of Standards (WCO, 2018). This framework of standards aims to support a harmonized approach by Customs towards safeguarding supply chain security without undue disruption to global commerce. First drafted in 2005, updated versions followed in 2007, 2012, 2015 and 2018. The framework follows the templates set by the United States and the EU's supply chain security programmes with recommendations for: advance cargo reporting; customs cooperation; and AEO-type partnership programmes between Customs and the business community. It also encourages the mutual recognition of such business partnership programmes.

WCO SAFE Framework of Standards stands on three pillars: customs-to-customs cooperation; customs-to-business cooperation; and customs-to-government cooperation.

1 CUSTOMS-TO-CUSTOMS COOPERATION

The first pillar concerns customs-to-customs cooperation. It holds that customs administrations must work cooperatively in line with common standards to safeguard supply chain security without disrupting it. High-risk goods are to be identified as early as possible and at or before the port of departure. To enable this, relevant information is to be shared expediently (see Chapter 2), preferably using standardized electronic formats. The use of modern scanning technologies, such as large-scale X-ray and radiation detection devices, to scan cargo before it is shipped is advised (Chapter 5). And the approach to customs-to-customs cooperation should be in line with common standards, such as those of the WCO Revised Kyoto Conventions and other related instruments (WCO, 2018).

2 CUSTOMS-TO-BUSINESS COOPERATION

The second pillar within the SAFE Framework of Standards concerns customs-to-business cooperation, where businesses involved in international trade are encouraged to tighten security across their supply chain in exchange for preferential treatment by customs – and in some countries by other government agencies as well (see box on the following page). The main vehicle for customs–business partnerships are the previously mentioned AEO programmes. For the period 2018–19 the World Customs Organization listed more than 80 operational AEO programmes. These do vary in scope and ambitions. In most countries AEO programmes are open to all businesses that import and export subject to any applicable eligibility criteria; in a few countries access to AEO programmes is restricted either to importers or exporters only. Policies about access to AEO programmes for intermediaries such as customs brokers and agents, or infrastructure service providers such as port and terminal operators, differ widely (WCO, 2019).

Criteria for authorization can also vary from programme to programme (Table 7.4). But amongst the qualifying criteria, businesses must usually be able to show that suitable safety and security provisions are in place. These tend to relate to:

- the use of qualified third parties;
- the management of boundaries (eg fences and access gates to company facilities);
- measures put in place to protect the integrity of cargo;
- controls to stop unauthorized shipments or the tampering of cargo;
- suitable storage provisions during storage and manufacture;
- security arrangements with suppliers and during transportation;
- the access to premises; and
- the training of staff (WCO 2018).

CUSTOMS–BUSINESS PARTNERSHIP PROGRAMMES: THE EXAMPLE OF THE EUROPEAN UNION AND THE UNITED STATES

European Union – Authorized Economic Operator (AEO)

Criteria: There are three types of AEO status. Authorization criteria differ depending on whether authorization is sought for 'Security and Safety' purposes, 'Customs Simplifications' or both. Conditions for AEO authorization depend on the type of authorization desired and relate to proof of: establishment in the EU customs territory; compliance with customs legislation and taxation rules; the absence of criminal offences related to the economic activity; appropriate record-keeping; financial solvency; practical standards of competence or professional qualifications; and appropriate security and safety provisions.

Benefits (depending on the type of AEO status): Easier admittance to customs simplifications; fewer physical and document-based controls; prior notification in the case of selection for controls; priority treatment if selected for controls; possibility to request a specific location for controls; and mutual recognition with third countries.

Mutual Recognition Agreements: China, Japan, Norway, Switzerland, USA.

United States of America – Customs and Trade Partnership against Terrorism (CTPAT)

Criteria: Satisfactory completion of a self-assessment security profile; validation visit by Customs and Border Protection (CBP) officers to check that appropriate security measures are in place; commitment to updating the security profile on an annual basis; and seek revalidation every four years or sooner where deemed necessary by CBP (subject to risk assessment).

Benefits: Reduced examination rates; eligibility to participate in other US government programmes, eg Free and Secure Trade (FAST); possible exemption from particularly burdensome examination practices (so-called stratified exams); front-of-the-line processing; business resumption priority after a major event (eg natural disaster or act of terrorism); shorter waiting times at the border; access to CBP security specialists; mitigated penalties; and mutual recognition with third countries.

Mutual Recognition Agreements: Canada; Dominican Republic; European Union; Israel; Japan; Jordan; Korea; Mexico; New Zealand; Peru; Singapore; Taiwan.

SOURCE Extracted and adapted from WCO, 2019

In many instances AEO programmes also overlap or tie into customs authorizations that provide for special customs arrangements. These might relate to accessing procedures that confer fiscal benefits, such as customs warehousing, or special procedures that confer operational and administrative benefits, such as inland clearance. Mutual recognition agreements between countries extend the benefits of AEO authorization at home to those of trade partners (Widdowson *et al*, 2014a, 2014b). Moreover, mutual recognition can also provide for eased compliance relationships between business partners. For example, US C-TPAT authorized businesses are obliged to check the security credentials of their suppliers. These checks have been described by some as very burdensome. However, if the supplier has an AEO certificate that is mutually recognized by the United States then the need for that detailed check no longer applies (Grainger, 2016). Often customs managers also view the AEO certification process as an opportunity for obtaining Customs' confirmation that the systems in place are fit for purpose. Such confirmation can be particularly useful for senior accounting officers of larger companies who are made personally liable for making sure that appropriate tax compliance systems (including those concerning import duties) are in place – as is the case in the United Kingdom under its Finance Act 2009.

3 CUSTOMS-TO-GOVERNMENT COOPERATION

The third pillar within the SAFE Framework of Standards concerns customs cooperation with other government and inter-government agencies. And in countries like Brazil, AEO-type business–customs partnership programmes include options to extend that partnership to non-customs border agencies, such as those responsible for quarantine controls (Coelho, 2019). There are also considerable efforts by customs agencies to collaborate with maritime and aviation agencies. These, subsequent to 9/11, were faced with similar political pressures to tighten security, albeit with a focus on ports, terminals, ships and aircraft. Initiatives here include the aviation-specific 'known shipper/consignor' programmes (ICAO, 2017) that have their roots in the 1988 Lockerbie disaster, predating 9/11. The International Maritime Organization (IMO), within just a few months of 9/11, adopted the

International Ship and Port Security Code (ISPS Code) (IMO, 2003) as an amendment to the Safety of Life at Sea 1974 Convention (SOLAS) (IMO, 1974). These two international security initiatives by ICAO and IMO overlap with customs controls when planes and ships carry cargo, traditionally controlled by Customs, and the specified security measures at ports and airports, which tend to be customs-controlled areas. Subsequently, the customs administrations in many countries will take transport security authorizations into account when granting the AEO status (Widdowson *et al,* 2014a, 2014b).

Control beyond the border along supply chains

There is considerable overlap between the subject of coordinated border management and supply chain security (WCO, 2018). They both draw on the supply chain metaphor with the former predominantly focusing on the horizontal and vertical interactions within and between border agencies at home and internationally. Supply chain security similarly concerns the coordination of activities between customs agencies along trade lanes, especially with regard to stopping risky goods before being shipped. Like the subject of coordinated border management, the WCO supply chain security framework also emphasizes the need for cooperation between Customs and non-customs agencies. In addition, it stresses the need for partnership arrangements with business operators. Through Authorized Economic Operator programmes these are encouraged to enhance their security provisions in exchange for access to advantageous treatment.

The image of the border as a boom barrier at which authorities stop and inspect goods no longer quite applies. Instead, border agencies are working towards integrating themselves into supply chains. The links of the 'control chain' are forged through the cooperation amongst border agencies at home and abroad as well as the partnership agreements between them and business operators. Furthermore, obligations by business operators (usually carriers) to share information in advance of shipment provide for opportunities to assess, stop and intercept cargo before arrival or shipment (Chapter 2). Increasingly, policy makers are exploring the case of voluntary information sharing that allows businesses and authorities to share information as soon as it becomes available (UN CEFACT, 2018).

Hesketh (2009) use the term 'data pipeline' to describe the volume of data generated by businesses in end-to-end operations of trade logistics; encompassing data generated when procuring, processing, transporting and selling goods. The voluntary sharing of such data, as and when captured along the supply chain, provides opportunities for authorities to continually assess risks as the picture about them evolves, and if need be, to make relevant interventions at the soonest possible moment. Hesketh (2009) also suggests that it would eventually be possible to replace the need for formal declarations to the border agencies, such those outlined in Chapter 2, and replace current control practices with self-assessment arrangements that are conducted under the surveillance of Customs and other border authorities.

Extensive data-sharing of supply chain data on a voluntary basis can also have other significant benefits for business operators. In a study conducted with the Dutch FloraHolland (a large global trader in cut flowers) the voluntary information sharing of commercial information (eg invoices) before it was formally required enabled Dutch Customs and phytosanitary authorities to take decisions about inspections before the aircraft lands, and thus enable FloraHolland to arrange collection for all released cargo (94 per cent on average) from the airport immediately upon landing without fear of any inspection-related delays (Rukanova *et al*, 2020).

Potentially, there is a future without the need for formally placing goods under customs control through declarations. Instead, regulatory control is assured through granting authorities access to relevant data as and when it is generated in the supply chain. That data is then assessed by the agencies working together under various cooperation agreements. The next chapter, Chapter 8, takes a closer look at the drivers for such policy reforms. Chapter 9 then looks at the many proposed solutions, of which several emphasize the need for improved coordination between all operators – business and government – and the electronic sharing of information to help speed up processes and reduce friction.

ACTIVITIES AND DISCUSSION POINTS

1 Discuss what reservations businesses might have about routinely sharing information containing commercial details with the customs administration.

2 Is a future without the need for businesses to make customs declarations realistic? Discuss.

3 Based on your personal experiences, draw a list of examples where government agencies at the ports and borders have not worked together. Discuss what it would take to get them to work together more effectively.

References

Aniszewski, S (2009) Coordinated border management: A concept paper, World Customs Organization, Brussels

CBP (2020) Customs Mutual Assistance Agreements (CMAA), US Customs and Border Protection, www.cbp.gov/border-security/international-initiatives/international-agreements/cmaa (archived at https://perma.cc/3Y68-U32H)

Coelho, F (2019) From 'red tape' to 'red carpet': How the Brazilian AEO Programme has brought Customs procedures to an entire new leve, *WCO News*, 88 (Feb), pp 18–21

European Commission (2010) Guidelines for Integrated Border Management in European Commission External Cooperation, EuropeAid, European Commisssion, Brussels

European Commission (2020) International Customs Co-operation and Mutual Administrative Assistance Agreements, ec.europa.eu/taxation_customs/business/international-affairs/international-customs-cooperation-mutual-administrative-assistance-agreements_en (archived at https://perma.cc/LX6W-S6GE)

European Union (1997) Agreement on Customs Cooperation Between the Kingdom of Norway and the European Communities, *Official Journal of the European Communities,* (L105), p 17

European Union (2005) Regulation (EC) No 648/2005 of the European Parliament and of the Council of 13 April 2005 amending Council Regulation (EEC) No 2913/92 establishing the Community Customs Code, *Official Journal of the European Union,* **48** (L117), pp 13–19

Flynn, SE (2000) Beyond border control, *Foreign Affairs,* **79** (6), pp 57–67

Flynn, SE (2002) America the Vulnerable, *Foreign Affairs,* **81** (1), pp 60–74

Grainger, A (2007) Supply chain security: Adding to a complex operational and institutional environment, *World Customs Journal,* **1** (2), pp 17–29

Grainger, A (2008) Customs and trade facilitation: From concepts to implementation, *World Customs Journal,* **2** (1), pp 17–30

Grainger, A (2015) Customs issues falling under INTA's new remit, European Parliament, Brussels

Grainger, A (2016) Customs Management in Multinational Companies, *World Customs Journal,* **10** (2)

Grainger, A and Hintsa, J (2017) The role of border management in implementing trade policy goals, Directorate-General for External Policies, European Parliament, Brussels

Hesketh, D (2009) Seamless electronic data and logistics pipelines shift focus from import declarations to start of commercial transaction, *World Customs Journal,* **3** (1), pp 27–32

ICAO (2017) Annex 17 to the Convention on International Civil Aviation: Security, International Civil Aviation Organization, Quebec

IMO (1974) International Convention for the Safety of Life at Sea (as amended), International Maritime Organization, London

IMO (2003) *ISPS (The International Ship and Port Facility Security) Code,* 2003 edn, London

Japan Customs (2020) CMAA (Customs Mutual Assistance Agreement), www.customs.go.jp/english/cmaa/ (archived at https://perma.cc/ZXD4-2UVM)

Polner, M (2011) Coordinated border management: from theory to practice, *World Customs Journal,* **5** (2), pp 49–64

Poutiainen, M (2015) Managing land borders, the innovative Finnish model, *WCO news,* February (76), pp 12–16

Rukanova, B, Tan, Y-H, Huiden, R, Ravulakollua, A, Grainger, A and Heijmann, F (2020) A framework for voluntary business-government information sharing, *Government Information Quarterly,* **37** (101501)

SARS (2020) Agreements on mutual administrative assistance: customs, https://www.sars.gov.za/legal-counsel/international-treaties-agreements/maas-on-customs/ (archived at https://perma.cc/T32G-M3W5)

UN CEFACT (2004) Recommendation 33: Single window recommendation, ECE/TRADE/352: 37, CEFACT. United Nations, Geneva

UN CEFACT (2018) Data Pipeline: White Paper, United Nations Economic Commission for Europe, Geneva

UNCTAD (2011) Technical notes on trade facilitation measures, United Nations, Geneva

WCO (2004) Model bilateral agreement on mutual administrative assistance in customs matters, World Customs Organization, Brussels

WCO (2006) Revised Kyoto Convention: International Convention on the Simplifications and Harmonization of Customs Procedures, World Customs Organization, Brussels

WCO (2015) Coordinated Border Managment Compendium, World Customs Organization, Brussels

WCO (2018) Integrated Supply Chain Management Guidelines, World Customs Organization, Brussels

WCO (2018) SAFE Framework of Standards (2018 edn), World Customs Organization, Brussels

WCO (2019) Compendium of Authorized Economic Operator Programmes (2019 edn), World Customs Organization, Brussels

Widdowson, D, Blegen, B, Kashubsky, M and Grainger, A (2014a) Review of accredited operator schemes, Centre for Customs and Excise Studies, Charles Sturt University, Australia

Widdowson, D, Blegen, B, Kashubsky, M and Grainger, A (2014b) Review of accredited operator schemes: An Australian study, *World Customs Journal*, 8 (1), pp 17–34

WTO (2005) Communication from Norway, Negotiating Group on Trade Facilitation, World Trade Organization, Geneva

WTO (2014) Agreement on Trade Facilitation (WT/L/931), Preparatory Committee on Trade Facilitation, World Trade Organization, Geneva

08

Logistics, supply chain management and borders

The strength of the supply chain management metaphor and the desire to weed out costs through coordination and cooperation has already been highlighted in previous chapters. Responsibilities for compliance operations between contracting businesses – suppliers and buyers – are dependent on the agreed commercial arrangements and the Incoterms® in particular. Inevitably, all parties involved in international trade have an interest in weeding out cost and improving outcomes – whether they relate to better control (especially for government agencies) or improved business competitiveness.

As outlined in earlier chapters, trade and customs policy – especially in the form of trade tariffs (Chapter 2) – can have a direct bearing on the cost of supply. Likewise, the cost of compliance can also add to the cost of supply. The image of the supply chain lends itself well to describing the relationship between business operators and the border agencies. Where both parties work hand-in-hand compliance costs need not be so high and regulatory control outcomes can be improved. Where the relationship between business operators and government agencies is one characterized by friction, costs can quickly undermine business competitiveness as well as any wider economic gains from participating in international trade.

Much of the logistics and supply chain management literature concerns itself with the forces that govern and control the physical movement of goods (including materials) within companies and production systems, and the operational strategies that improve a firm's competitive standing by addressing the challenges associated with the efficient flow of those goods. Research themes within the field tend to look at cost reduction and value in the hand of the end user (Christopher, 1992b). They frequently also focus on relational aspects within firms and between entities in production networks (Harland and Lamming, 1999; Lamming *et al,* 2000). This is also the focus of the emerging literature in trade facilitation, albeit on the specific challenges that arise where business operators and government agencies meet (Grainger, 2011).

This chapter gives an account of supply chain management and logistics practices, and the challenges that business operators frequently face at the ports and borders. This chapter also discusses the costs resulting from any friction between business operators and border agencies. The subsequent case for trade facilitation is made by reference to how business operators and border agencies may best collaborate. As such, it provides the necessary context for Chapter 9, which examines trade facilitation policy with specific focus on the main concepts and ideas about how cross-border logistics operations can be managed better.

Logistics and supply chain management theory and practice

The idea of collaboration between contracting businesses to weed out costs and delight customers is not new and is now a key feature in contemporary logistics and supply chain management literature. Peter Drucker (1962), an early commentator on the strategic significance of distribution-type activities for businesses, highlighted that by shipping goods to customers, their physical properties are converted into items of economic value. And costs are best managed through effective coordination between the various activities that relate to production, marketing and distribution. An outcome of lower costs, as emphasized by Martin Christopher (1992a), is improved business competitiveness. Moreover, improved cooperation between parties in the supply chain also enables superior customer value to be achieved, which further enhances competitiveness. Leaning on Michael Porter's (1985) seminal work, many authors will also use the term 'value chain' when emphasizing the need for competitive advantages, and 'global value chains' where chains takes advantage of global business and production opportunities (Gereffi, 1994).

The subject of logistics and supply chain management (SCM) is also a staple within the contemporary manufacturing and operations literature (Prasad and Babbar, 2000) as well as in marketing (Voorhees and Coppett, 1992) and business strategy (Christopher, 1992a). It has also evolved into a literature in its own right, now benefiting from a range of specialist academic journals. However, within that literature the terms 'logistics management' and 'supply chain management' are debated extensively (Fawcett and Magnan, 2002). For many, supply chain management concerns the configuration, planning and management of production systems that extend from suppliers' suppliers to customers' customers. Logistics management concerns the flow of goods and materials within such production systems. However, it is not uncommon for practitioners and academics to treat the terms logistics and supply chain management as synonymous (Cooper *et al*, 1997) – especially when questions about managing the movement of goods cannot be easily untangled from questions about how those goods are produced and where those goods originate.

A key feature within the logistics and SCM literature is the metaphor of the chain, where a string of interdependent activities leads to the transformation of raw materials into finished goods at the disposal of their customers. Oliver and Webber (1992) are often cited as one of the first to depict the supply chain as such, by linking suppliers with end users through a chain of enabling activities, which include procurement, manufacturing, production (the factory), distribution and customers – who are either the end users of the goods or who sell the goods on to the end users (Figure 8.1).

Figure 8.1 is of course an over-simplification, and although the term 'supply chain' is commonly used, it is usually understood to be a network of interacting businesses within which suppliers have their own suppliers and customers have their own customers in turn, and where

FIGURE 8.1 The supply chain from suppliers to end users

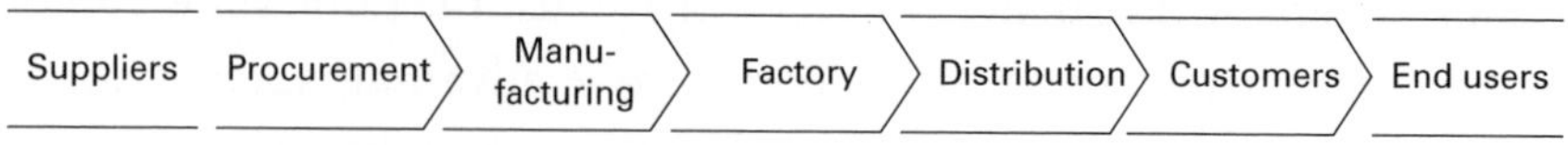

SOURCE Adapted from Oliver and Webber, 1992

competition allows for multiple configurations of all the parties involved. Competitiveness is derived from configurations that are either more cost effective or more responsive to customer needs (Figure 8.2).

Managing how such networks should be best configured in terms of costs, the flow of goods within and the responsiveness to customer needs is no small challenge. This is the focus of an increasingly rich literature in logistics and supply chain management. Much of that literature focuses on three themes:

- industrial dynamics and inventory costs;
- customer value and responsiveness to customers' needs; and
- the transaction costs between the many parties involved.

FIGURE 8.2 Supply chain networks

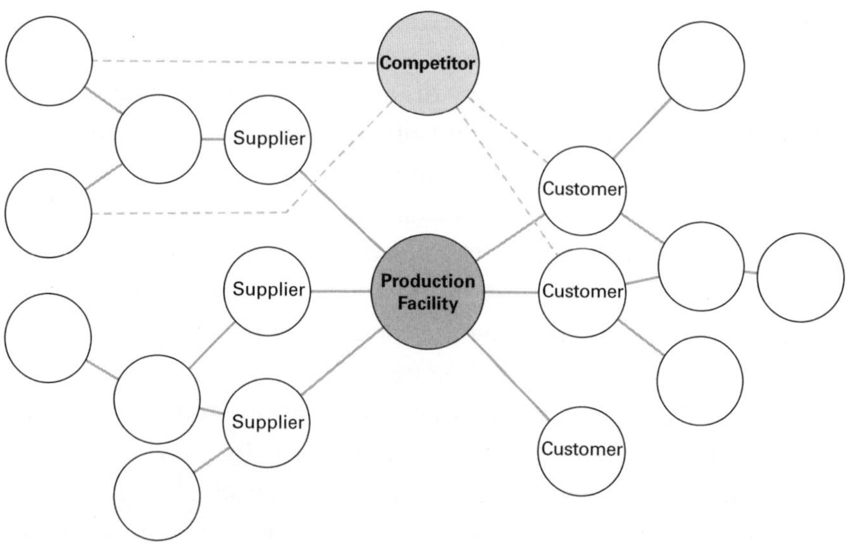

In tandem with these themes the literature also discusses relevant business strategies that help make supply chains more competitive. The main ones relate to lean thinking, just-in-time and similar time-related strategies, including agility.

Industrial dynamics

One of the more influential ideas underlying the logistics and SCM literature is Jay Forrester's model in industrial dynamics – also, frequently referred to as the Forrester or bullwhip effect. In his book, Forrester (1961) describes a model that illustrates the dynamics between orders and inventories held by contracting retailers, distributors and a factory. In this model, Forrester simulates how small changes in retail sales can lead to significantly larger swings in factory production that result from the uncoordinated management of inventory stock level. Such 'bullwhip effects' are highly disruptive and lead to production fluctuations and unnecessarily high levels of costly stock. Where inventory levels are insufficient and demand cannot be met because of stock-out, business opportunities are lost.

Figure 8.3 provides a simple example of such a bullwhip effect. The model presumes that demand for a given product in Period 1 is 100. The order for those 100 items is taken from the manufacturer's stock. To build up stock levels back to 100 items the manufacturer in turn needs to place an order for 100 items from the supplier. That order is fulfilled by drawing on the supplier's stock. The supplier in turn needs to replenish stock and places orders for 100 items from their suppliers. The second-tier supplier in turn places an order for 100 items from the third-tier supplier. Now, if demand were to fall in Period 2 from 100 to 95 it can be met by the manufacturer by drawing on the 100 items held in stock. A surplus of five items remains. To replenish stock levels to the new level of demand that is 95 only 90 items need to be ordered from the first-tier supplier. That supplier in turn is able to fulfil that order with a surplus of 10 items in stock, and assuming the new level of demand is 90 will only need to place an order of 80 to replenish stock. Repeating this pattern will yield a swing in production for the third-tier supplier of between 20 items in

FIGURE 8.3 An example of Forrester's 'bullwhip effect'

Period	Third-tier Supplier		Second-tier Supplier		First-tier Supplier		Manufacturer		Demand
	Produce	Stock	Produce	Stock	Produce	Stock	Produce	Stock	
1	100	100 100	100	100 100	100	100 100	100	100 100	100
2	20	100 60	60	100 80	80	100 90	90	100 95	95
3	180	60 120	120	80 100	100	90 95	95	95 95	95
4	60	120 90	90	100 95	95	95 95	95	95 95	95
5	100	90 95	95	95 95	95	95 95	95	95 95	95
6	95	95 95	95	95 95	95	95 95	95	95 95	95

Period 2 and 180 items in Period 3, and only to settle at the sixth iteration to the adjusted demand level of 95.

Although Figure 8.3 is only a simple illustrative model, it does demonstrate how minor changes without coordination between suppliers and the manufacturer can quickly escalate into big production swings. Good supply chain management practice thus dictates that there should be a high level of coordination and cooperation between various supply chain tiers in order to mitigate the risk of undue fluctuations. This can be achieved, for example, where the manufacturer shares demand and forecasting data as and when available to make sure that suppliers further up the chain are able to make more informed decisions about anticipated demands.

The value chain and competitive advantage

One of the prevailing assumptions within the logistics and SCM literature is that the business environment is inherently competitive. For firms to survive this environment, they need to seek competitive advantages. Michael Porter (1985) is one of the seminal authors writing about competitive advantage. He argues that it stems from the implementation of business strategies that focus on cost leadership, differentiation and focus. Porter also argues that competitive advantage arises from the value a firm is able to create for its buyers. Value may be defined by lower prices than competing offerings or the provision of extra benefits that offset a premium on price – such as product quality or on-time delivery.

At the heart of Porter's thesis is that the firm is not viewed as a single entity, but should be viewed as a value chain – which is an amalgamation of many discrete activities from designing, producing, marketing and delivering products, and to supporting those products once sold (Porter, 1985). The strategic aim is to ensure that each activity adds value and provides for a competitive product. The primary activities within such a value chain are performed by dedicated functional units, such as inbound logistics, operations, outbound logistics (or distribution), marketing and sales, and service. Those primary activities require support that cuts across the various units' boundaries. Supporting activities in Porter's model include those concerning the firm's infrastructure, human resources, technology and procurement. In many businesses, supporting activities usually also include tax and legal compliance – raising the question whether customs management activities fall within the sphere of logistics and transport (a primary business function) or falls within the wider supporting categories (such as tax and legal).

The principles of Porter's value chain concept may also be extended to the supply chain, where distinct activities are performed by different organizations – albeit not necessarily under the umbrella of a single firm. The challenge within the value chain perspective is to thus make sure that the chain delivers a competitive product and that it is configured in a way that creates the most value; for example, by being more cost efficient than competing supply chains or by being able to respond more effectively to customer needs.

Transaction cost

More often than not, it makes sense for businesses to outsource some or many of the activities outlined in Porter's value chain. Third parties often benefit from economies of scale or have specialist capabilities that cannot be developed easily within a firm. This is where the logistics and supply chain management literature draws on the ideas of Oliver Williamson (1981). Williamson holds that the study of economic organization regards the transaction as the basic unit of economic analysis. Decisions about producing goods in-house or outsourced are dependent on whether the cost of production inputs and services procured from the market are lower than what they would be if performed in-house.

While orthodox economic thinking at the time suggested that the price for goods and services is based on the forces of supply and demand, Williamson highlights that there are also transaction costs. Drawing on a mechanical metaphor, transaction cost may be found where gears turn against each other, where parts are insufficiently lubricated, where there is needless slippage or other loss of energy – friction, in other words. Such friction adds to costs and should be part of the consideration about whether to outsource specific activities or not. Friction can stem from failures to accommodate technical production interdependencies,[1] lack of knowledge,[2] incomplete contracts, opportunism and rent-seeking behaviour, the actual cost of contracting (including lawyer's fees), and conflicting priorities and performance failures – such as those stemming from Forrester's industrial dynamics.

Within the context of logistics and supply chain management, lower transaction costs between activities within a firm are undesirable and deserve due attention. And where transaction costs with suppliers can be minimized, it provides even greater scope for making supply chains more cost efficient and thus competitive.

Logistics and supply chain management strategies

In addition to describing logistics and supply chain management challenges the literature also offers strategic solutions to cost and value challenges. Many of these are born from observations about the Toyota production system and 'lean thinking'. It also includes time-focused business strategies – especially the just-in-time (JIT) concept. However, there is also a rich literature about designing 'agile' production systems that are able to respond rapidly to changes in demand – or any, for that matter, adverse impacts on the overall business environment that require businesses to quickly modify their supply chain arrangements.

LEAN THINKING

Researching the automotive industry, Womack *et al* (1990) describe in their book *The Machine that Changed the World* how car manufacturers can dramatically improve their performance by embracing the lean production approach pioneered by Toyota where 'more and more' is achieved with 'less and less'. In lean production the focus is on reducing waste, or to use the Japanese word *muda*. Common forms of waste as defined by Taiichi Ohno[3] are activities that add cost but no value for the customer. Waste includes the production of goods not yet ordered, waiting, rectification of mistakes, excess processing, excess movement, excess transport and excess inventory. Improving cost efficiency in production and market responsiveness requires the elimination of unnecessary steps, aligning all steps in any given activity into a continuous flow, re-combining labour into cross-functional teams dedicated to that activity and continually striving for improvements (Jones and Hines, 1997).

The success of applying 'lean thinking' is determined by the ability of organizational units, suppliers and customers to synchronize their operations in the most efficient and coordinated manner (including any industrial dynamics). And benefits can be dramatically improved if linked up and down the supply chain (Womack *et al,* 1990; Womack and Jones, 1994).[4] Collaborative relationships between business units and between contracting businesses is emphasized, and also reminiscent of Porter's value chain (see above). The idea that customers and suppliers are in the 'same boat' and share a 'mutual destiny' is central; some might even use the term 'lean supply' as opposed to 'supply chain' to stress the collaborative need for leanness (Lamming, 1996).

Those collaborative relationships require active management, for example, in the form of performance management systems, but also by building trust. And while it may be argued that there is a natural tendency towards trust (McKnight *et al,* 1998), which may in turn be dependent on variables of national culture (Doney *et al,* 1998), much of the required level of trust is the result of formal control mechanisms (Das and Teng, 1998) or the threat of penalties and sanctions (Hagen and Choe, 1998). It is also not uncommon for suppliers to adopt standard operating procedures to ensure that they deliver goods in line with contractual specifications. Often such procedures may also be part of a wider quality control system that is independently assessed.

JUST-IN-TIME AND SIMILAR TIME-FOCUSED STRATEGIES

One of the SCM challenges is that the nature of the business environment is in constant flux. Demand patterns change because products are seasonal, have short shelf lives, new competitors enter the market, or consumers change spending patterns that reflect the overall state of the economy. Consequently, many supply chain strategies give particular consideration to time – that is, to drive the movement of materials and goods to the end user before conditions of demand change. This aspect of SCM has been particularly widely discussed in terms of just-in-time (JIT) management along with similar ideas such as quick response (QR) logistics, efficient consumer response (ECR) (Vokurka and Lummus, 2000) and agility (Sharifi and Zhang, 1999).

The JIT concept is rooted in research that examined the Toyota production system (Sugimori *et al,* 1977) – just as was the case for lean management. Commonly, JIT is described as a 'pull' concept, where consumer demand determines the flow of products, rather than what was the traditional 'push' system, where products are manufactured or assembled in batches in anticipation of expected demand (Christopher, 1992a: 153). To be competitive it is imperative that cost efficiency, quality and responsiveness across the supply chain is assured (Vokurka and Lummus, 2000). This is achieved by managing inventories (a cost) effectively, minimizing them as much as possible and replenishing them at the point in time when they are needed. In the JIT approach, surplus buffer stock is considered an unnecessary cost that hides inefficiencies – such as those that arise from suppliers missing their delivery deadlines, operational bottlenecks (including unpredictable delays at the border), and inaccurate production and demand forecasts. Thus, any efforts to reduce inventory levels require management to actively address any of those inefficiencies.

Variant strategies to JIT have evolved from analysis of other industry sectors. Most notable is the quick response (QR) concept, which has its roots in the textile and apparel industry, where short-lived fashion cycles and fickle consumer behaviour demand speed and responsiveness. Similar problems are associated with grocery supply chains where shelf life for perishable goods is very short. Here, it is more common to use the term efficient consumer response (ECR) or continuous replenishment (CR) (Vokurka and Lummus, 2000). To meet and maximize on short-lived consumer demands, extensive collaboration between retailers and manufacturers is essential. Extensive use of technologies that quickly capture data about demand and that are able to feed that data up the supply chain is essential. One example of such technologies is retail bar codes which, once scanned at the till using electronic point of sale – EPOS – technologies, can be automatically set to initiate re orders. And the more responsive production and subsequent deliveries are, the less stock needs to be carried.

AGILE SUPPLY CHAINS

Technology and the ability to share market data across the supply chain is also the foundation for agile production approaches, where networks are configured in order to best react to the 'voice of the market' as and when it changes. In such 'pull' focused supply chains, failure to deliver as and when the need arises can have devasting consequences. On the other hand, a production system that can quickly respond to market demands should have little need for keeping inventories. For such business models where customers sit in the driving seat some will use the term 'demand chains' (Selen and Soliman, 2002).

Important to note is that companies are likely to subscribe to multiple supply chain strategies (Towill and Christopher, 2002). For example, they may procure the bulk of their goods from low-cost suppliers that benefit from economies of scale or enjoy factor advantages, such as low labour or energy costs. But if there is a sudden shortage, arising, for example, from a surge in demand or production disruptions, then that shortfall will be met by more agile supply chain arrangements. These might include procuring goods from suppliers closer to home who are able to respond to demand quickly – though their costs are likely to be significantly greater than those of the main suppliers.

Borders and the relevance of logistics and supply chain management

An understanding of supply chain management configurations and the flow of goods within is important for those who are concerned with border operations. The nature of modern production is that supply chains criss-cross borders extensively. At each link within the supply chain, trade and customs compliance considerations – such as those outlined in Chapter 6 – come into play. And where border agencies cooperate internationally, as is increasingly the case through trade and customs cooperation agreements or supply chain security programmes (see Chapter 7), border agencies also seek to insert themselves into those supply chains as an integral thread (Figure 8.4).

Within the supply chain network perspective an understanding of borders is also important (Figure 8.5). Customs tariffs can apply and

FIGURE 8.4 Government agencies at border: an integral thread across supply chains

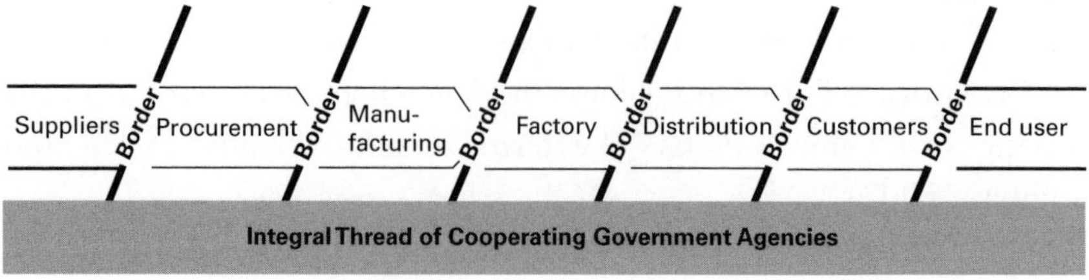

SOURCE Adapted from Grainger, 2007

there are also the border-related compliance costs. Depending on trade policy and the availability of preferential trade arrangements (Chapter 2) the impact of tariffs on supply chain configurations between suppliers and customers can differ from one country to the next. Inevitably, depending on location, different supply chain arrangements will be exposed to different levels of duty liabilities. And even where companies can take advantage of preferential trade agreements (ie where they are able to comply with preferential origin rules) significant compliance costs remain. These relate to declaring goods, but also to implementing and operating any special customs arrangements designed to support export manufacturing. These, as touched upon in Chapter 2, include duty drawback, inward processing relief, processing under customs control and the utilization of free zones (Box 8.1) Inevitably, the advantages of such trade and customs procedures need to be weighed against their associated compliance costs. And just like

BOX 8.1

Customs procedures with financial benefits frequently used to support export manufacturing

- Inward processing relief, where goods may be brought into the country free from duties and taxes on the basis that such goods are intended for processing, manufacturing or repair and subsequent exportation.
- Outward processing relief, where goods may be temporarily exported to another country for manufacturing, processing or repair and then re-imported with total or partial exemption from import duties and taxes.
- Drawback, where goods are exported and Customs refunds the import duties and taxes relating to the materials contained within those goods or consumed in their production.
- Processing for home use, where manufacturers import goods and materials and choose to pay duties and taxes on the finished goods in instances where the duties and taxes on the finished goods are lower than on their inputs.
- Entry into an approved customs free zone, where goods in terms of taxes and duties are considered to be outside the customs territory. Subsequently, any taxes and duties upon goods do not apply while held or processed in the free zone.

FIGURE 8.5 Supply chain networks and borders

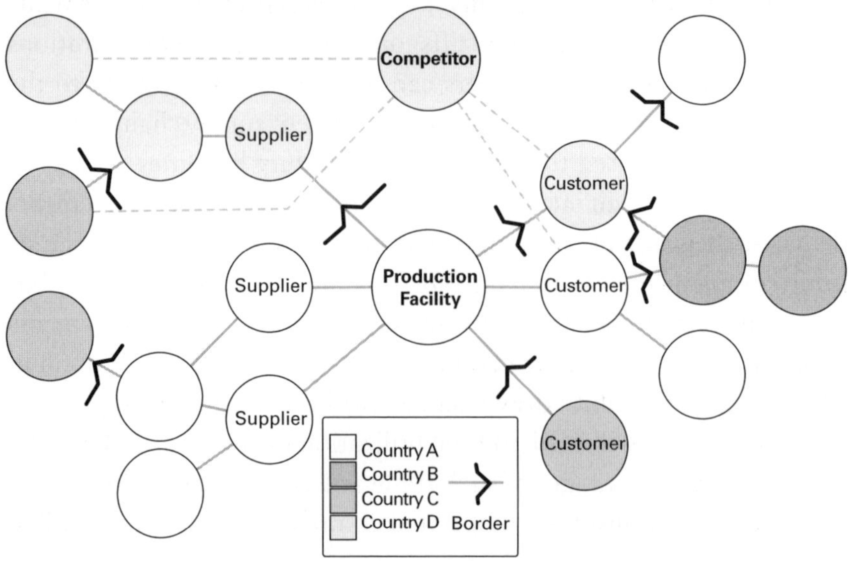

the friction between contracting supply chain partners, significant friction can also be found in the relationship between supply chain operators and the government border agencies. Much of that friction, as will be outlined, manifests itself in undermined supply chain performance (a cost) and inability to deliver goods in line with customer expectations – especially where goods are unduly delayed at the border. Standard supply chain strategies, such as lean thinking or just-in-time, do not quite work and businesses often have to resort to carrying additional stock as a buffer against unforeseen delays – or risk not being able to meet the customer's needs.

Costs and their resolution

Research into the nature of trade- and customs-related compliance costs along with any associated friction – transaction costs – is relatively new. Much of the work has been conducted by economists, concerned about how such costs might undermine the benefits that are derived from global trade, and building the case for implementing trade facilitation measures (Chapter 9) that might reduce those costs

(WTO, 2015). Complementing this work are a few macro-level studies, too. Andrew Grainger (2013), for example, described in detail the trade- and customs-related compliance costs experienced by UK meat importers. The World Bank, amongst others, conducts regular global surveys about border management performance; the two main ones are the Trading Across Borders Dataset (World Bank, 2021) and the Logistics Performance Index (World Bank, 2020). While useful, both datasets are prone to criticism (Sourdin and Pomfret, 2012), because sample sizes in both cases are insufficiently comprehensive, because the former relies on input from consultancy or law firms whose experience tends to be narrowly defined and largely of an indirect nature, and because the latter relies on perceptions that are subject to bias.

In many countries the customs administration conducts formal time release studies using a standardized methodology developed by the World Customs Organization (Matsuda, 2012). Although they do not provide a comprehensive account of experienced costs, they do provide an account of the time it takes to obtain customs release when importing or exporting goods. Sadly for researchers, few customs administrations make their time release studies public. And a focus on time should not be the only cost variable. The requirements of trade and customs procedures tend to have direct and indirect components (OECD, 2009). Direct costs are those incurred when interacting with the border agencies, for example, by making a declaration, while indirect costs are those subsequent to inefficient trade and customs procedures, which includes, for example, the loss of competitiveness and missed business opportunities (Box 8.2).

BOX 8.2

Direct and indirect compliance costs

Broadly, direct compliance costs for business operators can be associated with the following:

- The interactions with the applicable authorities, including the preparation and submission of relevant documents (whether electronic or paper) as well as any inspection arrangements, amongst others.

- The set-up of systems to ensure compliance with the applicable trade and customs procedures; this includes the costs associated with obtaining authorizations to take advantage of special procedures (such as customs warehousing or duty drawback) but also the development and implementation of appropriate standard operating procedures.
- The appointment and management of specialist intermediaries, including brokers and customs agents, and related transaction costs.
- The support of specialist staff, including their training, development of standard operating procedures, supervision and operational support (eg travel to border facilities).

Likewise, border agencies will also experience various direct costs that relate to their work. These include, to give a few examples, costs associated with:

- the administration of applicable procedures, including the employment of officers and implementation of appropriate systems;
- inspection, where staff need to be trained and deployed;
- infrastructure, where appropriate facilities for administration and inspection need to be put in place.

However, it is common in many countries for border agencies to pass on their costs to the private sector in the form of fees and charges.

Indirect costs for business operators, are commonly associated with:

- the loss of business competitiveness where customer expectations have not been met or where the burden of compliance costs make alternative product offerings more attractive;
- missed opportunities, where red tape ties up resources that could be put to better use;
- the risk of liabilities, where procedures have not been applied correctly or where officers challenge their correctness (thus necessitating expensive appeals and other legal responses);
- cascading activities made necessary because of inefficiencies and delay, including, for example, the need to make alternative transport arrangements and compensating customers for missed delivery deadlines.

Likewise, government agencies might experience indirect costs in the form of:

- inefficiency that adds to the cost of administration;
- undermined national competitiveness, especially where businesses choose to operate elsewhere or where complex trade procedures inhibit foreign investment;
- loss of tax revenue because trade-led economic growth is stunted or because businesses choose to operate outside the formal economy;
- societal costs where the authority of the state is brought into question, where controls are not effectively administered and where poor control practices lend themselves to corruption, smuggling and other crimes.

The nature and type of costs will also differ, depending on who has incurred them. In Chapter 6 we elaborated on the arrangements between sellers and buyers as well as the role of intermediaries, along with the services provided by transport carriers, port and terminal operators, and financial services (Box 8.3). Good logistics and SCM practice would dictate that managers seek to identify and address border-related costs across the supply chain, not just within their own organizations. However, there is considerable scope for gold-plating, especially where compliance requirements are not clear or those responsible for trade and customs compliance decisions lack relevant knowledge or experience.

Specialist customs agents or brokers often benefit from economies of scale that allow them to price their services at levels that are less than if they were performed in-house (Verwaal and Donkers, 2003). Nevertheless, any add-on costs, such as demurrage where goods are held in port because of extended delays at Customs and other border agencies, still tend to be passed on. Likewise, inefficient customs procedures can quickly compound costs elsewhere – for example, where delays require booked transport services to be rearranged or cancelled, or where uncertainty about border clearance demands higher stock levels to provide a buffer against such uncertainties.

BOX 8.3

Business operators involved in moving goods across borders

Traders: such as buyers, sellers, their agents and distributors.

Transport operators: such as shipping lines, airlines, railway companies, logistics and trucking companies.

Providers of trade services: such as banking, finance and insurance.

Operators of transport infrastructure: such as port terminals, airports, stevedores and handling agents, warehouses and port/business community systems.

Specialist service providers: such as freight forwarders, shipping agents and logistics service providers.

SOURCE Grainger, 2012

There remains much opportunity for more detailed research in the assessment of border-related costs and performance, especially when taking the specific needs of the various parties involved in cross-border operations into account (Grainger and Shaw, 2018). The phrase 'stuck in customs' is often used as an excuse for all kinds of costs and delays – whether customs- or non-customs-related (Grainger, 2017). Such an excuse is easy to make, where operational requirements are complex (see Chapters 3 and 4). Subsequent anecdotes by practitioners about operational frustrations are in abundance (Box 8.4)

BOX 8.4

Examples of common accounts about operational frustrations at the border

1 Excessive paperwork and multiple parties demanding documents that are similar or overlapping in content.

2 Long queues at the government offices responsible for stamping paperwork.

3 Checks at the border taking too long.

4 The office hours kept by officials fail to coincide with when the goods arrive at the border and there are no means to clear goods outside of office hours.

5 Customs officers may be unnecessarily heavy-handed in order to solicit payment for 'special' treatment.

6 Officers fail to appreciate how their actions impact on costs.

7 Published rules and procedures cannot be easily accessed or are out of date; compliance requirements are established through costly trial and error.

8 Officers at the ports and border interpret applicable rules and procedures differently, causing confusion and adding to cost.

9 The capacity of inspection facilities is constrained, resulting in significant backlogs and extended periods of delay.

10 The various border agencies fail to coordinate their controls, resulting in duplication of control activity, delay and additional costs.

11 Paper documents go missing, especially when travelling with the goods (for example, in the driver's cab).

12 Officers reject documents because of minor errors: for example, the number 8 can easily be confused with the letter B; the lower case L (l) and upper case i (I) along with the number 1 frequently look the same.

13 Correction and appeal mechanisms may not exist – or are very cumbersome unless 'facilitation monies' have been paid.

14 The operational practices of one government agency contradict those of another.

15 Government agencies fail to take adequate advantage of modern technologies, thus adding to cost.

SOURCE Adapted from Grainger, 2017

Many of those frustrations can be attributed to a mismatch between modern logistics and SCM expectations and the operational practices of the border agencies. Their resolution – just as within Porter's value chain model – is found through improved coordination and cooperation. This might be at the transactional level within the context of day-to-day interactions between business operators and the government agencies. It might also be in partnership, as already outlined in Chapter 8 within the context of supply chain security and trusted trade arrangements. It might also be at the environmental level, where regulators and the business community seek to improve the wider trade and customs control regime to make it more amenable towards modern logistics and supply chain management demands (Table 8.1).

Issues at the transactional level might be resolved through the implementation of electronic customs systems and shared electronic infrastructure, such as the development of port community systems (see Chapter 2). Experienced customs agents and freight forwarders can also be invaluable in navigating complexities and are often able to clear goods efficiently by being able to draw on extensive tacit knowledge, knowing relevant systems inside out, and benefiting from good relationships with the officials. Many companies may also invest in sophisticated electronic trade management systems in order

TABLE 8.1 Relationship categories between business operations

Transaction-focused	The focus is on the day-to-day interactions between logistics operators and the border agencies; it is where businesses declare goods to the authorities and where necessary arrange for the physical inspection of goods at inspection facilities, and seek clearance from the authorities. Declarations might be made directly to the border agencies, or indirectly via intermediaries such as brokers, agents, freight forwarders.
Partnership-focused	The focus is on regulatory procedures where logistics operators are encouraged to take on some of the enforcement burden in exchange for access to operational and fiscal benefits. One comprehensive example of such shared control responsibilities are the respective Authorized Economic Operator (AEO) programmes of the UK and Brazil, where business membership confers comprehensive access to preferential customs treatment.
Business environment-focused	The focus is on how public and private sector stakeholders in the cross-border environment interact when determining the form and shape of applicable trade and customs procedures. Within the spirit of trade facilitation this is very much about developing a regulatory environment within which transaction costs are minimized whilst ensuring that regulatory objectives are appropriately met.

SOURCE Adapted from Grainger and Morini, 2019

to help automate as many compliance processes as possible (Hausman *et al*, 2010).

Partnership arrangements are increasingly found between border agencies (see Chapter 8) as well as with trusted businesses that have a robust compliance record. For example, customs administrations in more and more countries permit businesses to make declarations in their own records as opposed to having to formally submit a full customs declaration. Those records are then audited by customs officers on a periodic basis – for example, every two to three years. Border formalities are kept to a minimum. Such arrangements significantly reduce the administrative burden for the business operator and for the customs authority. The European Union's procedure for 'Entry in the Declarant's Records' (EIDR) is one such example (Irish Revenue, 2021). The UK's de facto default import arrangements for the period immediately after its departure from the European Union offers another example (HMRC, 2021).

Governing regulations that determine the applicable trade and customs procedures tend to be the result of political discourse. And where business communities are able to suitably articulate their needs, improvements to governing trade and customs procedures might be found – which Grainger (2010) refers to as the 'trade procedures reform cycle' (Figure 8.6). Much inspiration may be taken from international trade facilitation recommendations (Chapter 9). Inevitably, it requires a healthy consultation culture that ensures that prevailing trade and customs procedures are consistently reviewed, and where necessary, appropriate actions are taken. Institutional vehicles to support such dialogue are becoming increasingly commonplace (Grainger, 2010; Belastegui, 2020). They draw on the requirements of the WTO Trade Facilitation Agreement (discussed in Chapter 9), the UN CEFACT Recommendation 4 for national trade facilitation bodies (UN CEFACT, 2015). The focus of such bodies might relate to the implementation of measures – including changes in regulations – to reduce transaction costs. Well-performing bodies will also hold government agencies to account, for example, by setting performance targets and evaluating their performance against them. One common target is to ensure that

FIGURE 8.6 Trade procedures reform cycle

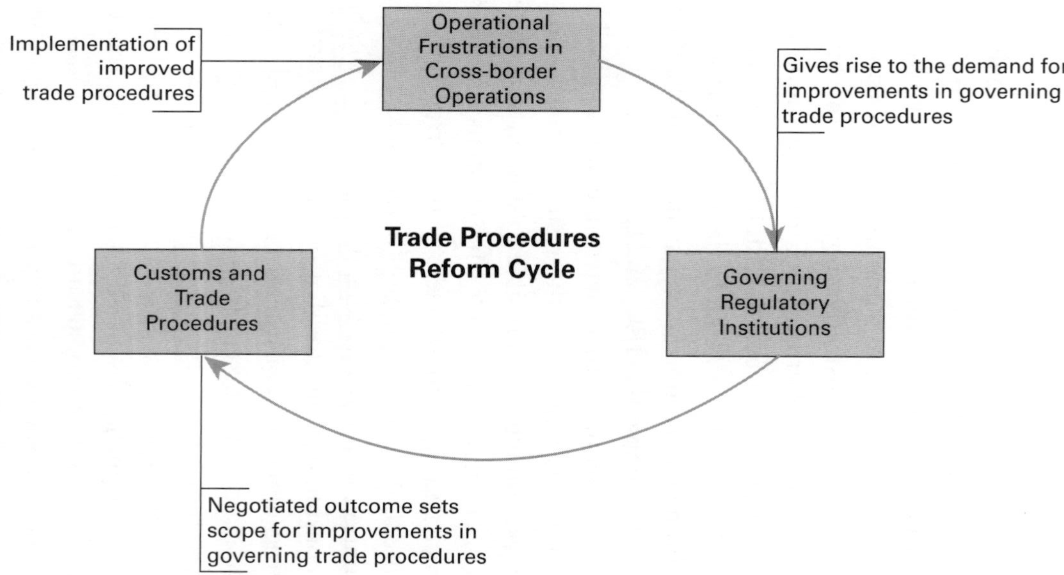

SOURCE Grainger, 2010

goods declared in line with requirements are cleared within a specific period of time.

Inevitably, since international trade always involves more than one country, it is often necessary to encourage improvements to the regulatory environment amongst trade partners, too. Such efforts have manifested themselves in the form of bilateral trade agreements as well as the work of international trade organizations. Thus, many bilateral trade agreements set requirements for measures that help improve control outcomes – for example, in the form of cooperation between border agencies (Chapter 8) – and reduce the cost of compliance, so-called trade facilitation (Chapter 9) – for example, by requiring inspections to be based on risk management principles or by encouraging the development of electronic compliance system (Chapter 3). The EU–UK Trade and Cooperation Agreement offers one such example (Box 8.5). But more and more countries choose even deeper models of cooperation by taking away or eliminating the impact of national borders on cross-border logistics operations (Table 8.2).

BOX 8.5

Example: EU–UK commitment to customs cooperation and trade facilitation

The customs and trade facilitation objectives specified in the EU–UK Trade and Cooperation Agreement are set out in Article 1 of Chapter 5, and are as follows:

(a) to reinforce cooperation between the Parties in the area of customs and trade facilitation and to support or maintain, where relevant, appropriate levels of compatibility of their customs legislation and practices with a view to ensuring that relevant legislation and procedures, as well as the administrative capacity of the relevant administrations, fulfil the objectives of promoting trade facilitation while ensuring effective customs controls and effective enforcement of customs legislation and trade-related laws and regulations, the proper protection of security and safety of citizens and the respect of prohibitions and restrictions and financial interests of the Parties;

(b) to reinforce administrative cooperation between the Parties in the field of VAT and mutual assistance in claims related to taxes and duties;

(c) to ensure that the legislation of each Party is non-discriminatory and that customs procedures are based upon the use of modern methods and effective controls to combat fraud and to promote legitimate trade; and

(d) to ensure that legitimate public policy objectives, including in relation to security, safety and the fight against fraud are not compromised in any way.

SOURCE EU and UK, 2020

Customs unions between partner countries, for example, are defined by a shared common external trade tariff. Goods moving within such a union may do so with considerable ease. Businesses taking advantage of customs union arrangements usually only need to prove that goods originate within the union (eg in the form of a movement certificate) and in cases where goods have been imported from outside the union, demonstrate that applicable tariff duties have been paid. Such procedures compare favourably with free trade agreements, which are subject to complex preferential origin rules (Chapter 2). The template of the European Union's single market, which incorporates a customs union, goes further and has largely removed the need for its internal borders. There are no border controls between Member States and imports, once cleared by Customs for free circulation, may move freely, too.

TABLE 8.2 List of WTO notified customs unions

Customs union name	Entry into force
Andean Community (CAN)	1988
Caribbean Community and Common Market (CARICOM)	1973
Central American Common Market (CACM)	1961
Common Market for Eastern and Southern Africa (COMESA)	1994

(continued)

TABLE 8.2 (Continued)

Customs union name	Entry into force
East African Community (EAC)	2000
Economic and Monetary Community of Central Africa (CEMAC)	1999
Economic Community of West African States (ECOWAS)	1993
EU – Andorra	1991
EU – San Marino	2002
EU – Turkey	1996
Eurasian Economic Union (EAEU)	2015
European Union Customs Union	1958
Gulf Cooperation Council (GCC)	2003
Southern African Customs Union (SACU)	2004
Southern Common Market (MERCOSUR)	1991
West African Economic and Monetary Union (WAEMU)	2000

SOURCE Extracted from WTO, 2020

ACTIVITIES AND DISCUSSION POINTS

1. Discuss what the transaction costs of working with a specialist customs broker might be. At what point would it make sense, if at all, to bring that function in-house?
2. Discuss the supply chain decisions that businesses might have to take when significant changes to trade and customs policy are made. If you like, consider various news stories about adjustments UK-based supply chains have had to make within the context of Brexit.
3. The bullwhip effect outlined in this chapter relates to minor fluctuations in demand. Its impact can be mitigated by sharing information with supply chain partners further up the chain. Could extended border disruptions (eg strikes, Brexit, Covid-19) create a similar bullwhip effect? Discuss.

Notes

1 For example, in earlier writings, Williamson (1971) cites thermal economies in the integration of iron-making and steel-making. If processes in the manufacture of iron and steel are separated, then these thermal economies are lost.

2 There are many examples. For instance, a buyer may have insufficient information to get the best price. See Simon, HA (1978) Rationality as process and as product of a thought, *American Economic Review,* **68** (2) p 1.

3 Taiichi Ohno of Toyota is credited by Womack *et al* (1990, 1996) as the pioneer of lean production.

4 A concept that Womack and Jones coin 'Lean Enterprise'.

References

Belastegui, AS (2020) National trade facilitation committees as coordinators of trade facilitation reforms, United Nations Conference on Trade and Development, United Nations, Geneva

Christopher, M (1992a) *Logistics and Supply Chain Management: Strategies for reducing costs and improving services,* Pitman, London

Christopher, M (ed) (1992b) *Logistics: The strategic issues,* Chapman and Hall, London

Cooper, MC, Lambert, DM and Pagh, JD (1997) Supply chain management: More than a new name for logistics, *International Journal of Logistics Management,* 8 (1), pp 1–14

Das, TK and Teng, B-S (1998) Between trust and control: Developing confidence in partner cooperation in alliances, *Academy of Management Review,* **23** (3), pp 491–512

Doney, PM, Cannon, JP and Mullen, MR (1998) Understanding the influences of national culture on the development of trust, *Academy of Management Review,* **23** (3), pp 601–20

Drucker, P (1962) The economy's dark continent, *Fortune,* April, **103**, pp 265–70

EU and UK (2020) Trade and Cooperation Agreement between the European Union and the European Atomic Energy Community, of the one part, and the United Kingdom of Great Britain and Northern Ireland, on the other part, *Official Journal of the European Union,* **63** (L444), pp 14–1462

Fawcett, SE and Magnan, GM (2002) The rhetoric and reality of supply chain integration, *International Journal of Physical Distribution & Logistics Management,* **32** (5), p 339

Forrester, JW (1961) *Industrial Dynamics*, Massachusetts Institute of Technology, MIT Press, Cambridge

Gereffi, G (1994) The organization of buyer-driven global commodity chains: How US retailers shape overseas production networks, *Commodity Chains and Global Capitalism*, eds G Gereffi and M Korzeniewicz, pp 95–122, Praeger, Westport

Grainger, A (2007) Supply chain security: Adding to an already complex operational and institutional environment, *2nd PICARD Conference,* World Customs Organization, Brussels

Grainger, A (2010) The role of the private sector in border management reform, *Border Management Modernization*, eds G McLinden, E Fanta, D Widdowson and T Doyle, pp 157–74, World Bank, Washington, DC

Grainger, A (2011) Trade facilitation: A conceptual review, *Journal of World Trade,* **45** (1), pp 39–62

Grainger, A (2012) Trade Facilitation, *Ashgate Research Companion to International Trade Policy*, eds K Heydon and S Woolcock, Ashgate, Aldershot

Grainger, A (2013) *Trade and customs procedures: The compliance costs for UK meat imports*, Nottingham University, eprints.nottingham.ac.uk/2143/ (archived at https://perma.cc/5W84-QLM8)

Grainger, A (2017) Trade and customs procedures in international transport: Requirements, issues and trends, *International Freight Transport: Cases, structures and prospects*, eds A Beresford and S Pettit, pp 57–75, Kogan Page, London

Grainger, A and Morini, C (2019) Disentangling cross-border interactions, *The International Journal of Logistics Management,* **30** (4), pp 958–73

Grainger, A and Shaw, D (2018) A method for measuring trade facilitation, *WCO News* (85), pp 21–23

Hagen, JM and Choe, S (1998) Trust in Japanese interfirm relations: Institutional sanctions matter, *Academy of Management Review,* **23** (3), pp 589–600

Harland, CM and Lamming, RC (1999) Developing the concept of supply strategy, *International Journal of Operations & Production Management,* **19** (7), p 650

Hausman, WH, Lee, HL, Napier, GRF, Thompson, A and Zheng, Y (2010) A process analysis of global trade management: An inductive approach, *Journal of Supply Chain Management,* **46** (2), pp 5–29

HMRC (2021) Making an import declaration in your records without authorisation, www.gov.uk/guidance/making-an-import-declaration-in-your-records-without-authorisation (archived at https://perma.cc/F99P-E4GT)

Irish Revenue (2021) Entry in the Declarant's Records (EIDR) – import, www.revenue.ie/en/customs-traders-and-agents/simplified-customs-procedures/entry-in-the-declarants-records-import.aspx (archived at https://perma.cc/2VG4-U6L6)

Jones, DT and Hines, P (1997) Lean logistics, *International Journal of Physical Distribution & Logistics Management,* **27** (3/4), p 153

Lamming, R (1996) Squaring: Lean supply with supply chain management, *International Journal of Operations & Production Management,* **16** (2), pp 183–96

Lamming, R, Johnsen, T, Zheng, J and Harland, C (2000) An initial classification of supply networks, *International Journal of Operations & Production Management,* **20** (5/6), p 675

Matsuda, S (2012) The time release study as a performance measurement tool for a supply chain and an international corridor, *World Customs Journal,* **6** (1), pp 79–92

McKnight, DH, Cummings, LL and Chervany, NL (1998) Initial trust formation in new organizational relationships, *Academy of Management Review,* **23** (3), pp 473–90

OECD (2009) *Overcoming Border Bottlenecks: The costs and benefits of trade facilitation*, Organisation for Economic Co-operation and Development, Paris

Oliver, RK and Webber, MD (1992) Supply-chain management: Logistics catches up with strategy, in *Logistics: The strategic issues*, ed M Christopher, pp 63–75, Cengage Learning, London, New York and Melbourne

Porter, ME (1985) *Competitive Advantage: Creating and sustaining superior performance,* Free Press, New York

Prasad, S and Babbar, S (2000) International operations management research, *Journal of Operations Management,* **18** (2), pp 209–47

Selen, W and Soliman, F (2002) Operations in today's demand chain management framework, *Journal of Operations Management,* **20** (6), pp 667–73

Sharifi, H and Zhang, Z (1999) A methodology for achieving agility in manufacturing organisations: An introduction, *International Journal of Production Economics,* **62** (1/2), pp 7–22

Simon, HA (1978) Rationality as process and as product of a thought, *American Economic Review,* **68** (2), p 1

Sourdin, P and Pomfret, R (2012) *Trade Facilitation: Defining, measuring, explaining and reducing the cost of international trade,* Edward Elgar, Cheltenham

Sugimori, Y, Kusunoki, K, Cho, F and Uchikawa, S (1977) Toyota production system and kanban system materialization of just-in-time and respect-for-human system, *International Journal of Production Research,* **15** (6), p 553

Towill, D and Christopher, M (2002) The supply chain strategy conundrum: To be lean or agile or to be lean and agile? *International Journal of Logistics: Research & Applications,* **5** (3), pp 299–309

UN CEFACT (2015) Recommendation 4: National Trade Facilitation Bodies, United Nations Centre for Trade Facilitation and Electronic Business, United Nations, Geneva

Verwaal, E and Donkers, B (2003) Customs-related transaction costs, firm size and international trade intensity, *Small Business Economics,* **21** (3), pp 257–71

Vokurka, RJ and Lummus, RR (2000) The role of just-in-time in supply chain management, *International Journal of Logistics Management,* **11** (1), p 89

Voorhees, RD and Coppett, JI (1992) Marketing–logistics opportunities for the 1990s, *Journal of Business Strategy,* 7 (2), pp 33–38

Williamson, OE (1981) The economics of organisation: The transaction cost approach, *American Journal of Sociology,* **87** (3), pp 548–77

Womack, J and Jones, D (1994) From lean production to the lean enterprise, *Harvard Business Review,* **72** (2), pp 93–103

Womack, JP, Jones, DT and Roos, D (1990) *The Machine that Changed the World*, Rawson Associates, New York; Maxwell Macmillan International, Oxford

World Bank (2020) Logistics Performance Index (LPI), lpi.worldbank.org (archived at https://perma.cc/BCZ4-HJQT)

World Bank (2021) Doing business: Trading across borders, www.doingbusiness.org/ExploreTopics/TradingAcrossBorders/ (archived at https://perma.cc/KK86-BD6M)

WTO (2015) World Trade Report 2015: Speeding up trade – benefits and challenges of implementing the WTO Trade Facilitation Agreement, World Trade Organization, Geneva

WTO (2020) Regional Trade Agreements Database, rtais.wto.org/UI/PublicMaintainRTAHome.aspx (archived at https://perma.cc/KT4E-7NWV)

09

Trade facilitation

The term trade facilitation is used in multiple contexts and definitions can vary in scope, but the main focus within contemporary trade and customs policy is the desire to reduce the transaction costs – friction – between business operators and the many government agencies with border control-related responsibilities (Grainger, 2011). The term trade facilitation is thus often used as simple shorthand for the reduction of red tape in cross-border logistics operations.

Its associated literature recognizes that friction between business operators and government agencies (B2G) is best avoided and undermines business competitiveness. Such transaction costs also undermine trade-related economic growth along with associated economic development (Mann, 2012). Friction is also detrimental to the ability of government agencies to effectively enforce border controls, especially where administrative practices tie up unnecessary resources or overly bureaucratic practices foster corruption and push businesses into the shadow economy.

It is important to note that many see trade facilitation within the wider context that also concerns the commercial procedures between interacting businesses across international supply chains. This is emphasized, for example, in the UN CEFACT's Buy–Pay–Ship model in which compliance with regulatory obligations is one of many activities in international logistics and supply chain operations (UN CEFACT, 2019). Occasionally, customs officers might (perhaps mistakenly) use the term 'trade facilitations' as a shorthand for special customs procedures that allow businesses to defer or suspend duties (Chapter 2). It is also not uncommon for governments to refer to their export promotion, trade finance and trade insurance programmes as trade facilitation (EBRD, 2021).

Within the context of contemporary trade and customs policy, trade facilitation is largely understood to be a collection of agreed best practice measures aimed at reducing trade and customs-related compliance costs. In some form or other these measures draw on the principles of transparency, simplification, harmonization and standardization (Table 9.1) and are the result of trade facilitation advocacy from two directions:

- The first is from the bottom up, where experienced operational frictions – as outlined in Chapter 8 – have been suitably articulated by those affected (whether working for globally operating businesses or for the border administrations) and subsequently addressed in formal recommendations to help get rid of their cost (Figure 8.6).
- The second is from the top down, where such recommendations have been adopted within international trade and customs cooperation

TABLE 9.1 The four UNECE principles of trade facilitation

Transparency	This principle promotes the openness and accountability of a government agency's actions. It invites business stakeholders to actively participate in the processes that shape the adoption and implementation of trade and customs procedures. It also holds that any details – such as legal instruments or administrative guidelines – are published and easily accessible.
Simplification	This principle seeks to eliminate all unnecessary elements and duplication of activities. This may be achieved, for example, by ensuring that information already declared to one border agency need not be declared again to another border agency.
Harmonization	This principle seeks to align various national trade and customs procedures with international conventions, standards and best practice recommendations – such as those of the WCO's Revised Kyoto Convention.
Standardization	This principle seeks to develop standard formats for the sharing of trade and customs-related information. This gives greater scope for electronic solutions and automation, which in turn help reduce compliance costs.

SOURCE Adapted from UNECE, 2012

agreements and then made binding within the framework of bilateral and multilateral trade and customs agreements.

SOURCE Grainger, 2011

International trade facilitation policy and its institutions

Internationally, considerable strides towards trade facilitation have been made (Box 9.1). Much of the World Customs Organization's (WCO) activities, for example, concern the harmonization of customs procedures between countries. The WCO's Revised Kyoto Convention now serves as template for customs legislation in over 120 countries and customs compliance requirements are similar from one country to the next (WCO, 2006). The WCO's 2019–2022 Strategic Plan also highlights trade facilitation – next to revenue collection (Chapter 2) and the protection of society (Chapters 4 and 7) – as one of the three main needs of customs administrations (WCO, 2019b). The adoption of trade facilitation principles is recognized as essential for economic growth. They also lend themselves well to utilizing customs resources in the most efficient manner. This is achieved, for example, through improved coordination at the border (as discussed in Chapter 8) and risk management practices (as discussed in Chapter 2) where inspection resources are targeted at those operators without a good compliance record.

Another international organization actively championing trade facilitation is the United Nations Economic Committee for Europe (UNECE). It was formed in 1947 and one of its primary goals is to encourage greater economic cooperation among its 55 European Member States. But, for the subject of trade facilitation the UNECE carries the global remit on behalf of the entire UN in the form of its Centre for Trade Facilitation and Electronic Business (UN CEFACT). The UNECE is also active in other areas of trade facilitation. For example, its Working Party No 7 has responsibilities for agricultural quality standardization, enforced in many countries by dedicated horticulture and marketing inspectors (UNECE, 2021). With the

International Road Transport Union (IRU), it maintains the TIR Convention of 1975 (TIR, 2005) which offers a significantly simplified customs control regime for road vehicles in transit through third countries.

Together with various international transport bodies, UNECE also helps set international standards for the transport, marking, packaging and handling of dangerous goods (UNECE, 2020). One of UN CEFACT's many recommendations worth highlighting is Recommendation 18 (UNECE, 2002). It reiterates that businesses face many obstacles in international trade which result in friction between operators across the supply chain. To reduce that friction, including the cost of compliance with government agencies, UN CEFACT recommends that:

- procedures should be kept to a minimum;
- procedures should be commercially oriented and relate more closely to trade and transport requirements;
- procedures should be simplified, harmonized and should comply with international standards;
- data requirements should be kept to a minimum;
- data requirements should be simplified, harmonized and standardized, to ease the information flow;
- Laws, regulations and other information regarding procedures and data requirements should be readily accessible to all parties concerned;
- documentary requirements should be kept to a minimum;
- documents should [follow a standardized layout]... in line with [the] UN Layout Key for Trade Documents (UNECE, 2017);
- the use of plain paper, documents produced or appearing to be produced by reprographic automated or computerized systems should be acceptable;
- the presentation of supporting documents should not be required;
- hand-written signatures and their equivalents should be avoided as far as possible (eg on invoices) on paper documents;

- the use of information and communication technology and the resulting electronic solutions should be encouraged;
- the use of electronic documents and standard format should be supported;
- the requirement for authentication can be fulfilled by means of technological solutions and need not be accompanied by a signed and/or authenticated paper document.

For most countries trade facilitation commitments also result from their membership of the International Maritime Organization (IMO). Its Convention on Facilitation of International Maritime Traffic (IMO, 1965) makes it mandatory for national governments to introduce systems that support the electronic information exchange between ships and ports. This requirement applies to all regulatory documentation needs, including cargo declarations, dangerous goods declarations, crew manifests and vessel details. To ease compliance, that information should be collated and submitted without duplication via a single portal (IMO, 2019).

Similar commitments also result from membership of the International Civil Aviation Organization (ICAO). Its Annex 9 of the ICAO Chicago Convention details a series of standards and recommended practices for the facilitation of regulatory formalities. They concern passengers and cargo and relate to the requirements of Customs, Immigration, Public Health and Agriculture authorities. As with the requirements for maritime cargo, information should ideally be submittable via a single entry point, to avoid the need for operators having to declare the information to each of the authorities individually (ICAO, 2017).

BOX 9.1

A short history of the main international organizations championing trade facilitation

One of the key international institutions governing the liberalization of trade is the **World Trade Organization** (WTO) and its predecessor, the General Agreement on Tariffs and Trade (GATT). The GATT came into existence in 1947 as a temporary substitute for the International Trade Organization, which was proposed under the Bretton Woods Agreement in

1944, but which failed to be established following the US Congress's failure to ratify it.

The GATT's overall objective was to prevent a repetition of the protectionist and discriminatory trade policies of the 1930s that are frequently seen as a significant contributory factor to the outbreak of World War II (Stubbs and Underhill, 1994; Appling and Archer, 1998; Braithwaite and Drahos, 2000). The GATT's purpose, as defined in the preamble to its Charter, is to promote economic well-being by enabling its members to enter into 'reciprocal and mutually advantageous arrangements' aimed at the 'substantial reduction of tariffs and other barriers to trade and to the elimination of discriminatory treatment' in international trade (GATT, 1947).

Originally founded with 23 member states, the GATT managed to attract a membership of 117 states by the end of the Uruguay Round in 1994. Following on from the Uruguay Round, members agreed to set up the more permanent WTO with its own secretariat. The WTO was established on 1 January 1995 and now has over 1,600 member countries.

Average tariff levels for goods, as discussed in Chapter 2, have fallen significantly. Not surprisingly, trade negotiators are now increasingly focusing on the non-tariff areas. At the 1996 WTO ministerial meeting in Singapore, trade facilitation, along with transparency in government procurement, investment and competition policy, was introduced as a new agenda item. In November 2001 these four 'Singapore Issues' were adopted formally as part of the Doha development agenda. In 2013 WTO members concluded the Trade Facilitation Agreement (WTO, 2014) which subsequent to the ratification by two-thirds of its membership entered into force on 22 February 2017 (WTO, 2017).

The origin of the **World Customs Organization** (WCO) dates back to 1947 when the 13 European governments represented in the Committee of European Economic Co-operation (CEEC)* agreed to set up a study group to examine the possibility of establishing one or more inter-European customs unions based on the principles of the GATT. In 1948, the study group set up two committees: an Economic Committee and a Customs Committee. The Economic Committee eventually evolved into the Organisation for Economic Co-operation and Development (OECD). The Customs Committee, with 17 founding members from various European countries, formalized itself in 1952 as the Customs Co-operation Council (CCC). In 1994, with increasing membership from outside Europe, the CCC was eventually renamed as the World Customs Organization (WCO). Today the WCO has a membership of 183 customs administrations (WCO, 2002; OECD, 2020; WCO, 2020).

The **United Nations Centre for Trade Facilitation and Electronic Business** (UN CEFACT) was established in 1996, replacing the UNECE Working Party No 4 which was formed in 1960 for the facilitation of international trade procedures. UN CEFACT has developed a series of some 30 recommendations and standards that are used worldwide in aid of trade facilitation and to simplify, standardize and harmonize applicable trade procedures – especially with regard to the flow and exchange of information between relevant parties (UNECE, 2020b). It has a global membership consisting of experts from inter-governmental organizations, individual countries, authorities and the business community. This community of experts was instrumental in helping define the many ideas about how trade and customs procedures could be improved.

*NOTE *The CEEC was a body established with US and Canadian aid to help with the implementation of the Marshall Plan and European reconstruction after World War II.*

The most significant multilateral trade facilitation instrument is the World Trade Organization's Trade Facilitation Agreement, which was concluded by members in 2013 (WTO, 2014). The WTO's objective of reducing 'other' barriers to trade, those next to trade tariffs, is explicitly highlighted in the original preamble of GATT (GATT, 1947). Much of the drive to foster trade facilitation initiatives amongst its member countries comes from the shared desire to enable developing and emerging economies to more actively participate in global trade opportunities, and thus improve global economic growth (WTO, 2015). Subsequent to the ratification by two-thirds of the WTO membership, the Trade Facilitation Agreement entered into force on 22 February 2017 (WTO, 2017).

Many of the measures specified in the Trade Facilitation Agreement focus on trade and customs-related administrative practices, specifying:

- minimum benefits for trusted traders (Article 7);
- advance customs rulings (for tariff classification and origin, but also recommended for customs value, duty relief and quotas (Article 3);
- the right to appeal (Article 4);

- pre-arrival processing of customs declarations (Article 7);
- electronic payment of duties, taxes and fees (Article 7);
- the adherence to risk-based controls (Article 7);
- post-clearance audits by Customs (Article 7);
- the implementation of the special customs procedures, such as inward processing and outward processing relief (Article 10);
- and expedited clearance for air cargo and perishable goods (Article 7).

TABLE 9.2 Summary of measures in the WTO Trade Facilitation Agreement: Articles 1–12 and 23 (paraphrased)

Article/Heading	Trade facilitation obligations for the WTO member country
ARTICLE 1: PUBLICATION AND AVAILABILITY OF INFORMATION	
1. Publication	To publish applicable trade and customs-related information promptly in an easily accessible manner
2. Information available through internet	Produce practical compliance guides
	Make trade documents available for download
	Publish applicable trade laws
	Publish the contact details for the below enquiry points
3. Enquiry points	Implement a contact services where relevant parties (including business operators) can obtain information about the applicable trade and customs procedures
4. Notification	Inform the WTO about where the above points have been published
ARTICLE 2: OPPORTUNITY TO COMMENT, INFORMATION BEFORE ENTRY INTO FORCE AND CONSULTATIONS	
1. Opportunity to comment and information before entry into force	Ensure that traders and other interested parties have the opportunity to comment about any new trade and customs-related laws before they are implemented
2. Consultations	Border agencies must regularly consult with traders and other stakeholders
ARTICLE 3: ADVANCE RULINGS	
Advance (binding) rulings	To provide, upon application by the trader, advance (binding) tariff classification or origin rulings before goods are imported

(continued)

TABLE 9.2 (Continued)

Article/Heading	Trade facilitation obligations for the WTO member country
ARTICLE 4: PROCEDURES FOR APPEAL OR REVIEW	
Appeals	Traders shall have the right to appeal decisions made by Customs in an administrative or judicial proceeding
ARTICLE 5: OTHER MEASURES TO ENHANCE IMPARTIALITY, NON-DISCRIMINATION AND TRANSPARENCY	
1. Notification for enhanced controls or inspections	Temporary enhanced control arrangements (eg in response to public health risk) shall be based on risk Relevant information and guidance must be published Any enhanced controls shall be in proportion to risk and removed when the risk no longer applies
2. Detention	Where goods are detained for inspection, relevant business operators are to be informed promptly
3. Test procedures	Business operators shall have the right to a second test where the first led to an adverse outcome Publish/share the contact details of laboratories where tests can be caried out
ARTICLE 6: DISCIPLINES ON FEES AND CHARGES IMPOSED ON OR IN CONNECTION WITH IMPORTATION AND EXPORTATION AND PENALTIES	
1. General disciplines on fees and charges imposed on or in connection with importation and exportation	Any fees and charges shall be applied in line with WTO Principle (see GATT, 1994) Fees and charges shall be published along with details about how they can be paid Any applicable fees and charges shall be periodically reviewed and reduced where possible
2. Specific disciplines on fees and charges for customs processing imposed on or in connection with importation and exportation	Customs fees and charges shall be in proportion to the cost and service provided by the administration Any fees not specific to an import or export operation must be closely related to Customs' processing of goods
3. Penalty disciplines	Penalties are only to be imposed on the person(s) responsible and proportionate to the degree of violations; prior disclosure shall be considered as a potential factor for mitigating the penalty sum Penalties are to be issued with a written explanation Any conflicts of interest in the assessment of penalties are to be avoided

(continued)

TABLE 9.2 (Continued)

Article/Heading	Trade facilitation obligations for the WTO member country
ARTICLE 7: RELEASE AND CLEARANCE OF GOODS	
1. Pre-arrival processing	Traders shall be permitted to submit import documents and related information in advance and prior to the arrival of the goods in order to expedite their release
2. Electronic payment	Electronic payment options for duties, taxes, fees and charges shall (as far as practical) be implemented
3. Separation of release from final determination of customs duties, taxes, fees and charges	Subject to financial guarantee, goods may be released by Customs prior to the payment of duties and taxes
4. Risk management	Risk management principles shall apply to the control of goods
	Administrations shall concentrate their controls on high-risk goods and expedite the release of low-risk goods
5. Post-clearance audit	Post-clearance audit methods (eg by auditing relevant records at the trader's premises) shall be applied in order to expedite customs release
	The outcome of those audits shall inform risk management evaluations
6. Establishment and publication of average release times	Conduct studies to measure the average time it takes to release goods at the borders and publish those studies
7. Trade facilitation measures for authorized operators	Special or preferential customs treatment is to be provided to reliable (trusted) traders
	Qualifying criteria for trusted trader or authorized economic operator programmes is to be published
	WTO members shall seek to provide mutual recognition of their respective trusted trader programmes
8. Expedited shipments	Air express delivery operators and similar types of companies may benefit from special procedures for expedited customs release
9. Perishable goods	Allow for release in the shortest possible time
	Priority treatment for examination and clearance
	Where appropriate, to accommodate clearance outside normal office hours
	Allow goods to be stored in conditions appropriate for their conservation (eg temperature-controlled) and where practical to conduct examinations at those facilities

(continued)

TABLE 9.2 (Continued)

Article/Heading	Trade facilitation obligations for the WTO member country
ARTICLE 8: BORDER AGENCY COOPERATION	
Border agency cooperation	Border agencies shall cooperate and coordinate their controls and procedures to facilitate trade Countries with common land borders shall cooperate and coordinate procedures
ARTICLE 9: MOVEMENT OF GOODS INTENDED FOR IMPORT UNDER CUSTOMS CONTROL	
Imports under customs control	Allow goods to be moved under a simplified customs procedure to an inland office, and permit the importer to clear goods at the destination rather than at the border crossing or port of arrival
ARTICLE 10: FORMALITIES CONNECTED WITH IMPORTATION, EXPORTATION AND TRANSIT	
1. Formalities and documentation requirements	Regularly review the number of documents and formalities required with a view towards reducing or simplifying them Document requirements and formalities should be as fast and as efficient as possible; eliminated where no longer needed; and should not be adopted if less restrictive solutions are available (eg automation)
2. Acceptance of copies	Where border agencies require supporting documents to complete their control (eg commercial invoice or transport documents) they need not be originals The export declaration (original or copy) shall not be required for importation If the original document has been provided to one government authority, other government authorities shall accept any authenticated copy by that agency holding the original
3. Use of international standards	Relevant international standards for trade and customs procedures are to be adopted (eg for electronic data-sharing) WTO members shall participate in the regular review of those standards

(continued)

TABLE 9.2 (Continued)

Article/Heading	Trade facilitation obligations for the WTO member country
4. Single window	Efforts towards the implementation of a 'single window' facility which allows traders to submit all trade-related information via one single entry point
	The one-time submission principle shall apply whereby information already shared shall not be requested again
	As far as possible, modern information and communication technology shall be utilized
5. Pre-shipment inspection (PSI)	In countries where PSI procedures apply (ie inspection by private companies before shipment), they shall be phased out
	New PSI regimes are not to be introduced
6. Use of customs brokers	Mandatory requirements for the use of customs brokers should not be introduced
	Where their use is mandatory any broker licensing rules shall be transparent and objective
7. Common border procedures and uniform documentation requirements	The release of goods and clearance shall be based on common customs procedures and uniform document requirements (but different customs treatment and risk management practices are permitted)
8. Rejected goods	The importer has the right to return (eg to the exporter) or re-consign any rejected goods in circumstances where the prescribed sanitary, phytosanitary or other technical regulations could not be met
9. Temporary admission of goods and inward and outward processing	These procedures shall be provided for. Temporary admission allows for goods to be imported fee of duties on condition that they are returned within a specific period of time. Inward processing relief allows for goods to be imported free of duties where they form part of export manufacturing or repair. Outward processing relief allows for duties and taxes to be collected only on the value added by foreign processing
ARTICLE 11: FREEDOM OF TRANSIT	
1–3. Transit charges, regulations and formalities	Transit formalities shall be eliminated or reduced if no longer required or a less trade restrictive solution is available; charges may only relate to the cost of administration and services provided

(continued)

TABLE 9.2 (Continued)

Article/Heading	Trade facilitation obligations for the WTO member country
4. Non-discrimination	Goods in transit shall not be treated less favourably than if they had not been in transit
5–10. Transit procedures and controls	Allow pre-arrival declarations; only apply formalities necessary for transit control; not apply charges, formalities or inspections at locations other than at the office of departure or destination; not apply technical regulations and market conformity assessments; promptly release goods from transit once they reach the office of exit
	Separate clearance lanes for transit traffic are encouraged
11–15. Guarantees	Transit guarantees shall be proportionate, discharged without delay, and applied in a consistent manner
	Information about how guarantees are set must be made available
	Customs may only insist on accompanying transit goods in convoy where they are high risk or where the requirement is specified by national law
16–17. Cooperation and coordination	Countries shall cooperate and coordinate to enhance the freedom of transit
	A national transit coordinator to accommodate enquires and proposals should be appointed
ARTICLE 12: CUSTOMS COOPERATION	
Customs cooperation	Customs cooperation between countries is to be encouraged along with obligations to respond to information requests
ARTICLE 23: INSTITUTIONAL ARRANGEMENTS	
1. Committee on Trade Facilitation	The WTO Committee on Trade Facilitation is to review the operation and implementation of the Agreement every four years
	The Committee shall maintain close contact with other international organizations (eg WCO)
	Best practice experiences and insights are to be exchanged
2. National committees on trade facilitation	National trade facilitation committees are to be established in order to facilitate both domestic coordination and implementation of the provisions of this Agreement

SOURCE Adapted and paraphrased from WTO, 2014

Several of the Agreement's articles address the need for authorities to cooperate with each other at home and internationally (see Chapter 7). This includes:

- the adoption of common border procedures and uniform document requirements (Article 10);
- the adoption of the single window principle (enabling importers to submit all relevant information for declaration to the authorities via one single interface (Article 10);
- and a mechanism for the exchange of information between customs administrations (eg copies of the import and export declaration) (Article 12).

The Agreement also states that WTO Member States shall not introduce the mandatory use of customs brokers (Article 10). In countries where customs brokers are a licensed profession, applicable rules governing their use must be transparent and objective. Likewise, the introduction of pre-shipment inspection requirements (a costly aspect of trade compliance in some developing countries) is to be discouraged (Article 10).

Furthermore, the Trade Facilitation Agreement sets requirements for ensuring that business operators have access to relevant legislation and related information (Article 1). It also provides for business consultation whenever rules and procedures are changed or amended, and whenever new rules and procedures or systems are implemented (Article 2). Last but not least, the Agreement contains provisions for the coordination of trade facilitation activities between the authorities and business interest groups (Article 23).

However, it is worth noting that the bulk of the WTO's trade facilitation measures draw on ideas and concepts already developed elsewhere, especially the WCO's Revised Kyoto Convention (Wolffgang and Kafeero, 2014) and the recommendations of UN CEFACT. What makes the WTO Trade Facilitation Agreement special is that it holds countries accountable for the implementation of such measures. It also contains extensive provisions to make sure that developing and least developed countries are offered meaningful technical and financial support when implementing those trade facilitation measures (UNCTAD, 2017; WTO, 2021).

Trade facilitation themes and objectives

Most trade facilitation measures within contemporary trade and customs policy can be attributed to four guiding themes:

1. the simplification and harmonization of applicable rules and procedures;
2. the modernization of trade compliance systems;
3. best practices in the administration and management of trade and customs procedures; and
4. the institutional mechanisms to safeguard ongoing commitment to reducing trade-related compliance costs.

SOURCE Grainger, 2011

Trade facilitation measures and ideas now also benefit from an extensive literature that has largely been produced by the organizations outlined above (UN ESCAP, 2004; De Wulf and Sokol, 2005; UNCTAD, 2006a, 2006b; Rege *et al,* 2007; McLinden *et al,* 2010). The body of work has been further substantiated with extensive online resources, ranging from databases and repositories to training materials and case studies. This includes the UNECE's Trade Facilitation Implementation Guide (UNECE, 2020c) and the WTO's Trade Facilitation Agreement Facility (WTO, 2021) which have been designed to help raise awareness about trade facilitation opportunities, their underlying principles and practices, and the coordination of their implementation.

Inevitably, there are many ways by which measures and ideas can be discussed and summarized – whether by reference to the WTO's Trade Facilitation Agreement's specific articles (WTO, 2021), the domains, itineraries, instruments and organizations involved (UNECE, 2020c) or underlying ideas and concepts (Grainger, 2011). For the purposes of a broad overview (without focus on the details, which could merit a book in its own right) it is probably worth holding onto trade facilitation's wider underlying **objectives.** These are seldomly expressed explicitly within international recommendations or instruments, but in the most general of terms can be attributed to the following four objectives:

1. Make international trade and cross-border processes more efficient, less costly and easier.
2. Harness data-sharing technologies to best effect.
3. Improve coordination and cooperation between the various parties involved in cross-border logistics operations.
4. Assess and evaluate frictions in cross-border logistics operations, hold parties accountable to their promises and obligations, and to learn and innovate.

All four themes draw in some way or other on the wider objective of wanting to improve applicable trade and customs procedures within the legal, regulatory and operational setting that define them.

Make international trade and cross-border processes more efficient, less costly and easier

Efficient cross-border processes that are easy to comply with have less of an impact on cost and subsequently improve business competitiveness. Likewise, unbureaucratic practices lend themselves to businesses taking advantage of global trade opportunities. Wider economic gains follow. Government agencies tasked with the administration of trade and customs procedures can put their resources to more effective use. The scope for improvements inevitably depends on the level of frustrations already suffered by business operators.

KNOWING HOW TO COMPLY

A key concern frequently highlighted by business operators, especially those with little or no experience in international trade, are the challenges associated with working out what the specific requirements of the border agencies are and then how to best comply with them. Support for formal training and awareness-building type activities is often recommended. Governments may also help foster formal training at universities and professional colleges or adopt professional training standards such as those of the WCO PICARD programme (WCO, 2019a), and the EU Customs Competency Framework (European Commission, 2019). Often, especially when new procedures or electronic systems are introduced by relevant government agencies, the business community may also be offered dedicated training at free or subsidized rates. Without such training, it is likely that mistakes will happen, compliance is not assured and unnecessary friction between business operators and officials is created.

More and more countries around the world now also maintain dedicated websites and information portals where all information about how to be compliant can be easily found (LTP, 2021). Some of these websites may also contain detailed guides with step-by-step instructions that make it easier for businesses to be compliant (UK Government, 2021). Some free government web services also contain a wide range of additional support material designed for users at home and those who wish to trade with the country (EU, 2021). Complementing their online presence, border agencies may also offer dedicated telephone and email support services where traders may ask for detailed information. In the European Union the need to cater for such services is also made explicit in its customs law, the Union Customs Code (EU, 2013), which specifies that customs authorities must respond to information requests made by any person (Box 9.1).

BOX 9.1

Extract from the EU's Union Customs Code, Article 14

Article 14

Provision of information by the customs authorities

1. Any person may request information concerning the application of the customs legislation from the customs authorities. Such a request may be refused where it does not relate to an activity pertaining to international trade in goods that is actually envisaged.

SOURCE Union Customs Code: EU, 2013

SERVICE PROVISIONS

Many administrations commit to service standards, for example by promising not to hold goods for longer than 12 or 24 hours unless there is a good reason to do so. Likewise, customs legislation in line with the Revised Kyoto Convention usually allows genuine mistakes to be corrected. Mistakes can easily be made. Perhaps the wrong reference number was used, perhaps a typing or communication error led to a misdeclaration, perhaps the shipment made had the wrong paperwork attached. This should not lead to undue delay. In practice, though, there are significant variances in the extent to which corrections are permitted, and often there is also concern about corrupt practices where procedures for corrections are abused. At the risk of over-generalization, non-customs agencies are often more stringent, especially where prohibitions and restrictions are concerned.

In instances where the correct interpretation or rules and procedures are ambiguous – for example, within the context of tariff classification and origin (Chapter 2) – business operators can usually also ask for binding decisions or rulings in advance. Often referred to as Binding Tariff Information or Binding Origin Information, these may take time to obtain, but will normally eliminate any risk of goods being delayed at the border because of ambiguity about the correct interpretation of tariff classification or origin rules.

Given the scope for variances in interpretation by officials, fast-track appeal procedures are also desirable. Rather than having to challenge decisions in court, which can take time, many administrations offer the option of a review – for example, by a more experienced officer with advanced technical training or a dedicated review team. Depending on the nature of the review, erroneous decisions by officers at the border may be overruled at a considerably faster pace than that offered by the courts.

ALIGNMENT OF BORDER PROCEDURES WITH BUSINESS REQUIREMENTS

Border processes are often described by logistics and supply chain practitioners as 'bottlenecks' where goods do not move as efficiently as they should. This has implications for costs and how supply chains should be best configured, including procurement and location decisions. It is often found that processes are needlessly duplicated and that opportunities to make compliance significantly easier or to develop economies of scale are missed.

That said, more and more countries, in line with the recommendations of the WCO Revised Kyoto Convention and the recommendations of the WTO Trade Facilitation Agreement, permit suitably authorized traders to clear goods away from the border and at their own premises.

Such practices significantly reduce the operator's exposure to congestion at ports and borders. They also reduce the risk of any related expenses, such as handling and demurrage charges.

Significant operational efficiencies can also be achieved where regulatory regimes allow for audit-based controls. Rather than having to declare a declaration for each and every shipment, declarations are made in the operator's own records (as is, for example, permitted in the EU and the UK). Those records are then audited by customs officers on a periodic basis (eg every two to three years). Likewise, it is usually more efficient if procedures allow for the payment of duties, taxes and fees on a periodic basis as opposed to for each and every shipment – a procedure sometimes also referred to as 'periodic entry'. Such payments may even be combined with the payment of other taxes. For example, the United Kingdom, Ireland and Poland permit import value added tax (VAT) payments to be accounted for within regular VAT returns (usually every two to three months), instead of linking payment demands to the customs declaration.

Trade and customs procedures may also be designed to enable operators to develop economies of scale. In the European Union, for example, authorized operators may take advantage of centralized clearance procedures (EU, 2013). These allow the operator to lodge a customs declaration for anywhere within the territory of the European Union at one single office rather than in each member state. Economies of scale may also be achieved where compliance systems draw on the same information, such as the commercial invoice and standard transport documents. It thus becomes possible to develop cost-effective document management solutions with a wide range of applications that include regulatory compliance.

AVOID DUPLICATION

Amongst trade facilitation advocates there is also a lot of concern about unnecessary duplication within contemporary compliance requirements. For example, each and every trade between two countries is exposed to at least one customs export declaration and one import declaration. Lean thinking (Chapter 8) would dictate that both processes (with suitable harmonization and cooperation between the regulatory authorities) could be brought into one. Indeed, in

Chapter 7 several examples of coordinated border management have already been outlined. However, examples of where one country's export procedures feed into or replace another country's import procedures, are rare. More common are practices that allow some trade documents to be put to multiple use. The EU–UK Trade and Cooperation Agreement, for example, allows origin statement to be made on the commercial invoice (EU and UK, 2020). Arrangements between the EU and New Zealand allow, amongst others, the origin certificates of the New Zeeland Meat Board to serve as the EU import licence (New Zealand Meat Board, 2021).

Another successful example of cutting out duplicate procedures can be found in Montenegro. There, authorized express parcel operators are permitted to submit one consolidated electronic manifest in advance. Thus, in most cases, the need for multiple individual declarations to Customs for each and every parcel falls away. Moreover, such advance sharing in an electronic format also makes it significantly easier for customs officers to process and release goods – usually within less than one hour upon arrival (DAfTF, 2020).

CUT OUT UNNECESSARY PROCESSES

As outlined in Chapters 3 and 4 import clearance is often conditional upon importers presenting documents that have been issued by authorities in the country of export. This frequently applies to documents evidencing proof of origin. It usually also applies to animal and plant health certificates.

The process for obtaining and presenting such documents can be rather complex and usually requires an application to the relevant government agencies in the country of export. Once obtained, the exporter must then send that document to the importer. The importer in turn must then present that document to the authorities there. There is no direct link between the two government agencies; thus it is a rather lengthy government-to-business-to-business-to-government (G2B2B2G) process. Significantly more efficient would be for the documents to be shared directly between the agencies in the country of export and import (G2G). An example of such arrangement is the ePhyto procedure developed for the flower trade between Kenya and the Netherlands. Here phytosanitary authorities share the document in an electronic form directly. Reliance on the importer and exporter to share the certificate falls away (Grainger *et al*, 2018).

Harnessing data-sharing technologies to best effect

Significant cost and efficiency gains can also be achieved through the use of modern information and communication technologies (ICT). Most trade and customs procedures were originally developed with paper documents in minds (Box 9.2). This, when compared to the widespread use of modern ICT, looks outdated, especially when so much of modern logistics and supply chain operations has been enabled though the use of ICT. The big trade facilitation idea is that these technologies allow processes between business operators and with government agencies to be radically redesigned with significant scope for automation and more streamlined arrangements. Some might also use the term 're-engineered' (Hammer, 1990), but to enable such opportunities it is first necessary to agree on standards that allow for the information traditionally captured in trade documents to be shared in an efficient manner.

BOX 9.2

Document families associated with international trade operations

- **Authorizations**, certificates and licences, such as those issued by Customs and other government agencies where control is conditional on additional requirements – including those that apply to preferential origins, permit the shipment of restricted goods or are needed for SPS-type controls (eg veterinary health certificate, phytosanitary certificate, fumigation certificate).
- **Cargo-handling documents**, such as packaging lists, labels, dangerous goods declarations, loading lists, loading plans.
- **Commercial documents**, especially commercial invoices.
- **Customs documents,** such as an import, export and transit declaration, pre-departure or pre-arrival notifications, and accompanying transit documents.

- **Financial documents**, such as payment instructions, guarantees and letters of credit.
- **Insurance documents**, including certificates, whether arranged on an open policy basis, annual basis, single voyage basis, or under a freight forwarder's open cover facilities.
- **Terminal instructions (port or border)**, such as slot applications, arrival notifications and departure confirmations.
- **Transport documents**, such as the bill of lading, standard shipping notes, consignment notes, cargo receipts and cargo manifests.

An early driver for standardizing trade documents was the idea of a master document, which with the use of stencils and photocopiers could be used to generate a full set of trade documents. It is now common for trade documents as well as many documents used by government agencies to follow the UN Layout Key for Trade Documents set out in UN Recommendation 1 (UN CEFACT, 1981). Adherence to this layout key makes it easier for software providers to develop electronic document management solutions that draw on a single master dataset from which all relevant documents can then be automatically produced. Often such software solutions also have the capability to automatically submit the generated electronic documents directly to the relevant government agencies.

BOX 9.3

Two examples of the use of trade standards

One example for data standardization is the UK Location Codes (UN CEFACT, 2021). They are used to describe over 100,000 key transport and logistics locations around the world in an unambiguous manner. They incorporate IATA location codes and ensure that, irrespective of language or spelling, locations are always clear. Air travellers will thus recognize LHR code as London Heathrow, LAX as Los Angeles and GVA as Geneva – or Genève in French, Genf in German and Ginevra in Italian.

Another example is the European Union's Single Administrative Document (SAD) that was discussed in Chapter 2 and is also used in many other countries for customs declarations. It follows the UN Layout Key for Trade Documents and also incorporates a multitude of international UN standards, amongst others.

FIGURE 9.1 SAD and international standards

International standards incorporated into the EU's Single Administrative Document (SAD)

United Nations Layout key for trade documents (Rec 1)	**UN CEFACT Rec 7** Date formats	**UN CEFACT Rec 16** Location codes	**UN CEFACT Rec 24** Logistics status codes
UN CEFACT Rec 3 Country codes	**UN CEFACT Rec 8** UNIC (Reference numbers)	**UN CEFACT Rec 20** Units of measurement	**UN CEFACT Rec 28** Means of transport codes
UN CEFACT Rec 5 ICC Incoterms®	**UN CEFACT Rec 9** ISO currency codes	**UN CEFACT Rec 21** Packaging type codes	**WCO HS** Commodity codes

SOURCE Adapted from presentation slides by Sue Probert, Chair, UN CEFACT

Indeed, where regulatory systems such as those of customs are electronic (see Chapter 3), business operators must normally subscribe to specialist software that interfaces with those electronic systems. Permission to submit electronically may also be subject to authorization requirements, sometimes also referred to as Direct Trader Input (DTI) authorization. For the border agency, electronic declarations enable processes to be automated. They also enable advanced risk management techniques (Chapter 3) where the declared data is automatically analysed against set inspection profiles and algorithms to explore and identify unusual patterns worthy of further investigation.

Yet, despite the widespread use of electronic customs systems, the need for supporting paper documents prevails in most parts of the world. Customs declarations usually still need to be supported by other documents, such as copies of the commercial invoice and transport documents or for the presentation of veterinary and phytosanitary certificates. These may need to be submitted as paper copies to the Customs office. Linking paper documents to electronic customs clearance processes can often be tricky (Grainger, 2013). However, the use of fax- and email-based systems in the absence of full electronic systems is becoming more widespread (especially during the Covid-19 pandemic) and serve as a helpful stop-gap measure.

A significant operational challenge is that most government agencies have their own compliance systems, and business operators are obliged to declare similar information to each one of them. Subsequently, one of the more ambitious trade facilitation measures within the WTO Trade Facilitation Agreement is the Single Window.

Defined by UN CEFACT Recommendation 33, a single window '... allows parties involved in trade and transport to lodge standardized information and documents with a single entry point to fulfil all import, export and transit-related regulatory requirements. Individual data elements should only be submitted once electronically' (UNECE, 2020a). The list of all parties (often also referred to as stakeholders) is extensive (Table 9.3). The single entry point serves as a hub through which they can exchange all relevant information (Figure 9.1); this is preferable to trade and custom environments where information is declared directly to each agency without the opportunity to explore streamlined processes, weed out duplicate information requests and retain data for repeat use (eg authorization numbers, permits and licences).

TABLE 9.3 Single window stakeholders as per UN Recommendation 33

Government parties	Private-sector parties
• customs authorities; • tax authorities; • border regulatory agencies; • licensing authorities (non-tariff regulation); • national statistics authorities; • state authorities carrying out transport control; • state authorities carrying out veterinary control; • state authorities carrying out phytosanitary control;	• exporters, importers, exporting companies, central purchasing companies and their representative associations; • carriers, non-vessel operating common carriers (NVOCC), ship agents, global service and sales agents (GSSA), express carriers, handling agents, stevedores and their respective representative associations; • logistics companies, freight forwarders, forwarding agents and their representative associations;

(continued)

TABLE 9.3 (Continued)

Government parties	Private-sector parties
• state authorities carrying out sanitary and quarantine control; • control (supervision) over compliance of technical regulations; • export, radiation, foreign exchange and other forms of state control; • governmental port authorities; • organizations authorized to issue permits, including chambers of commerce, certification bodies and testing laboratories (centres) performing the work in the field of assessment (confirmation) and compliance with technical regulations.	• customs brokers, customs agents, customs carriers, owners of temporary storage warehouses, owners of customs warehouses, owners of free warehouses, owners of duty-free shops and their representative associations; • certification companies; • chambers of commerce and industry; • banks, second-tier banks (branches), non-banking credit and finance institutions, insurance companies, patent organizations (patent attorneys), postal operators and other organizations; • single submission portal operators.

SOURCE UNECE, 2020a

FIGURE 9.2 Comparison of non-single window arrangements vs single window operating through one single point of entry

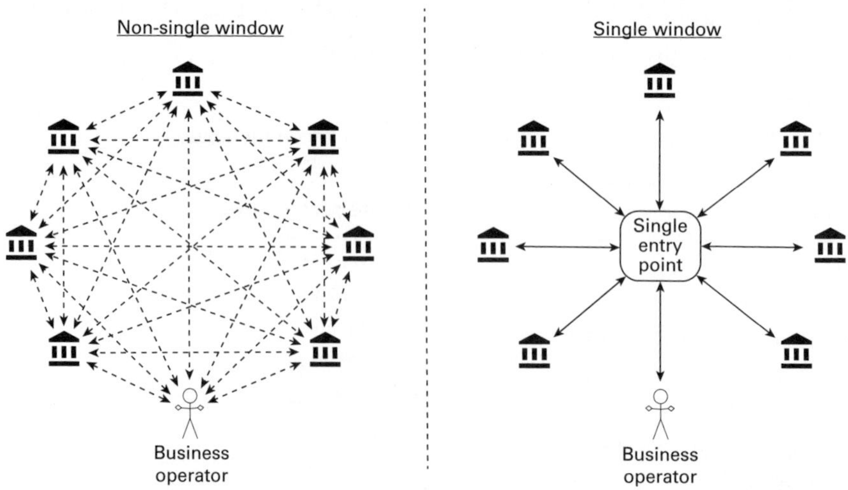

Much of the information shared through the single window will be based on details derived from the commercial arrangements between trading businesses (Chapter 3). However, the demands of control and coordinated border management (Chapter 7) also require extensive

FIGURE 9.3 Data-sharing processes via the single window

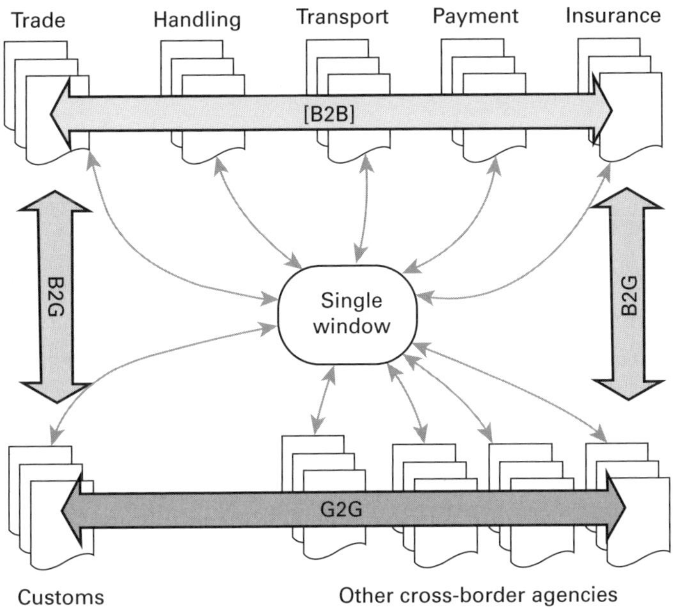

SOURCE Adapted from presentation slides by Sue Probert, Chair UN CEFACT

data-sharing between government agencies. The latter, in addition to control and authorization decisions, may also include details about risk management and intervention instructions. Single windows thus serve both B2G and G2G processes (Figure 9.2). Though some countries, such as Singapore, are developing their single window environment to also accommodate the trade processes amongst businesses (B2B) – such as insurance, payment and shipping – and automatically capture derived data for regulatory compliance, too (Singapore Customs, 2018).

Not too dissimilar to the single window environment idea is the 'trade data pipeline' (Hesketh, 2009). It stresses the utility that information derived from commercial processes has for regulatory controls. By tapping into that pipeline government agencies may access information as and when it is created (for example, when arrangements for shipments are being made) as opposed to when it is declared. This provides for more streamlined decision making, ensures data is captured at source rather than second hand – which currently often is the case, for example, when pre-arrival information from the shipping line to Customs is (in many countries) based on information provided by the shipper; or where a health certificate issued by a government agency in the country of export is handed to the exporter who in turn passes on to the importer for presentation to the authorities there.

Improve processes amongst the various parties involved in cross-border logistics operations

As outlined in Chapter 8, cooperation and coordination is a central theme within the logistics and transport literature and may be found at the transaction, partnership and business environment level. Good relationships between business operators along the supply chain and with government agencies enable opportunities for weeding out many cross-border logistics-related operational challenges. Undesirable friction in the form of transaction costs is reduced. Likewise, as outlined in Chapter 7, coordination between border agencies at the border or across borders as well as with business operators also provides for opportunities to improved border control outcomes.

COORDINATION AND COOPERATION AT THE DAY-TO-DAY TRANSACTIONAL LEVEL

The daily interplay between business operators and border agencies entails all operational steps necessary to place goods under their control as well as any subsequent inspection and release activities (Chapters 2 to 6). Inevitably, as in any type of business operation, there are opportunities to make improvements. To help identify these it is common for business operators and border staff to meet regularly – eg at the beginning of the week – to coordinate staffing arrangements and shift patterns, operating hours, and the management of traffic flows, especially where they are prone to alternation between inward- and outward-bound movements. Early advance notifications by operators also enables officers to prepare and be on standby, which can often significantly speed up processes and prevent congestion at facilities.

In busy operational environments the appointment of a 'boundary spanner' or dedicated contact persons can also help speed up decision making. It provides operators with quick access to operationally sensitive decisions, including, for example, the differentiation between urgent and less urgent operational tasks. Clear communication and subsequent coordination also provide scope for operational models that allow certain goods to be fast-tracked, such as express parcels or perishables.

COORDINATION AND COOPERATION AT THE PARTNERSHIP LEVEL

Coordination and cooperation can reach deeper than within the day-to-day operations context. In Chapter 7 reference has already been made to supply chain security programmes where suitably trusted businesses benefit from preferential treatment. Businesses that tend to have a good compliance record should normally also benefit from significantly less disruptive experiences at the border. At some ports and borders business operators and government agencies may also come together to develop dedicated infrastructure. This might be an electronic system, such as the port community system outlined in Chapter 3. It might also relate to the development and provision of dedicated inspection infrastructure to enable officers to conduct checks more efficiently.

Often, coordination and cooperation activities also concern the sharing of intelligence. This enables officers to be more selective, thus ensuring that resources are put to best use. It also means that in the case of maritime ships only parts of the cargo are detained and not the entire vessel. Agreements between businesses operators and the border agencies may also extend to active assistance in investigations, for example, by providing access to customer data.

COORDINATION AND COOPERATION AT THE BUSINESS ENVIRONMENT LEVEL

A big theme here is consultation about whenever new procedures are implemented, but also about sharing insights about how processes and procedures can be better managed and improved. The WTO Trade Facilitation Agreement, for example, requires government agencies to reach out and consult the business community whenever implementing new trade and customs procedures. This is essential for enabling business operators to prepare for those new requirements. It also provides an opportunity for the business community to advise on how those procedures might be best implemented without adding unnecessarily to the compliance burden. Ideally, business operators are also given the opportunity to regularly feed back to the border agencies about their operational experiences and frustrations. Resulting dialogue provides an opportunity for identifying solutions about how those inefficiencies might be best remedied.

A common model for business consultation is to publish relevant initiatives in a public gazette within a dedicated business consultation database. Sometimes officers will also seek views informally. Some border agencies may also maintain dedicated consultation groups. The UK's Joint Customs Consultative Group (JCCC), for example, has been active for over 50 years and draws a membership base from over 20 business interest groups (Box 9.2). The secretariat is staffed by UK Customs (HMRC). Members and customs officials meet formally at least three times per year. Specialist subgroups may be created where the topic of concern is of a more specialist nature. The minutes of meetings are published and can be freely accessed on the UK Government's Gov.uk website.

BOX 9.2

UK Joint Customs Consultative Committee's terms of reference

The purpose of the Joint Customs Consultative Committee (JCCC) is to:

- discuss and advise upon proposed strategic changes to customs policies, procedures and business models;
- share information and act as a consultative group for EU, international and national customs initiatives, and obtain industry views to ensure coherence and a common understanding in influencing negotiations;
- understand industry and regulatory impacts;
- horizon scan;
- review progress against agreed aims and objectives, and to suggest remedial action for objectives that are not being achieved.

SOURCE HMRC, 2021

In line with the obligations of the WTO Trade Facilitation Agreement, more and more countries now also operate dedicated national trade facilitation committees. They concern all government agencies and their interactions with the business community. Many are still in their infancy, though are likely to be staffed by a dedicated secretariat with a focus on coordinating the implementation of WTO trade facilitation measures (WTO, 2016). Many will also focus on trade facilitation related to transport and port operations. They can also be a good vehicle for capturing the business community's insights into unnecessary transaction costs experienced in export markets so that appropriate action through diplomatic channels and trade policy can be taken.

Well-functioning national trade facilitation bodies will draw their membership from all relevant business stakeholder groups as well as relevant border agencies (Table 9.4). In addition to the requirements

TABLE 9.4 Recommended membership for national trade facilitation bodies

Government authorities/agencies	Traders	Related trade service providers
Commerce or trade and their agencies (eg export development agency)	Importers and their associations	Carriers or transporters
Transport/roads railways/waterways/infrastructure and their agencies including sea and land port agencies and others	Exporters and their associations	Freight forwarders
Finance/planning/economic development/industry ministries and their agencies including central banks and others	Small and medium-sized exporters and importers and their associations	Chambers of commerce and their federations
Customs agencies		Private laboratories or certification agencies
Government foreign trade institutes and think tanks		Technical software providers
Standards and accreditation organizations		Banks, insurance companies
		Customs agents
		In all the cases above, their associations
		Academic institutions, non-public think tanks

SOURCE UN CEFACT (2015b)

of the WTO Trade Facilitation Agreement they may also play an active role in the development of other trade and customs policy initiatives, contribute to the drafting and development of governing trade and customs legislation, provide input into the drafting and adoption of applicable trade and customs procedures, develop proposals for improvements, lend a hand to the drafting and development of electronic system specifications and assist in the coordination and implementation of trade facilitation measures (UN CEFACT 2015b).

Ideally any form of consultation should be based on the six basic principles outlined in UN CEFACT Recommendation 40 (UN CEFACT 2015a):

- partnership and trust;
- transparency;
- managing differences of opinion and interests;
- results orientation;
- consultations as an iterative process with respect for time and timing;
- accountability and responsibility.

Assess and evaluate, hold parties accountable, learn and innovate

There has been considerable effort by policy makers to assess and evaluate the performance of border agencies. Much of these, such as the WCO's Time Release Study methodology or the World Bank's trading across borders dataset were discussed in Chapter 8. The motivation for understanding experienced compliance costs and friction can have multiple sources, be it to: identify opportunities for trade facilitation-type improvements; measure the performance of respective government agencies and operators; evaluate the cost and benefits of specific trade facilitation-type initiatives; research; or simply to help understand the cost impact associated with trade and customs procedures (Grainger *et al,* 2018).

Armed with cost and performance figures it is possible to hold relevant parties accountable. The old adage that 'what can't be measured can't be managed' applies. The challenge is to work out what to measure and whether any figures or insights provided are robust enough to act upon. Inevitably, different stakeholders will perceive costs and their impacts differently. They are also likely to have different evaluation needs. Subsequently, the assessment of trade facilitation initiatives can prove tricky when accommodating the various stakeholder perspectives.

Studies by trade economists often focus on the macro-level impact of trade facilitation-type measures, especially with regard to trade-related economic growth (Wilson *et al,* 2003; Mann, 2012). Business operators, by contrast, are more concerned about competitiveness, and the ability to serve their customers well. In an environment where friction at borders undermines competitiveness, it should be weeded out. On the other hand, not all business operators experience the same types of costs. As already outlined, some might have developed superior compliance capabilities, maybe even benefit from economies of scale. Others do not have these and might consider trade and customs procedures to be a bigger cost. Thus, some early research strongly suggests that a score-card approach might be merited (Kaplan and Norton, 1992). Categories as identified by Grainger *et al* (2021) in their evaluation of a trade facilitation initiative in Montenegro include:

- alignment with international obligations (eg those of the WTO) and other strategic needs;
- operational improvements for business operators and the border agencies;
- learning;
- evidence of benefits for the economy and society (eg through trade-related economic growth or improved control capabilities).

Inevitably, any evaluation needs to take account of the respective stakeholder's assessment needs and ideas about what success might look like.

ACTIVITIES AND DISCUSSION POINTS

1 See if you can find the minutes of the most recent national trade facilitation meeting in a country of your choice. What did they discuss?

2 Much of the reviewed trade facilitation measures in this chapter relate to B2G improvements. Discuss what role, if any, government should play in improving processes between businesses (B2B).

3 How can businesses best articulate their trade facilitation needs so that government agencies take action? Discuss.

References

Appling, G and Archer, A (1998) *Creating the International Trade Organization*, ed D Moss, Harvard Business School, Boston, MA

Braithwaite, J and Drahos, P (2000) *Global Business Regulation,* Cambridge University Press, Cambridge

DAfTF (2020) Montenegro's success model, Deutsche Alliance für Trade Facilitation

De Wulf, L and Sokol, JB (eds) (2005) *Customs Modernization Handbook,* World Bank, Washington, DC

EBRD (2021) Trade Facilitation Programme: Overview, European Bank for Reconstruction and Development, www.ebrd.com/work-with-us/trade-facilitation-programme.html (archived at https://perma.cc/N7RB-EU2S)

European Commission (2019) The CustCompeu, EU Customs Competency Framework, European Union, Brussels

EU (2013) Regulation (EU) No 952/2013 of the European Parliament and the Council of 9 October 2013 laying down the Union Customs Code (recast), *Official Journal of the European Union,* **56** (L269)

EU (2021) Access2Markets, trade.ec.europa.eu/access-to-markets/en/content/ (archived at https://perma.cc/2DT7-W284)

EU and UK (2020) Trade and Cooperation Agreement between the European Union and the European Atomic Energy Community, of the one part, and the United Kingdom of Great Britain and Northern Ireland, on the other part, *Official Journal of the European Union,* **63** (L444), pp 14–1462

GATT (1947) The General Agreement on Tariffs and Trade, World Trade Organization

GATT (1994) The General Agreement on Tariffs and Trade, World Trade Organization

Grainger, A (2011) Trade facilitation: A conceptual review, *Journal of World Trade*, **45** (1), pp 39–62

Grainger, A (2013) *Trade and customs procedures: The compliance costs for UK meat imports*, University of Nottingham, nottingham-repository.worktribe.com/output/718068 (archived at https://perma.cc/N3BC-QGUY)

Grainger, A, Bartels, K, Boskovic, T, Milosevic, S, Rackovic, M, Sowinski, C and Pope, S (2021) What the example of Montenegro's new pre-arrival processing capabilities tell us about customs performance measurement, *WCO news*, March

Grainger, A, Huiden, R, Rukanov, B and Tan, Y-H (2018) What is the cost of customs and borders across the supply chain? ... and how to mitigate the cost through better coordination and data sharing', *World Customs Journal*, **12** (1), pp 1–28

Hammer, M (1990) Reengineering work: Don't automate, obliterate, *Harvard Business Review*, **68** (4), p 104

Hesketh, D (2009) Seamless electronic data and logistics pipelines shift focus from import declarations to start of commercial transaction, *World Customs Journal*, **3** (1), pp 27–32

HMRC (2021) Joint Customs Consultative Committee (JCCC), www.gov.uk/government/groups/joint-customs-consultative-committee#jccc-newsletters (archived at https://perma.cc/F69V-3W9K)

ICAO (2017) Annex 9 to the Convention on International Civil Aviation: Facilitation (15th edn), International Civil Aviation Organization, ICAO, Montréal

IMO (1965) Convention on Facilitation of International Maritime Traffic (FAL) (as amended), International Maritime Organization, London

IMO (2019) Explanatory Manual to the Convention on Facilitation of International Maritime Traffic, 165, as amended, International Maritime Organization, London

Kaplan, RS and Norton, DP (1992) The balanced scorecard: Measures that drive performance, *Harvard Business Review*, **70** (1), pp 71–79

LTP (2021) Lao PDR Trade Portal, www.laotradeportal.gov.la (archived at https://perma.cc/VGH9-VKHT)

Mann, CL (2012) Supply chain logistics, trade facilitation and international trade: A macroeconomic policy view, *Journal of Supply Chain Management*, **48** (3), pp 7–14

McLinden, G, Fanta, E, Widdowson, D and Doyle, T (eds) (2010) *Border Management Modernization*, World Bank, Washington, DC

New Zealand Meat Board (2021) Guidance note to EU sheepmeat and goatmeat quota allowance allocation system, www.nzmeatboard.org/main.cfm?id=40#19 (archived at https://perma.cc/7VRA-YG5N)

OECD (2020) The OECD at 60, Organisation for Economic Co-operation and Development, Paris, https://read.oecd-ilibrary.org/view/?ref=1059_1059103-whi5k2wv7w&title=OECD-at-60 (archived at https://perma.cc/9V7Y-JBXU)

Rege, V, Kataric, I and Commonwealth Secretariat (2007) *Trade Facilitation: A handbook for trade negotiators*, Commonwealth Secretariat, London

Singapore Customs (2018) Going beyond the national single window, *WCO news*, 87

Stubbs, R and Underhill, GRD (1994) *Global Issues and Historic Perspectives: Political economy and the changing global order*, eds R Stubbs and GRD Underhill, pp 145–62, Macmillan, London

TIR (2005) The TIR Convention, 1975 (2005 version)

UK Government (2021) Import goods into the UK: step by step, www.gov.uk/import-goods-into-uk (archived at https://perma.cc/G3B8-B6TV)

UN CEFACT (2015a) Recommendation 40: Consultation approaches: Best practices in trade and government consultation on trade facilitation matters, United Nations, Geneva

UN CEFACT (2015b) Recommendation 4: National trade facilitation bodies, United Nations Centre for Trade Facilitation and Electronic Business, United Nations, Geneva

UN CEFACT (2019) Business Requirements Specification: Buy–ship–pay reference data model, United Nations, Geneva

UN CEFACT (2021) UN/LOCODE since 1981, unece.org/trade/uncefact/unlocode/history-1981 (archived at https://perma.cc/M2VG-5SQP)

UN ESCAP (2004) ESCAP Trade Facilitation Framework: A guiding tool (ST/ESCAP/2327), United Nations, Bangkok

UN CEFACT (1981) Recommendation 1: United Nations Layout Key for Trade Documents, UN ECE/TRADE/137: 11, United Nations, Geneva

UNCTAD (2006a) *Trade Facilitation Handbook Part I: National Facilitation Bodies – Lessons from experience*, UNCTAD/SDTE/TLB/2005/1

UNCTAD (2006b) *Trade Facilitation Handbook Part II: Technical notes on essential trade facilitation measures*, UNCTAD/SDTE/TLB/2005/2

UNCTAD (2017) Next steps upon the entry into force of the WTO Trade Facilitation Agreement (Technical Note No 24), UNCTAD, Geneva

UNECE (2002) Recommendation 18: Facilitation measures related to international trade procedures, United Nations, Geneva

UNECE (2012) Trade facilitation: Principles and benefits, tfig.unece.org/details.html (archived at https://perma.cc/3BSR-2KGJ)

UNECE (2017) Recommendation 1: United Nations Layout Key for Trade Documents Recommended Practice and Guidelines, United Nations, Geneva

UNECE (2020) Dangerous Goods, unece.org/transport/dangerous-goods (archived at https://perma.cc/TC3X-VJ5L)

UNECE (2020a) Recommendation 33: Recommendation and Guidelines on Establishing a Single Window, United Nations Centre for Trade Facilitation and Electronic Business, United Nations, Geneva

UNECE (2020b) Summary of UNECE Trade Facilitation Recommendations: 2019 revised edn, United Nations Centre for Trade Facilitation and Electronic Business, United Nations, Geneva

UNECE (2020c) Trade Facilitation Implementation Guide, tfig.unece.org/ (archived at https://perma.cc/Q8V9-THVV)

UNECE (2021) Working Party 7, unece.org/trade/working-party-agricultural-quality-standards-wp7 (archived at https://perma.cc/HDE2-6NUS)

WCO (2002) 1952–2002 World Customs Organization

WCO (2006) Revised Kyoto Convention: International Convention on the Simplification and Harmonization of Customs Procedures, World Customs Organization, Brussels

WCO (2019a) PICARD Professional Standards, World Customs Organization, Brussels

WCO (2019b) Strategic Plan 2019–2022, World Customs Organization, Brussels

WCO (2020) World Customs Organization Annual Report 2019–2020, World Customs Organization, Brussels

Wilson, JS, Mann, CL and Otsuki, T (2003) Trade facilitation and economic development: A new approach to quantifying the impact, *World Bank Economic Review,* **17** (3), pp 367–89

Wolffgang, H-M and Kafeero, E (2014) Old wine in new skins: Analysis of the Trade Facilitation Agreement vis-à-vis the Revised Kyoto Convention, *World Customs Journal,* 8 (2), pp 27–37

WTO (2014) Agreement on Trade Facilitation (WT/L/931) Preparatory Committee on Trade Facilitation, World Trade Organization, Geneva

WTO (2015) Annual Report 2015, World Trade Organization, Geneva

WTO (2016) National Committees on Trade Facilitation: Current practices and challenges, World Trade Organization, Geneva

WTO (2017) WTO's Trade Facilitation Agreement enters into force, www.wto.org/english/news_e/news17_e/fac_31jan17_e.htm (archived at https://perma.cc/46ZR-JQF6)

WTO (2021) Trade Facilitation Agreement Facility, www.tfafacility.org (archived at https://perma.cc/K277-TT8Z)

10

Borders and disaster relief logistics operations

The image of goods being held or delayed at the border is not a good one, especially when it relates to disaster relief efforts and lives are at stake (BBC, 2015). Border management within the context of disaster responses is of increasing concern within trade and customs policy (World Bank Group, 2014), and a number of internationally recommended procedures and measures have been designed to help assist disaster relief efforts. The World Customs Organization's Revised Kyoto Convention's Annex J, Chapter 5 concerning the control and administration of relief consignments is one such example (WCO, 2006).

The increased attention on developing appropriate trade and customs measures is merited not only because it is the right thing to do, but also because a number of global trends make the impact of disasters more urgent. Climate change certainly plays a big factor with regard to the frequency of disasters (USGS, 2021). But factors relating to human geography are of urgent significance, too. Compared to just a few decades back, the world's population has increased markedly. In 1960 the world had 3 billion human inhabitants. This increased to almost 4.5 billion in 1980, 6.1 billion in 2000, and 7.7 billion in 2019 (UNDP, 2020). The greater the human population, the greater the number of people that could be affected by disaster.

Likewise, the world has seen considerable economic growth over the last few decades. Although that wealth is not distributed evenly

(World Bank, 2020), greater wealth overall does suggest that more is at stake should disaster strike. The last few decades have also been subject to considerable increases in urbanization. In 1960 the world's share of urban population was 33.6 per cent. This increased to 39.4 per cent in 1980, 46.7 per cent in 2000, and 55.7 per cent in 2019 (UNDP, 2020). Thus, compared to the past, the human population overall is increasingly dependent on extended production and supply networks to support urban populations. Logistics disruptions, including those at borders, are keenly felt.

Of course, the impact of a disaster is defined by its nature and context. Some parts of the world – especially those developed countries that are prone to disasters (eg fire, earthquakes, flooding) – are often very prepared and the overall impact of the event is quickly contained. Other parts of the world might be less prepared, and sudden disasters give rise to large-scale human suffering. The scale of disaster also differs. Many types of disasters are local or national in nature and may even struggle to gain global attention (OCHA, 2021). Some have a wider geographic footprint, such as the 2004 tsunami across the Indian ocean (Banomyong *et al,* 2011). Disasters can also be global in nature, such as the outbreak of Covid-19 in 2020. Common to all disasters is that when countries are caught off-guard the demand for relief is urgent. The logistics mission, however challenging, is to help by providing goods and services that are critical to life. Depending on the nature of the disaster, those goods and services often relate to the immediate need for shelter, nourishment, medical treatment and care, search and rescue, communications, energy, transport and equipment (Box 10.1).

BOX 10.1

Typical types of disaster relief goods and equipment

- battery generators;
- blankets;
- clothing;
- foods;

- household hygiene items and kits (soap, sanitary napkins, etc);
- household kitchen sets (pots, pans, cutlery, etc);
- laboratory equipment;
- latrines;
- means of transport;
- medical equipment;
- medicines;
- mosquito nets;
- plastic sheets (tarpaulins);
- prefabricated houses;
- search and rescue trained animals;
- shelter repair tool kits (hammer, nails, rope, etc);
- solar lights;
- surgical equipment;
- telecommunications equipment;
- tents;
- vehicles;
- water purification units;
- water storage (buckets, jerry cans, transport bladders, tanks, etc).

SOURCE UN CEFACT, 2021

Some types of disasters might see regulators respond with added border controls and restrictions on the flow of goods and people. For example, much of the global Covid-19-related efforts placed significant restrictions on the movement of people (including transport workers). Many countries also responded by controlling the export of goods deemed to be essential at home, such as personal protective equipment (PPE) and medical devices (WTO, 2021).

Some disasters are foreseeable and mitigating activities can be planned, for example by stockpiling critical goods for when they are needed. Speed may not be quite so urgent, and the operational characteristics are likely to be similar to regular commercial logistics and supply chain operations, including concern for costs, as discussed in Chapter 8. Rapid onset disasters, by contrast, are likely to be characterized by the need for speed and when delayed will cost lives.

Given the described trends, the subject of disaster logistics is fast evolving along with an extensive literature (Tomasini *et al*, 2009; Logistics Cluster, 2021). However, just like regular cross-border logistics operations, that mission is impacted by the demands of border agencies and the form and shape of applicable trade and customs procedures, including those designed to support relief shipments.

This final chapter of the book thus offers a practical illustration of logistics operations and border management practices including yet more pressing and urgent scope for trade facilitation.

Touchpoints with trade and customs procedures

Supply chains to enable relief efforts can differ from one response to the next. Where practical, goods may be procured locally and concern for cross-border logistics operations is less urgent. However, given the global nature of production there are usually considerable customs touchpoints in international disaster relief operations (Grainger *et al*, 2019).

They start at the procurement stage with concern for the applicable trade tariffs (Chapter 2) along with any storage arrangements that allow customs duties and taxes to be suspended. Customs touchpoints in relief operations also concern the export procedures to wherever the goods are needed. They also concern transit through any countries en route and via hub ports and airports. Transit procedures can also apply to movements between customs-controlled facilities, such as from land border posts to inland customs terminals. The import procedures in the country of destination need to be considered, too, especially those that grant exemption from import duties and taxes for humanitarian relief consignments. Where relief goods are not utilized, or where they can be reused elsewhere, there are also likely to be considerable reverse logistics operations. The re-export and return to storage creates yet further touchpoints with the border agencies (Figure 10.1).

As described by Grainger *et al* (2019) it is common for disaster relief goods (such as those described in Box 10.1) to be procured in advance and stored in a warehouse until they are needed. Stockpiling can ensure that the goods are immediately available for when the need arises. It also allows operators to secure competitive prices which might not be available during periods of sudden demand, as would be the case for most disasters. Stockpiling, however, does require goods to be stored in warehouses. The use of customs free zones or a customs warehousing arrangement ensures that goods do not have to be subject to import duties and taxes while in storage.

Alternatively, where goods are procured from countries that benefit from preferential trade agreements and import duties rates are very low or zero, operators may have no need for customs warehousing or free zone arrangements. However, it is likely that they will have to make sure that they have obtained the necessary proof in the form of preferential origin documentation to take advantage of those preferential trade agreements (Chapter 2).

When disaster strikes and goods are exported to relevant locations, customs export procedures apply. This entails a customs export declaration. Pre- or advance notification procedures often come into play as well. The customs export clearance might prove particularly tricky at locations where goods are handled by the military and not ordinarily subject to customs control. For non-military parties this can prove problematic not only from a trade compliance point of view, but also where proof of export is necessary when reclaiming taxes on exports, such as for value added tax.

Transit arrangements via third countries or between customs locations within the country of arrival are usually subject to financial securities and a customs seal (Chapter 3). Once goods arrive, customs import procedures apply. The challenge for those delivering relief is that they may not necessarily be familiar with the specific requirements in the country to which goods are destined. The support from experienced local customs agents or brokers is often essential. Alternatively, suppliers of relief items may consign their goods over to a local partner, NGO or government agency that benefits from customs import duty suspension and other types of preferential treatment. Just as for regular cross-border logistics operations, the Incoterms® 2020 matter (Chapter 6) so that there is clarity about who is responsible for the various parts of the logistics operations – including the import responsibilities.

It is likely that much of the equipment – non-consumables such as vehicles, generators, mobile hospitals, cargo-handling equipment, containers – is imported on a temporary basis. Most countries allow for temporary import procedures which provide relief from duties and taxes. The condition is that the goods are indeed returned (re-exported) within a specific period of time (eg 12 or 24 months). In line with the WCO's Revised Kyoto Convention, Annex G, Chapter 1 (WCO, 2006) temporary admission approval usually requires proof of entry and export along with a financial guarantee. Documents used for temporary import declarations also need to clearly identify the good. For vehicles, for example, customs and supporting documents thus often have to give explicit reference to the vehicle's chassis or frame number.

At the end of the relief operations, some of the equipment may be returned. Failure to return (re-export) items brought in under temporary import arrangements is likely to expose their importers to belated import duties and taxes, perhaps even fines. All returned goods should be appropriately declared for export. And once they arrive at the designated storage facility, operators may choose to enter them back into temporary storage arrangements, such as customs warehousing or into a customs free zone.

In addition to the customs procedures just described, certain types of goods commonly used in relief efforts are subject to additional controls and restrictions (Chapter 4). Licences and permits are needed. Control requirements for medicines can be particularly strict. Handling is usually also restricted to suitably qualified personal. Often shelf life and temperature control stipulations apply, too. Personal body armour, such as bullet-proof vests, are frequently

FIGURE 10.1 Touchpoints with trade and customs procedures in international relief operations

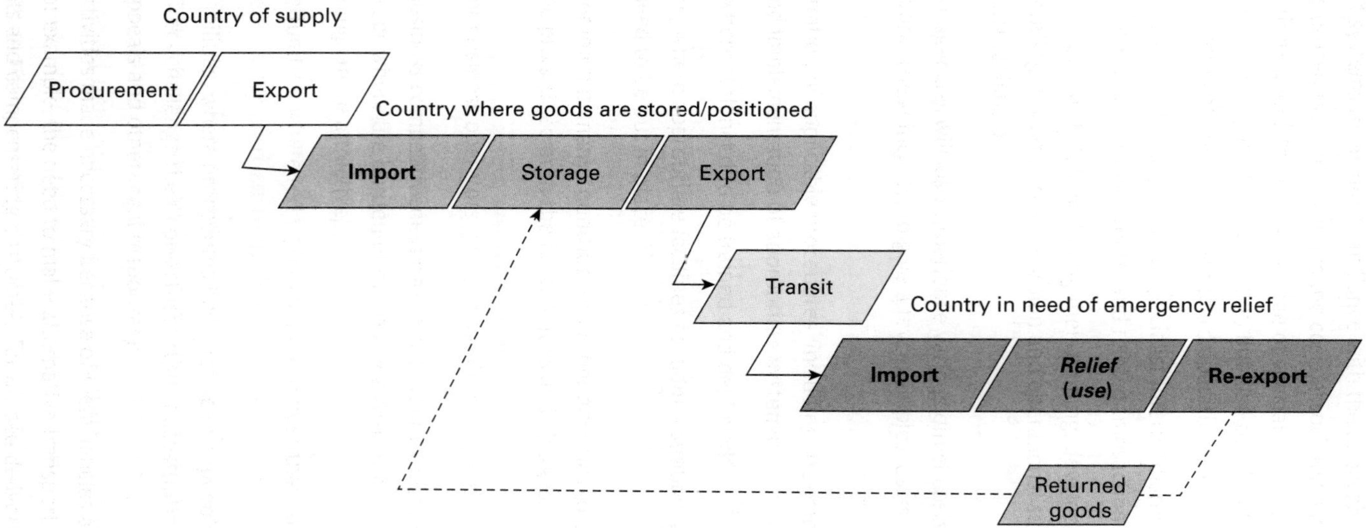

subject to export controls and may only be shipped with the right export and import licences in place. Food shipments, unless emergency measures are put in place, are likely to be subject to sanitary and phytosanitary controls (amongst others). Health certificates issued by suitably qualified authorities in the country of export before such goods are shipped, are frequently necessary.

Some countries, especially in the developing world (as touched upon in Chapter 3) might set stipulations for pre-shipment inspection (PSI). While procedures vary, they usually apply in the country of export and necessitate the service of an officially appointed PSI company. Often countries stipulate conditions for supporting documents needed by Customs for import clearance. Common stipulations relate to translations into the national language or demands for a specific format. In many countries there may also be a demand for non-preferential certificates of origin. The Arab Certificate of Origin is needed for imports into countries that are members of the Arab League. Some countries also stipulate that relevant documentation must be certified by their embassy or consulate before goods are exported (Grainger *et al*, 2019).

Instruments and standards

Given the importance of relief, the international community has produced a number of instruments to help support disaster relief operations. The UN CEFACT's Recommendation No. 44 for 'Cross-Border Facilitation Measures for Disaster Relief' is one such example. That recommendation also includes a helpful cross-reference to key reference documents, including many that have been frequently cited in this book, such as the WCO's Revised Kyoto Convention (Chapter 3) and the World Trade Organization's (WTO) Trade Facilitation Agreement (Chapter 9) as well as the WCO's SAFE Framework of Standard (Chapter 7). Naturally, instruments and measures designed to help improve regular cross-border logistics operations also have considerable utility within the humanitarian context.

However, there are also a number of instruments and measures with explicit concern for international relief operations. Annex J, Chapter 5 in the WCO's Revised Kyoto Convention, for example, recommends that relief consignments received as gifts by approved organizations for relief distribution under their control should be admitted free of import duties. It calls for procedures that allow for simplified customs declarations and even incomplete declarations on the provision that missing details are declared at a later point in time. Furthermore, declarations may be lodged, registered and checked by Customs before goods arrive to enable their release upon arrival. Clearance outside regular working hours or away from the customs offices shall be accommodated along with a waiver of any associated charges. Physical examinations and the taking of samples should only take place in exceptional circumstances.

The WCO Trade Recovery Guidelines (2018) concern plans for the recovery of trade flows after a major incident, such as from a natural disaster. They include, amongst others, recommendations for:

- advance preparations by the customs administration;
- Customs' response to the incident, its impact and repair;
- the resumption of operations, including collaboration with Customs in exporting countries; and
- the review of actions during the incident.

The 'Model Act for the Facilitation and Regulation of International Disaster Relief and Initial Recovery Assistance' is another noteworthy instrument (IFRC *et al,* 2013). Published by the International Federation of Red Cross and Red Crescent Societies (IFRC), the Office for the Coordination of Humanitarian Affairs (OCHA) and the Inter-Parliamentary Union (IPU), it is intended as a reference tool that is aimed at assisting legislators and policy makers in the development of domestic legislation, regulation and procedures concerning the management of international disaster assistance. It builds on the IDRL 'Guidelines for the Domestic Facilitation of International

Disaster Relief and Initial Recovery Assistance' (IFRC, 2011) and addresses, amongst many other issues, the arrangements for:

- providing relief from duties, tools and taxes on relief items;
- expedited entry and use of restricted items, such as medications, food, search dogs and telecommunications equipment;
- the disposition of unused equipment and goods, including re-export;
- the procedures for declaring the means of transport; and
- transit arrangements.

Challenges

Often, those tasked with delivering goods across borders to provide emergency relief will describe a picture that reflects some degree of chaos. Border agencies might be overwhelmed with the sudden influx of goods and materials. Bottlenecks are likely – perhaps even further compounded by large volumes of unsolicited aid or unnecessary shipments that do not meet the immediate needs. The operations of the border agencies might themselves be impacted by the disaster, with facilities destroyed, systems broken and without access to communications. Essential guidance from senior levels at headquarters might not be forthcoming. Border officials might be preoccupied with immediate concerns for the welfare of their families.

In such an operational environment, it might not always be easy for operators to work out who is in charge and what emergency procedures, if any, apply. Moreover, there is also a high risk that in the haste of offloading aircraft and vehicles, goods are misplaced along with any accompanying documentation (Grainger *et al,* 2019). Cargo-handling equipment to move goods, including to customs and storage facilities, might be inadequate. The customs-related challenges upon arrival are often described as severe (Turner, 2015), and are the subject of many international workshops (WCO *et al,* 2012a, 2012b, 2013, 2016; World Bank Group, 2014;). The findings of these workshops are summarized in Box 10.2.

BOX 10.2

Customs-related challenges to humanitarian logistics

- additional regulatory burdens for goods subject to additional controls, such as for medicines and foods;
- border-related hurdles in transit countries;
- capacity constraints and congestion at border points, including infrastructure constraints (such as for customs warehousing);
- capacity constraints within the private sector to comply with requirements, and within the public sector to administer requirements when faced with a sudden influx of goods at the ports and borders;
- complex bureaucratic and administrative requirements;
- corruption and abuse of procedures;
- delays in the communication of information necessary for customs clearance;
- disproportionate or excessive testing of goods;
- disruption and congestion caused by shipments of unplanned or inappropriate goods;
- failure to adopt temporary emergency measures for customs and border control requirements;
- insufficient or poor coordination between border agencies; including unclear jurisdictions about responsibilities;
- lack of clarity amongst donors and officials regarding regulatory procedures;
- misaligned and non-harmonized procedures and standards;
- poor preparedness amongst officials and insufficient support (including lack of training).

SOURCES WCO *et al*, 2012a, 2012b, 2013, 2016; World Bank Group, 2014

But in addition to the customs challenges already listed in Box 10.2, emergency relief practitioners can offer anecdotes of further issues (Grainger *et al*, 2019). They arise, for example, when consigning goods over to another party. This makes sense where that partner benefits from special emergency-related exemptions. However, once that control over the goods is lost, it is much more difficult to reclaim them for re-export in the event that they have not been used.

Particularly challenging might also be the switch from emergency border arrangements to regular border arrangements. What might have been possible within the general chaos at the onset of the disaster is no more. Confirmation of what has been landed may need to be obtained retrospectively. Backlogs and bottlenecks are likely to occur, support from experienced brokers and agents is often thought to be essential. Perhaps key is also the challenge of having to accommodate non-standard document requirements at very short notice, often also necessitating official translations. Such challenges already apply to regular cross-border logistics operations (Chapter 6), but the need for urgency makes them so much more pressing. Any mistakes or errors in trade documents – such as an insufficient description of the declared goods, disputed customs valuations or a mistyped reference number – further compound the challenge.

Scope for trade facilitation

Just as it is for regular cross-border logistics operations, the scope for trade facilitation is extensive. Broad trade facilitation themes, as outlined in Chapter 9, concern:

- the simplification and harmonization of applicable rules and procedures;
- the modernization of trade compliance systems;
- best practices in the administration and management of trade and customs procedures; and
- the institutional mechanisms to safeguard ongoing commitment to reducing trade related compliance costs.

SOURCE Grainger, 2011

Examples of trade facilitation opportunities within the disaster relief context that concern the simplification and harmonization of applicable rules and procedures are plenty. For instance, the WCO's Harmonized System used for classifying goods for customs purposes (outlined in Chapter 2) contains the option for additional codes (HS Chapters 98 and 99) that can be used to distinguish disaster relief items for easy identification and prioritization. A number of EU countries, for example, use the HS heading 9919 for that purpose.

Leniency by the border agencies for retrospective declarations and corrections, especially for trusted operators – and perhaps bearing a recognized Authorized Economic Operator or 'trusted trader' status (Chapter 7) – could also make operations significantly easier. Likewise, the harmonization of document requirements would ensure that any necessary paperwork can be completed using standard trade compliance software and systems. Non-standardized documents frequently necessitate manual, time-consuming and costly interventions. Given that so many relief items are subject to additional controls by non-customs agencies (Chapter 4) – such as medicines, radio equipment, foods and medical devices – the case for coordinated border management (Chapter 7) is particularly compelling. Likewise, cooperation between authorities in the country of export and at destination could be very helpful, too.

Modernized trade and customs systems help facilitate regular cross-border logistics operations and their efficiency when compared to paper-based systems will also be of considerable utility to humanitarian relief efforts. In Chapter 3 reference was made to ASYCUDA customs software that is used in over 90 countries. An enhancement of that software, the ASYREF Modul is also available for the processing of relief consignments (Bohl, 2017). Key features, amongst others, include:

- support for simplified procedures;
- functionality for duty relief on qualifying goods;
- the ability to lodge declarations prior to arrival;
- processing, management and risk assessment of relief shipments;

- support for post-audit assessment of humanitarian relief operators;
- the ability to set and manage the list of eligible priority goods.

SOURCE ASYCUDA, 2021

There are other useful technologies, national trade information portals, for example, that give detailed information about applicable rules and procedures, and how to be compliant (LTP, 2021). Such portals could also be used to share relevant information specific to unfolding disaster situations.

There are also many best practice administrative measures in aid of trade facilitation to consider. As highlighted in the work of Grainger *et al* (2019) some concern measures for the exemption of customs duties. Some aim to ensure there is adequate support for relief logistics operators, for example by appointing dedicated liaison and information officers and contact points. Furthermore 'one-stop-shop' facilities at major entry points, where the various border agencies are co-located and work in an integrated manner, can also help to rapidly fast-track coordinated border clearance (Turner, 2015).

Institutional measures in aid of disaster relief specific trade facilitation could include support for better training and support for officials to help them deal with and prepare for emergency situations. It would not be farfetched to recommend regular exchanges of experiences amongst operators and officials. This could be at an international level. The 'Get Airports Ready for Disaster' is one such initiative by the United Nations Development Programme and Deutsche Post DHL (UNDP, 2021). It has involved more than 50 airports around the world, incorporating training, on-site capacity evaluations and practical disaster exercises. Disaster relief subgroups with a focus on special border arrangements during crises would also have merit at the national level – for example within the framework of National Trade Facilitation Committees (UNCTAD, 2020a). Further suggestions for adopting trade facilitation measures to support disaster relief operations are also highlighted in UN CEFACT Recommendation 44 (2021).

Covid-19

The global Covid-19 pandemic is a global disaster with a worldwide death toll that in early 2021 amounted to almost 2.5 million; the total number of people infected exceeded 100 million (Johns Hopkins, 2021). Mitigating measures necessitated extensive restrictions on mobility (Oxford University, 2021), some of which are also enforced at borders. The resulting economic impact is also severe. The Committee for the Coordinating of Statistical Activities (CCSA, 2020) reported, amongst other grave issues, a fall in global manufacturing output by 20 per cent in April 2020 compared to the same period of the previous year. Global foreign direct investment was projected to fall by as much as 40 per cent in 2020. The first quarter of 2020 saw a loss of the equivalent of 155 million full-time jobs. That number increased to 400 million in the second quarter, with lower- and middle-income countries hardest hit. The CCES also highlighted that an additional 71 million to 100 million people have been pushed into extreme poverty.

The WTO's Goods Trade Barometer (2020) reported that the seasonally adjusted volume of world merchandise trade dropped in the second quarter of 2020, with a 17.2 per cent year-on-year decline and a 14.2 per cent drop between the first and second quarters. Container shipping was also impacted and took a significant dip at the beginning of the Covid-19 crisis (especially in China, where most of the world's largest container ports are located). As highlighted by the United Nations Conference on trade and development (UNCTAD), the disruptions to global maritime trade plunged in 2020 by 4.1 per cent in value (UNCTAD, 2020b). For airfreight, which is predominantly shipped in the bellies of passenger aircraft that are no longer in operation, the picture is grimmer. The IATA's Cargo Chartbook for the third quarter in 2020 reported that in April 2020 industry-wide cargo tonne-kilometres was 26 per cent lower than in the previous April. In July 2020 the decline, when compared to the previous year, was still 16.9 per cent (IATA, 2020). At the time of writing this book, recovery is expected, although it is likely to be unevenly distributed and dependent on the gravity of the overall Covid-19-related impact.

Border staff have witnessed significantly altered traffic flows. Their inspection and control facilities (Chapter 5) had to be quickly adapted to reflect changed trade flows as well as socially distanced handling and operating practice. Staff also had to accommodate new control demands. Many countries around the world, for instance, introduced measures to provide duty relief for critical goods, such as personal protective equipment (PPE), medical devices, medicines and equipment used for their production (WTO, 2021). However, many countries have also put in place measures to restrict or even ban the export of key items (WTO, 2021). Some actions taken were particularly controversial. Sought-after medical equipment destined for Latin America, for example, was seized by border officials during refuelling stops in the United States and Europe. To mitigate that risk, some shippers switched flights to Ethiopian Airlines to use its hub airport in Addis Ababa (Schipani and Pilling, 2020).

Many countries also put in measures to temporarily ease the border-related compliance burden, for example by allowing for expedited clearance or offering wider electronic services. Anecdotal reports, for example, suggest that countries that had previously set strict demands for original paper documents now permit emailed electronic scans. Given how severely economic activity and global production has been affected, policy makers are well advised to consider actions that help streamline border operations and reduce the compliance burden (Chapter 9). This does not have to be at the expense of control capabilities, especially when considering reports of counterfeit medicines and PPE (WCO, 2020). Trade facilitation and effective border management can go hand-in-hand.

ACTIVITIES AND DISCUSSION POINTS

1 Research what conditions, licensing and certification requirements apply specifically to the export of medicines (eg antibiotics, anaesthetics, vaccines) from one country of your choice to another of your choice. List the requirements and discuss any scope for making their trade easier within the context of humanitarian relief operations.

2 Reflecting on Chapter 6, what could a customs manager do to make sure that border-related disruptions within a disaster relief-type operation are minimized? Make practical recommendations and justify your reasoning.

3 By reference to Chapter 9, consider which procedures might be particularly useful for disaster logistics operations. State your reasoning. If you like, draw on recent insights that have been made within the context of Covid-19.

References

ASYCUDA (2021) About ASYREC, www.asyrec.asycuda.org/about (archived at https://perma.cc/CZL4-6D2Q)

Banomyong, R, Pettit, S, Beresford A and Whiting, M (2011) The 2004 Thailand tsunami reviewed: lessons learnt, in *Humanitarian Logistics: Meeting the challenge of preparing for and responding to disasters,* eds M Christopher and P Tatham, pp 103–19, Kogan Page, London

BBC (2015) Nepal quake: Airport customs holding up aid relief – UN, 3 May, www.bbc.co.uk/news/world-asia-32564891 (archived at https://perma.cc/UWW7-VSEE)

Bohl, V (2017) A new module in ASYCUDA speeds up the processing of relief consignments, *WCO News*, **82** (February)

CCSA (2020) How Covid-19 is changing the world: a statistical perspective, Volume II, Committee for the Coordination of Statistical Activities, Geneva

Grainger, A (2011) Trade facilitation: A conceptual review, *Journal of World Trade,* **45** (1), pp 39–62

Grainger, A, Rundle, JM and Ahsen, SR (2019) Customs and Humanitarian Logistics, *Global Trade and Customs Journal,* **14** (4), pp 154–68

IATA (2020) Cargo Chartbook Q3 2020, www.iata.org/en/iata-repository/publications/economic-reports/cargo-chartbook—q3-2020/ (archived at https://perma.cc/6YQX-9BAR)

IFRC (2011) Introduction to the guidelines for the domestic facilitation and regulation of international disaster relief and initial recovery assistance, International Federation of Red Cross and Red Crescent Societies, Geneva

IFRC, OCHA and IPU (2013) Model Act for the Facilitation and Regulation of International Disaster Relief and Initial Recovery Assistance (with commentary), International Federation of Red Cross and Red Crescent Societies, Office for the Coordination of Humanitarian Affairs, Inter-Parliamentary Union

Johns Hopkins (2021) Johns Hopkins University and Medicine—Coronavirus Resource Centre Dashboard, coronavirus.jhu.edu/map.html (archived at https://perma.cc/8MWM-D7HK)

Logistics Cluster (2021) Logistics Operational Guide (LOG), dlca.logcluster.org/display/LOG/Logistics+Operational+Guide+%28LOG%29+Home (archived at https://perma.cc/DYZ9-JGPD)

LTP (2021) Lao PDR Trade Portal, www.laotradeportal.gov.la (archived at https://perma.cc/8JL8-9WA3)

OCHA (2021) 'reliefweb', reliefweb.int (archived at https://perma.cc/BP48-L9UW)

Oxford University (2021) *Our World in Data: Government Response Stringency Index*, Oxford University, Oxford

Schipani, A and Pilling, D (2020, 22 May) Ethiopia steps in to deliver respirators to Latin Americans, *Financial Times,* London

Tomasini, R, van Wassenhove, L and van Wassenhove, Luc (2009) *Humanitarian Logistics,* Palgrave Macmillan, London

Turner, R (2015) Barriers to customs entry at the time of disaster in developing countries: mitigating the delay of life-saving materials, *World Customs Journal,* 9 (1)

UN CEFACT (2021) Recommendation No. 44: Cross-border facilitation measures for disaster relief, United Nations, Geneva

UNCTAD (2020a) National trade facilitation committees lead reforms, respond to COVID-19, unctad.org/news/national-trade-facilitation-committees-lead-reforms-respond-covid-19 (archived at https://perma.cc/4B6J-BGDY)

UNCTAD (2020b) *Review of Maritime Transport 2020*, United Nations Conference on Trade and Development, Geneva

UNDP (2020) *Population, total*, United Nations Population Division, United Nations, New York

UNDP (2021) Well prepared to respond: Get airports ready for disaster, https://www.europe.undp.org/content/geneva/en/home/partnerships/get-airports-ready-for-disaster--gard-.html (archived at https://perma.cc/7WHF-G5XZ)

USGS (2021) How can climate change affect natural disasters? www.usgs.gov/faqs/how-can-climate-change-affect-natural-disasters-1 (archived at https://perma.cc/FQY4-Q4EX)

WCO (2006) Revised Kyoto Convention: International Convention on the Simplifications and Harmonization of Customs Procedures, World Customs Organization, Brussels

WCO (2018) WCO Trade Recovery Guidelines, World Customs Organization, Brussels

WCO (2020) COVID-19 Urgent Notice: counterfeit medical supplies and introduction of export controls on personal protective equipment, www.wcoomd.org/en/media/newsroom/2020/march/covid_19-urgent-notice-counterfeit-medical-supplies.aspx (archived at https://perma.cc/4VDQ-H66K)

WCO, OCHA and IFRC (2012a) Regional Seminar on the Role of Customs in Natural Disaster Relief (Bangkok, Thailand), 19 February

WCO, OCHA and IFRC (2012b) Regional Seminar on the Role of Customs in Natural Disaster Relief (Santo Domingo, Dominican Republic), www.wcoomd.org/~/media/wco/public/global/pdf/topics/facilitation/activities-and-programmes/natural-disaster/report-on-the-regional-seminar-on-the-role-of-customs_edited.pdf?db=web (archived at https://perma.cc/K98E-KM7Y)

WCO, OCHA and IFRC (2013) Regional Seminar on the Role of Customs in Natural Disaster Relief (Astana, Kazakhstan), www.wcoomd.org/~/media/wco/public/global/pdf/topics/facilitation/activities-and-programmes/natural-disaster/regional-seminar-on-the-role-of-customs-in-natural-disaster-relief-_-final-report.pdf?db=web (archived at https://perma.cc/ZN5U-DCNE)

WCO, OCHA and IFRC (2016) Regional Seminar on the Role of Customs in Natural Disaster Relief (Addis Ababa, Ethiopia), www.wcoomd.org/-/media/wco/public/global/pdf/topics/facilitation/activities-and-programmes/natural-disaster/seminar-report-africa-march-2016-final-en.pdf?db=web (archived at https://perma.cc/3BSF-2CFT)

World Bank (2014) *Trade and Humanitarian Emergencies : A survey of trade policy issues affecting disaster response, recovery and reconstruction,* World Bank, Geneva

World Bank (2020) Atlas of Sustainable Development Goals 2020, datatopics.worldbank.org/sdgatlas/ (archived at https://perma.cc/36RL-SU9H)

WTO (2020) Goods Barometer signals trade resilience amid ongoing COVID concerns, *Goods Trade Barometer,* World Trade Organization, Geneva,

WTO (2021) COVID-19: Measures affecting trade in goods, https://www.wto.org/english/tratop_e/covid19_e/trade_related_goods_measure_e.htm (archived at https://perma.cc/A8MP-TVAK)

INDEX

NB: page numbers in *italic* indicate figures or tables

TABLE 9.2 (Continued)

Article/Heading	Trade facilitation obligations for the WTO member country
ARTICLE 8: BORDER AGENCY COOPERATION	
[illegible]	[illegible]
	[illegible] and coordination procedures.
ARTICLE 9: MOVEMENT OF GOODS INTENDED FOR IMPORT UNDER CUSTOMS CONTROL	
Moving under customs control	Allow goods to be moved under [illegible] customs procedure to an inland office, and permit the importer to clear goods at the destination rather than at the border crossing or point of arrival.
ARTICLE 10: FORMALITIES CONNECTED WITH IMPORTATION, EXPORTATION AND TRANSIT	
1. Formalities and documentation requirements	Regularly review the number of documents and formalities required with a view towards reducing or simplifying them.
	Document requirements and formalities should be as fast and as efficient as possible; eliminated when no longer needed; and should not be adopted if less restrictive solutions are available (eg, substitution).
2. Acceptance of copies	Where border agencies [illegible] to complete their [illegible] [illegible].
	The export declaration [illegible] required for [illegible].
	If the original document [illegible] government [illegible] shall accept [illegible] authenticated copy [illegible] similar [illegible].
3. Use of international standards	Relevant international standards [illegible] procedures [illegible] data sharing.
	WTO members shall participate in the regular review of those standards.

(continued)